DAN WALTERS

CALIFORNIA

FACING THE 21ST CENTURY
2nd Edition

CALFORNIA JOURNAL PRESS
Sacramento

John F. Hogan

ISBN: 0-930302-79-6

Contents

Preface

POLITICS IS ESSENTIALLY A REACTIVE BUSINESS. POLITICAL DECISIONMAKERS react to socioeconomic change and instant events, if they react at all. And political journalists, in turn, react to what politicians do. Political journalism, then tends to be at least two steps removed from reality—and probably two steps behind it as well.

This book was born of my desire to leap ahead of the traditional process by which political information is filtered, to figure out where California was headed in a socioeconomic and demographic sense and from that make some hopefully intelligent appraisals of the state's political future as well.

Originally, I conceived it to be a rather simple process. In the time-honored journalistic fashion, I would talk to demographers and other authorities on social change and draw together their views. From that I envisioned a series of columns for The Sacramento Bee and other newspapers would emerge. It was to be timed to set the stage for the 1986 elections.

As I began that process, however, I was struck by two things: there was very little coordination of research into the state's demographic present and future and even less application of that research to real life, in the form of political policy. At the same time, it became evident that California was undergoing enormous socioeconomic change and was looking at an acceleration of that evolution as the state approached the 21st century. A new kind of California was emerging, but one that few in private or public life were acknowledging.

1

What had been conceived as a simple journalistic exercise, therefore, evolved into a more fundamental and sweeping look at the state at it neared the end of the century and the millennium and what had been planned as a series of columns evolved into a series of longer articles for *The Sacramento Bee*. The editors of *The Bee*, fortunately, were willing to underwrite an extensive series of visits to every corner of California, one that involved some 9,000 miles of travel by automobile, airplane and even helicopter and eventually touched every one of the state's 58 counties. My goal was to match the information from data banks about what was happening in California to the on-the-ground reality.

My wife, Diana, accompanied me on many of those sojourns in the autumn of 1986 and provided her own insights into what we saw happening. I thank her and also the late C.K. McClatchy and Gregory Favre of *The Bee* for their support and assistance.

Although I tried to make the series and the book as timely as possible, I knew that with California's fast-changing social landscape, they would become obsolescent eventually and I always envisioned an update sometime after the 1990 census, which would provide more timely data. This second edition is that update.

I revisited all of the regions of the state during the half-decade that followed publication of the first edition, although I didn't quite get back to every county. The results of those visists and additional data collection is a book that's about 50 percent longer than the first edition and, I believe, a more complete protrait of California.

Dan Walters
Sacramento
January 17, 1992

Introduction
By Larry L. Berg

W HEN VETERAN COLUMNIST AND AUTHOR, DAN WALTERS, FIRST AUTHORED *THE New California: Facing the 21st Century* in 1986, he wrote in the preface:

> ....it became evident, California had undergone an
> enormous socioeconomic change in the past generation
> and was looking at even more change in the future. A new
> kind of California was emerging but one that few in
> private or public life were acknowledging.

Less than six years later, there is a growing acknowledgment by some Californians of the changes, but the paralysis in the public and private sectors, noted in the first edition, continues. California voters still object to most tax increases that would provide revenue to help meet the challenges. They also have continued to vote for divided control of the legislative and executive branches of government with the accompanying partisan and personal bickering. In short, California in the 1990's continues to experience political gridlock and a lack of accountability, accompanied by increasing social, economic, and environmental challenges.

Fourteen of the chapters in this book deal with specific areas of the state. However, in every region, to a greater or lesser extent, the socioeconomic stratification discussed in the mid 1980's, is even more apparent in the 1990's. Whether in the gap between the overcrowded, unsafe housing of the poor and people of color in the inner cities and the proliferation of $1 million plus "guard-gated estates" for mostly whites in the outlying areas, or between the residences of the under-or-unemployed in rural timber and agricultural areas and the nearby vacation homes of the urban affluent, the author provides evidence of an emerging two-tier society.

Compounding the problem is the out-migration of predominantly affluent, middle-aged residents while the population continues to swell with younger immigrants from Mexico, Central and South America, and Asia. Additionally, the preponderance of births is now occurring in the non-anglo population. Walters states:

.... it may set the stage for a 21st century political climate that pits "haves" against "havenots," with the political middle declining along with the economic middle. Lewis Butler and Bruce Kelly of California Tomorrow...use a brash term to describe what is happening: segregation.

The changing demographics in California also have produced changing policy needs and growing disparities among the population in areas such as health and education. Walters points out that 20% of Calfiornia's 30 million people lack any kind of health insurance coverage. Although California contains 12% of the national population, this number represents 20% of the nation's uninsured. Not surprising, as Walters observes, the overall status of California's children has deteriorated. A quarter of the State's mothers are unwed and a disproportionate number of babies suffer low birth weights, drug addictions, and other preventable maladies. Vaccination rates are declining, and diseases which we thought had been eradicated, such as measles, are making a comeback.

Walters also suggests, correctly, that the projected population growth and its ethnic and racial makeup will place tremendous burdens on an already strained infrastructure. However, as our society grows more complex and revenue needs increase, the base of taxpayers shrinks, and California voters, predominately middle-class and middle-aged whites, become less and less representative of California's disparate population.

These are but a few examples of the dramatic transitions evolving in California which Dan Walters sets forth. Each of the chapters eloquently delineates the problems, and the potential for dealing with those problems, in the 13 political regions of the State. Taken together, the chapters constitutue a challenge to California and to all Californians to create a "..larger sense of command purpose out of social diversity."

Public officials, community leaders, concerned residents, and voters would do well to reflect on what Walters has so effectively described in this book. Perhaps it is time to examine the basic governmental structures and processes established in the 19th century. If they are found to be inadequate to meet the challenges facing California in the 1990's, they will surely fail the State in the rapidly approaching new century.

Although much of the national media's focus on California is what Peter Schrag, Walter's colleague at the *Sacramento Bee,* calls "...a seizure of doomed California Stories, Walters suggests that:

"There is some evidence that California's crushing social and economic problems are sinking in on both the State's civic leadership and the larger population."

If this is true, the challenges Dan Walters has presented in *The New California* may, once again, call forward those described decades earlier, by Carey McWilliams in *California: The Great Exception*, as "..men and women who can match, in the scale of their imagination and the depth of their insight, the extraordinary diversity, power, and challenge which is implicit in this immense and fabulous province which sprawls along the Pacific like a tawny tiger." And it, with their leadership, the people of California meet these challenges, perhaps the 21st century needs of the nation, with a changing population in which believers in Islam already outnumber Episcopalians, can also be met.

The New California:
Egalitarianism to stratification

CALIFORNIA HAD SCARCELY 2 MILLION CITIZENS IN 1909 WHEN LORD BRYCE, THE British ambassador to the United States, visited the state and asked a prophetic question:

"What will happen when California is filled by 50 millions of people and its valuation is five times what it is now? There will be more people—as many as the country can support—and the real question will be not about making more wealth or having more people, but whether the people will then be happier or better than they have been hitherto or are at this moment."

Eighty-plus years later, California is more than halfway toward that 50 million mark and has become America's most diverse, most populous and most economically, culturally and politically potent state with superpower-like impact that reaches around the globe.

But without knowing it, Californians are still seeking answers to Lord Bryce's question as they careen toward the 21st century, thrilled and frightened—sometimes simultaneously—by the economic and cultural currents sweeping through their state, without fully understanding causes and effects, sensing that what they experienced in the 1980s is merely a prelude to what is likely to happen in the 1990s and beyond.

From San Ysidro to Susanville, from Ventura to Volcano, from Moreno Valley to Moraga, no region of the state is being left untouched as California fashions a 21st century civilization like nothing ever seen on the North American continent, or perhaps in mankind's history—a more ethnically

7

complex society, a society of more distinct socioeconomic classes, a more competitive society, a more technologically sophisticated society, an older society, a more harried society and perhaps, unless a cadre of new civic and political leadership emerges, a society that loses its communal identity and evolves into a collection of mutually hostile tribes.

A once-powerful industrial economy, created during the emergency of World War II and later expanded to serve both Cold War and civilian demands, gave way to a post-industrial hybrid economy that rests on multiple bases and resembles that of a major nation more than that of a typical American state.

In a single generation, hundreds of lumber mills, auto and tire factories, steel plants, canneries, railroad yards, shipyards and other basic industries have closed their doors. Many of those that remain have downgraded their wage structures to meet foreign competition. Deregulation of trucking, telephone service and airlines has made them more competitive but has forced their employees to accept restructuring of wage scales downward. And the new industrial jobs that have been created, especially those in high-tech and services, are overwhelmingly non-union with non-professional wage scales in the sub-$12 per hour range.

At the same time, whole new industries emerged, based on trade with the burgeoning Pacific Rim nations, on highly sophisticated technology and on information, new industries that created 3 million jobs during the 1980s and allowed California to absorb a record increase in population while lowering its unemployment rate before a severe recession took told in 1990.

Within those twin trends, traditional industry's contraction and new industry's expansion, lie the seeds of socioeconomic stratification. Opportunities for the offpsring of the postwar industrial middle class have reduced, or at least become more contrasting. They and the young immigrants who continue to pour into California must either prepare themselves for expanding opportunities in technical, managerial, creative and professional fields or be content with relatively low-paying service industry jobs.

California's workforce, therefore, is being squeezed like a tube of toothpaste—an expanding overclass at the top, earning the $40,000-plus salaries, buying the homes, living the California good life, and an exploding underclass at the bottom, ill-educated, ill-served by overburdened social services, struggling to find affordable housing, forgoing medical care and seeing the doors of opportunity become more difficult to open, while the economic and social middle stagnates or even declines. And it is a change that is punctuated by the state's rapidly evolving ethnic structure, one in which today's minorities will soon become the collective majority, but the economic and social differences are likely to become more distinct as California continues to move away from the egalitarian ideal.

Economists Leon Bouvier and Philip Martin, in a mid-1980s peek into California's future for the Washington-based Population Reference Bureau, described that scenario as "the possible emerging of a two-tier economy with

Asians and non-Hispanic whites competing for high-status positions while Hispanics and blacks struggle to get the low-paying service jobs..."

"Since 1970," they noted, "employment growth has shifted from high-wage manufacturing and government sectors to the lower-wage trade and service firms that are most likely to hire unskilled immigrants...

"Large-scale immigration reinforces this two-tiered occupational structure because many immigrants eagerly accept low-wage jobs by comparing their first United States wages to the poverty and unemployment they experienced at home."

End-of-decade economic data verified their prediction. Between 1982 and 1990, California's manufacturers added about a quarter-million jobs, but the service and trade sectors created nearly 2 million. Between 1972 and 1989, manufacturing dropped from nearly 21 percent of the state's jobs to about 17 percent. Jobs at the lower end of the scale, $5,000 to $15,000 a year, and those at the upper end, $40,000 to $50,000 per year, grew two to three times faster than middle-income jobs, $25,000 to $30,000 per year. Increasingly, California families have achieved or clung to middle-class status only by merging paychecks of two or more workers—especially if they sought to buy homes in inflated urban or suburban markets.

"This tells the story of California in the 1980s," an analysis of 1990 census data by the state Office of Planning and Research concluded, "a continuing decline in older, heavy industry manufacturing—the kind of jobs once found in Oakland and San Francisco—and the increase in newer, high-technology manufacturing jobs—mostly in the suburbs and even in the exurbs."

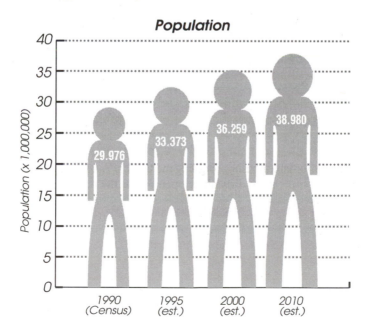

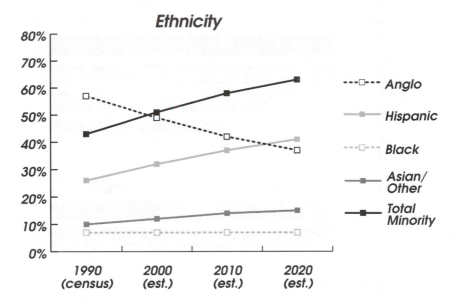

There are strong indications that these trends will continue in the 1990s as service and trade fields increase their dominance of the employment market and as manufacturing jobs continue to stagnate. The state Employment Development Department estimates that total California employment will increase by nearly one-third between 1987 and 2000, from 11.7 million to 15.4 million jobs, with above-average increases in trade, finance and services and sub-par growth in manufacturing, transportation, communication mining and government categories.

The Center for the Continuing Study of the California Economy is even more optimistic, seeing employment in the state approach 17.5 million by 2000 with job and personal income growth rates in the 1990s that are far above those of the nation as a whole and outstripping even population growth. In effect, these projections are that the economic and population explosions that occurred in California in the 1980s will be replicated in the 1990s, although the situation beyond 2000 is much cloudier.

"This is probably California's last great growth surge," said economist Stephen Levy of the Palo Alto-based economic study center. "It is entirely possible that the state's population, which will go from 30 million to 40 million in 20 years, may never reach the 50 million mark." Levy says that lower birth rates should slow California's population growth after 2010.

There is, however, some dissenting view among economists who believe that California peaked out in the 1980s and now faces a bleak economic future because of its deteriorating infrastructure and a competitive posture vis-a-vis other states and nations. They have noted a seemingly accelerated abandonment of California by major employers—especially manufacturers—who shift or expand plants in other states and nations because of California's above-average operational costs. Several states have set up recruiting offices in California with the specific mission of luring away payroll-heavy employers by offering lower taxes and labor and fringe benefit costs.

George Salem, a banking analyst for Prudential Securities, created a stir in California economic circles in 1991 when he circulated a report suggesting that the state "shows new evidence of structural weakness" and could face the kind of severe economic dislocation that struck Massachusetts and Texas during the 1980s.

"In short," he wrote, "a long era of growth and prosperity has ended in California."

At the time that Salem delivered his startling verdict, the state was experiencing a severe recession with unemployment having jumped more than two percentage points since the go-go days of the 1980s. During the first year of the recession, from mid-1990 to mid-1991, the state lost an astonishing 380,000 jobs—roughly a year's employment growth during the expansive years of the 1980s. And despite the recession, which economists said was exacerbated by such localized factors as a record freeze and cutbacks in military procurement spending, California continued to experience huge levels of migration and child birth that drove its population upward by some 800,000 persons a year, thus raising doubts whether the state could continue to absorb newcomers or would face a future of continued economic uncertainty.

At the very least, the recession accelerated the evolution from an industrial to a post-industrial economy and thus the stratification of California society. The physical clues of an emerging two-tier society already are evident in California, especially in the larger metropolitan areas.

And if it happens, it may set the stage for a 21st century political climate that pits haves against have-nots with the political middle declining along with the economic middle and both major parties being compelled to realign themselves to the new socioeconomic reality. Lewis Butler and Bruce Kelley of California Tomorrow, an organization devoted to worrying about California's future, used a harsh term to describe what is happening: segregation.

"Only if more and more people of different classes, colors and cultures choose...to live, work and go to school together can California reverse its divided fate," they wrote in the organization's magazine in 1989.

The data of change, gleaned from a variety of public and private sources, are staggering:

California's population, less than 16 million in 1960, grew by nearly 50 percent to 23.8 million by 1980, hit 30 million by 1990 and is expected to top 36 million by 2000 and climb to more than 40 million by 2010.

The Anglo population (what demographers call "non-Hispanic white") is virtually stagnant with little in-migration from other states and a less-than-replacement birth rate among Anglo women. In fact, the Anglo population may begin to decline before the turn of the century and the low Anglo birth rate means that its portion of the population is growing older faster than others, with median age at least 15 years higher already than the non-Anglo population.

Some three-quarters of the near-term population growth and nearly all longer-term growth are among Hispanics and Asians. There is a continual flow of Asians into the state, with Filipinos comprising the largest single sub-group and likely to increase even more if the Philippines are wracked by long-term political dissension. California already is home to more than a third of the Asians who live in the United States and the proportion of Californians who have Asian ancestry swelled from 4 percent to 10 percent in just a decade, replacing blacks as the state's third-largest major ethnic group.

The Hispanic population, meanwhile, is being expanded by a high level of legal and illegal immigration from Latin America, mostly Mexico, and a birth rate that is nearly twice that of Anglos. Demographers expect the continued political unrest and economic chaos in Latin America to push millions of Latino immigrants across a porous border into California and even economic reform in Mexico will not have a major impact on that trend for years.

The black population is relatively stagnant, fixed at under 8 percent of the total; it's not shrinking but grows only at the rate of the overall population.

Sometime before 2000, perhaps as early as 1996, California will become what a former black lieutenant governor, Mervyn Dymally, called a "Third World state" in which Anglos will be a minority for the first time—a decade earlier than demographers had expected in the mid-1980s.

A generation later, Hispanics and Anglos will be about equal in population, approximately 38 percent each.

Despite an evening-out of population among the state's large ethnic groups, there are growing disparities in education and economic attainment. Hispanics and blacks are far more likely to drop out of high school and less likely to obtain college educations than either Anglos or Asians, thereby becoming less able to compete for the well-paying professional and technical jobs that California is continuing to produce. The state, some demographers believe, may experience a labor shortage in skilled fields in the early 21st century.

With high birth rates among recent immigrants, the overall status of California's children has deteriorated markedly in recent years. A quarter of California's mothers are unwed and disproportionately high numbers of newborn babies suffer from low birth weights, drug addictions and other maladies and as vaccination rates for children decline, once-conquered childhood diseases such as measles are staging alarming comebacks.

Some 20 percent of California's 30 million residents lack any kind of health insurance coverage, either private or public. Those 6 million uninsured Californians are also about 20 percent of the nation's total, even though the state contains just over 12 percent of the American population.

But the signs of change are to be found in more than numbers. They are to be found in the changing California landscape.

They are found in such places as Moreno Valley, a small community in the semi-desert in Riverside County, which was the state's fastest-growing county in the 1980s.

Moreno Valley just became a city in the mid-1980s and within a few months had a population of more than 100,000, mostly young families who had bought into dozens of subdivisions that bloomed in the sandy soil, a growth so dramatic that it brought nationwide media attention. It was dramatically graphic evidence of one of the most important social trends of the 1980s, a dispersal of the economy and population from the coastal enclaves to the interior valleys and hills. Interior California is growing faster than coastal California and what were small towns a generation ago have blossomed into small cities.

That phenomenon was fueled, in part, by the changes in the economy, especially the advent of portable jobs in burgeoning technical and service fields, jobs that are not dependent on proximity to raw materials or even to transportation centers, jobs that can be moved out of the traditional urban employment centers and into the suburbs, thus allowing their workers to move even further into the countryside as they seek more pleasant surroundings and less expensive housing. The evolution of California's internal Sun Belt—employment centers in the older suburbs that evolved after World War II, such as Orange County in the south and Contra Costa County in the north and new residential suburbs even further inland—has created its own backlash of resentment among those who moved there first to get away from congestion.

The move to the interior is evident from Escondido in northern San Diego through San Bernardino and Riverside counties to the Central Valley as far north as Redding.

It is largely, however, a movement of Anglos. And it contributes, as do continued high rates of immigration from other nations, to radical social surgery on the face of California's cities. As whites flee the cities, their places are taken by the new immigrants who are packing themselves ever more densely into stocks of housing that are not expanding.

Los Angeles, the new American melting pot, lost 500,000 Anglos between 1970 and 1980 and is headed for a 60 percent Hispanic population by the turn of the century. There are more than 100 separate languages spoken at Los Angeles area schools, three-fourths of them at Hollywood High School alone.

San Francisco, once a polyglot, is becoming a Beverly Hills-like enclave of the Anglo-Asian affluent, driving its middle classes to the suburbs and its blacks across the bay to Oakland by development policies favoring high-income professionals.

One-time farm towns of the Central Valley are diversifying their economies and flirting with metropolitan status.

But the movement to the interior and the arrival of immigrants, the twin demographic phenomena, are not being universally experienced. Whole regions of the state, especially those north of the San Francisco-Sacramento axis, have seen their basic industries of timber and agriculture decline and nothing emerge to replace them. They are seeing economic and social stagnation that forces their young to flee to the growing areas for economic opportunity. One facet of California's stratification is a growing socioeconomic gap not only between those booming Sun Belts and older cities, but between Sun Belt areas and the rural outback.

The growth in and changing composition of California's population during the next 30 to 40 years will put an incredible strain on transportation systems, water supplies, sewage treatment, housing supply, educational facilities—what those in the public policy trade call "infrastructure." The California Economic Development Corp. has warned that without a massive overhaul of transportation policies, traffic congestion will increase by 15 percent a year.

Local officials throughout the state, especially in high-growth areas, already are feeling the strain and are being compelled to take extraordinary steps to deal with it. But as they and state officials seek the billions of dollars needed to build and staff public facilities, they collide with another phenomenon that evolved in 1980s California: the resistance to new taxes among voters who are themselves not representative of the diverse new California but carryovers from an earlier era. At the precise moment that California's political leaders confront a society that grows more complex as it grows numerically, California's voters are numerically stagnant, overwhelmingly white, middle-aged and middle class with conservative attitudes towards taxes, first felt with the passage of Proposition 13 in 1978 but still being expressed in the 1990s.

The effect of these twin, contradictory pressures is to contribute to the political confusion and deadlock that marked the 1980s.

Politicians explicitly fear voter backlash if they propose new government programs, or even if they push to supplement old programs feeling the pressures from expanded caseload. And both the state and local governments have direct restraints on spending imposed by a Proposition 13 aftermath, approved by voters in 1979 and modified only slightly in 1990.

The Legislature, moreover, has become preoccupied with internal power struggles and a series of image-bending scandals. Both it and the governor of the 1980s, Republican George Deukmejian, seemed disinterested in dealing with the far-reaching public policy issues that dynamic socioeconomic change creates and instead they played games of political one-upsmandship. That led to an explosion of initiative ballot measures that also contributed to the state's political paralysis. As the 1990s dawned, many were openly saying that California may have become ungovernable, at least in traditional terms.

That was what Stu Spencer, a veteran Republican political strategist, told U.S. Sen. Pete Wilson when Wilson, fresh off a Senate re-election victory in 1988, began thinking about running for governor in 1990. But Wilson, pressured by state and national Republican leaders to run and keep the Capitol in GOP hands for the all-critical reapportionment that was to follow the 1990

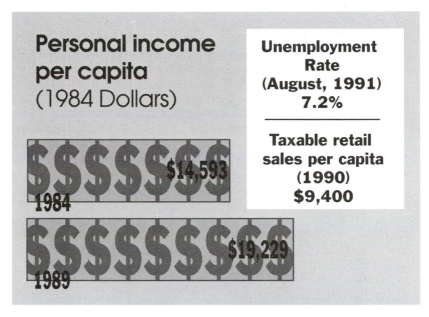

Personal income per capita (1984 Dollars)

$$$$$$$$ $14,593
1984

$$$$$$$$$ $19,229
1989

Unemployment Rate (August, 1991) 7.2%

Taxable retail sales per capita (1990) $9,400

Graphic courtesy *The California Journal*

census, decided to run anyway.

Wilson had a clear shot at the Republican nomination but there was a monumental battle beween Dianne Feinstein, the former mayor of San Francisco, and Attorney General John Van de Kamp for the Democratic nod. Feinstein, who had almost withdrawn from the campaign, came from behind to win on the strength of a brilliant media strategy, settng up a runoff struggle between two centrists who, until 1990, had been close political allies. Wilson won, albeit by a small margin, as the state's voters continued to demonstrate their top-of-the-ticket preference for Republican candidates. But the fact that both candidates came from the political middle—in some respects, interestingly, Wilson was to the left of Feinstein—indicated that voters yearned for new leadership that would tackle California's mounting social problems, not merely engage in ideological battles or indulge personal ambitions, as recent governors had done.

Wilson came into office in 1991 with a gritty determination to make California's government work again by such steps as shifting emphasis from remedial to preventive in education and social services and proposing a first-ever statewide growth management program aimed at bringing some order to the state's chaotic development patterns. But Wilson faced a monstrous state budget crisis born of recession and of a decade of ignoring the conflict between anti-tax fever and huge levels of population growth, and a Legislature that was beset by scandal and torn apart by factional and partisan infighting.

As the traditional forms of governance lock up, what may be emerging is a new form of quasi-public, quasi-private governance in which local economic and civic interests, working in concert with local governments, create new vehicles for the improvement of infrastructure.

In Santa Clara County, for example, the high-tech industry supported a successful drive to persuade local voters to raise sales taxes to finance better highways after it became apparent that more aid would not be forthcoming from Sacramento. Dozens of other counties followed suit and in a rare major policy action in the Capitol, Deukmejian and legislators agreed on a comprehensive transportation financing plan and saw it enacted by voters in 1990.

Bond issues, lease-purchase contracts and other forms of creative financing have been used by local officials to finance infrastructure improvements.

But as with other aspects of California culture, it's widening the gap between the haves and the have-nots and lessening the sense of broader community that, while never highly developed in such a mobile, immigrant-populated state, had propelled post-World War II policy-makers to enact sweeping public works programs.

Affluent, growing areas can afford to make such improvements while poor areas with stagnant economies cannot. In 21st century California, what kind of highways serve motorists, how crowded the schools, how dependable the water supply may depend on where one lives.

The incipient division of California into a two-tier society is evident in other ways too. Markets catering to upscale yuppies and warehouse-style operations catering to the masses are thriving while the ordinary supermarket is disappearing in many communities.

The demands of affluent parents for better elementary and high school education got results in Sacramento. New laws were passed that toughen high school graduation requirements and provide the money to meet them. But California has continued to lag behind in its overall educational performance, especially in services to the non-affluent, non-Anglo and non-English speakers, as it struggled to cope with record growth in school enrollment. By 1990, the average Latino adult in California had three fewer years of education than Anglo, Asian or black adults and Pacific Bell has reported a 68 percent failure rate on its test for prospective operators—a test that is geared to an eighth-grade education.

Dropout rates among minorities showed little, if any improvement in the 1980s, and tougher graduation requirements do nothing for those who couldn't meet the old ones. The community college system, once California's traditional educational ladder for the economically disadvantaged, drifted in the 1980s, a victim of post-Proposition 13 budget restraints and a seeming lack of purpose. Finally, in the late 1980s, there was an effort to revive the system and redirect it back to its original purpose, but no one was certain the reforms would work.

Although California's minority population is growing faster than the

Anglo population, the state's public and private universities and colleges remain bastions of Anglo and Asian aspirations.

Hispanics, now more than 25 percent of the population, represented less than 10 percent of the undergraduate enrollment at the University of California in 1988 while blacks were less than 5 percent and both numbers were even lower among graduate students. Asians were nearly 30 percent of UC's undergraduate enrollment, three times their proportion of the overall population.

California "is at a crossroads where we must make certain we include all parts of this family in this state in its educational system or else we will be setting an example that everyone else will follow in this country," said Joshua Smith, former chancellor of the state's community college system.

"It appears to me that we're moving into a de facto educational apartheid," Assemblyman Tom Hayden, D-Santa Monica, said during a 1985 legislative hearing into educational trends.

Little occurred in the ensuing years to change the situation and in some respects it got worse as the budget squeeze hit the schools. By 1990, California was spending about $4,000 per year on each student, slightly more than half of what New York was spending. Private school enrollments have soared, meanwhile, as affluent white and Asian parents abandoned the troubled public school system.

Keith Pailthorp of the California Postsecondary Education Commission co-authored a report on the near future of education in the state and concluded that, "We're going to end up with a less-educated generation of young people. And it is this generation that must drive the marvelous machine that we call California. It's a serious message. We're saying that we think something should be done."

California's public schools, anticipating the change that will occur in the larger population a decade later, acquired a non-Anglo student population in the late 1980s even as they absorbed growth rates that approached 200,000 a year—rates that required the construction of 20 new classrooms every 24 hours and billions of new dollars for teachers and other support activities.

But the public school system is producing widely disparate results.

According to the California Postsecondary Education System, only 3.6 percent of 1985's black high school graduates and 4.9 percent of Hispanic high school graduates were eligible for University of California admission—while 13 percent of Anglo graduates and 26 percent of Asians were qualified.

Asians, even those who only recently migrated from Southeast Asia, are doing very well in the state's schools—a byproduct, sociologists believe, of the Asian cultural impetus to excel that may be missing from other minorities.

"I believe what is happening now to Asian students is like what happened to Jewish students in the '20s and '30s," said UC-Santa Cruz history professor Sucheng Chan. "In the case of both Jewish and Asian students, the fear comes not because they're perceived as inferior, but because they're perceived as too smart, too successful...that they might take over."

Indeed, the high levels of Asian enrollment in the UC system led to demands that it be depressed and that more slots be set aside for Hispanics and blacks. The pressure became even more intense in 1991 when UC officials, citing budget constraints, cut overall enrollment by several thousand students by raising admission requirements.

The high level of Asian education and economic achievement, markedly above those of the population as a whole, has led many demographers to see them as part of an Anglo-Asian overclass that will dominate California's two-tier society of the 21st century.

And if the elementary and high schools become dominated by Hispanic and black students while an aging and stagnant Anglo population produces relatively few school-age children—and sends many of them to private schools—it's questionable whether the overclass will be willing to invest the money in public school buildings, teachers' salaries and other operational expenses. One poll taken for the California Teachers Association indicates that older, white voters are less supportive of public education than other groups; by one estimate, fewer than 20 percent of California voters are parents of public school students and the percentage is declining.

Some Hispanic and black leaders fear that public education—and especially programs geared to the needs of their children—will be neglected in the 21st century by a dominant class that has little direct interest in it. Indeed, some see Proposition 13 and its anti-government, anti-tax aftershocks as the first indications of growing disinterest.

Because of Proposition 13 and other legal restrictions on fiscal policy, because of the professionalization of the Legislature, because of rising partisanship and, most of all, because of the daunting pressures from population growth and socioeconomic change, the Capitol in the 1980s evolved into a place of political gridlock in which the petty concerns of internal politics came to dominate the more pressing matters of the real world. In the largest context, political leaders could not simultaneously meet the needs of the state's large and diverse population and obey the mandates of its politically active and somewhat conservative middle and upper-middle classes. That tension, which increased steadily during the decade, resulted in an explosion of ballot measures whose fate, both positive and negative, did little to clarify the situation. The Capitol remained paralyzed, beset by factional and partisan infighting, and discredited because of a series of corruption scandals, and voters demonstrated their disgust in 1990 by passing a tight limit on the terms that legislators can serve, a symbolic and perhaps actual retreat from the professional Legislature that voters had sanctioned a generation earlier.

If California is evolving into a two-tier society as present trends indicate, it will have vast political consequences.

There seems to be an overall swing toward conservatism and the Republican Party in California already.

No Democratic presidential candidate won in California between 1964 and 1988 and as measured by other statewide elections, a conservative-GOP tilt emerged in the late 1970s and early 1980s and continued to assert itself in elections throughout the decade, culminating in George Bush's California victory in 1988 and Pete Wilson's in 1990.

As the state was voting overwhelmingly for Ronald Reagan's re-election in 1984, for example, it also was giving a plurality of its votes to Republican congressional candidates—despite the fact that a partisan congressional redistricting plan enacted in 1982 handed firm control of the congressional delegation to Democrats.

Pollster Mervin Field reported in 1985 that his survey of voter identification showed the GOP having drawn even with the Democrats for the first time in recent history, and that, too, held firm as the 1980s evolved into the 1990s. Democratic voter registration, which approached 60 percent in the mid-1970s, slipped below 50 percent for the first time in more than 50 years.

What seems to be happening is that Anglo voters and middle- to upper-income Asians and Hispanics are identifying more strongly with the Republican Party. And while they may be outnumbered in the overall population, they are most likely to be politically active—to register and vote.

Lower-income Hispanics and Asians are not participating in California's political process. Asians have the overall lowest levels of political activity of any ethnic group; by 1990, they were 10 percent of the state's population but scarcely 2 percent to 3 percent of the dependable voters. Blacks are more politically active—and identify overwhelmingly with the Democratic Party—but they are a stagnant or even declining portion of the state's population. The industrial middle class, the traditional backbone of the Democratic Party, is shrinking because of economic changes.

These trends create a huge dilemma for the Democratic Party that it has not been willing to face as yet. It probably will continue to decline, drifting into minority status, unless it either woos back the disaffected middle- and upper-income voters who are realigning themselves with the Republicans or organizes the state's burgeoning underclass.

Either strategy is fraught with peril.

To appeal to the overclass, it would have to move its ideological identity to the right, putting more stress on such themes as crime control and economic development and less on providing government programs to the poor. In doing that, it would, in effect, have to turn its back on some of its most active current consti-u-encies and the liberal ideological bent of its current leaders. But to organize the un-organized also is perilous. It would run the risk of further alienating Anglo, middle-income voters and it would face enormous barriers of language, non-citizenship and a lack of political tradition among newly arrived immigrants. Such a massive organizational effort, too, would be hampered by a lack of traditional tools.

Earlier waves of European immigrants—Italians, Irish, Poles, Jews—became politically influential in such places as New York and Chicago because the political systems in those areas were heavy with patronage. Politicians could promise those blocs something specific in return for their votes. But the political reform movement that swept through California in the early 20th century made local offices non-partisan and eliminated virtually all patronage by creating strong civil service systems. And constitutional constraints make it almost impossible to launch vast new government programs. If California politicians try to organize the state's underclass, therefore, they will be hard-put to offer any tangible rewards—jobs, programs or status.

The state's Democrats have been unable to decide on either course—or any course—to stem their party's erosion of position. They have preserved their control over the Legislature and the state's congressional delegation by artificial means such as gerrymandered districts (that also froze out minority aspirations as they preserved Anglo Democrats in office) and voter registration laws that create a false picture of partisan alignment by leaving non-voters on the rolls.

With its series of losses in top-of-the-ticket contests, the Democratic Party continues to debate its future without coming to a conclusion. Ex-Gov. Jerry Brown became state party chairman in 1989 on the promise to expand the ranks of its voters, but despite spending millions of dollars he saw Democratic voter ranks continue to drop and he dropped out himself to re-enter electoral politics with a third bid for the White House. Brown has suggested that the party needs to move to the populist/left with new organizational drives aimed at minorities and dispossessed Anglos while other party leaders, such as 1990 gubernatorial candidate Feinstein, believe that it must become more centrist and appeal to defecting middle-class voters.

As the Democrats debate, there are unmistakable signs that the long-term drift to the right in California politics will make itself fully felt in the 1990s, especially if the reapportionment of legislative and congressional districts cannot be skewed by either party. And the election of Republican Wilson to the governorship meant that Democrats could not control the process as fully as they did after the 1980 census.

The most likely political scenario for California in the 1990s and at least the early years of the 21st century is for dominance by an affluent, politically active overclass using its position to protect its privileges against the larger but weaker underclass. It's a social situation that benefits the Republican Party, which itself has undergone a quiet evolution into a decidedly more moderate institution as it has expanded its reach. That shift is personified by Wilson, the one-time party pariah for his centrist views who won a U.S. Senate seat in 1982, re-election in 1988 and then retained the governorship for the GOP in 1990. If the Wilsonite philosophy—tough on crime, conservative on taxes and spending, and liberal on abortion and environmental issues—becomes the dominant image of the Republican Party, Democrats may be doomed to minority party status in the nation's largest state.

Evolving political power, however, is just one aspect, and probably not the most important one, of a unique culture that continually redefines itself as it expands and diversifies. Clearly, some of California's golden sheen has been tarnished by its social and economic complexities: tangled freeways, high housing prices, rising fear of crime and congested public facilities. A 1989 attitudinal poll by the Field Institute revealed a sharp drop in Californians' sense of pride about living in the state. In previous polls, about 75 percent of those responding had rated California "one of the best places to live." But the 1989 poll saw that drop to under 60 percent—a finding that coincided with the onset of a significant migration of Californians to other Western states, especially from Southern California, where pessimism was found by the Field poll to be the strongest.

There is some evidence that California's crushing social and economic problems are sinking in on both the state's civic leadership and the larger population. Newspapers have begun, belatedly, to explore the unpredictable evolution of their state through detailed articles that go beyond the daily events, although most television stations continue to feed their viewers steady diets of tabloid-style crime and sleaze and, if anything, have reduced their coverage of politics and public policy.

Cadres of civic leaders have been formed, both statewide and at regional and local levels, to explore workable approaches to such pithy issues as education, water, growth and, most of all, rising levels of social friction. Splashy blue- ribbon reports laying out developmental scenarios for the 21st century have been produced in both Los Angeles and San Francisco, laying the groundwork for regional governments. One statewide blue-ribbon commission of business leaders called for a "new societal compact" aimed at creating a larger sense of communal purpose out of social diversity.

Seminars on California's future have become staples in the state's colleges and universities with the promise of putting arguably the planet's most concentrated brainpower to work on home-grown issues that had hitherto been ignored. But all of these efforts are just beginnings. None has resulted yet in concrete policies that would materially mitigate what many see as an apocalyptic future for the state.

"California is just entering what may be its most crucial decades since the Mexican War ended in the 1840s," Bouvier and Martin conclude in their study of the state.

"The state will never be the same; yet, as with the nation, it remains unfinished. This could have been said in the 19th century, however. The important question is: How will the state adjust to these demographic changes and all their repercussions?"

It's a question whose answer, if anything, is becoming more elusive.

Los Angeles:
Dreams and Extremes

You can say anything about Los Angeles and it's true.

It's a pulsating metropolitan monster that will surpass New York to become the nation's largest supercity by the turn of the century.

It's the cultural arbiter of the world, emitting a torrent of music albums, movies and television shows that enthrall millions—and entice them into believing in a land of make-believe.

It's a place where the fictional violence of the movie screen is often surpassed by the real violence of the streets, where drug gangs wearing different-colored headbands stage nightly firefights, where 2,000 people die violently each year.

It's the new American melting pot, a fifth of whose population was born in another nation and whose schools try to educate children speaking more than 100 separate languages.

It's a place where entertainment idols, masters of the financial universe and fabulously wealthy refugees from the world's revolutions live in sybaritic splendor. And it's a place where poor, undocumented aliens live 10 to a room, dodge immigration agents and provide the cheap labor for the restaurants, hotels, sweatshops—and the homes of the rich on the other side of town.

It's a city that began as a frontier outpost of the Spanish empire and centuries later is becoming the most Hispanic of the nation's large cities—as much as 60 percent by the early 21st century.

It's the place that invented freeways, demonstrated that it's possible to create a metropolitan conglomerate without a distinct downtown core and exported that questionable urban model to the rest of California and the rest of the nation.

It's a land of dreams and a land of extremes, a throbbing monument to mankind's urge to reshape the environment, to abandon the old and to embrace the new.

It's the butt of comedians' jokes. It's the envy of the world. It's loved and hated in equal measure, even by those who live there.

And it's the engine that is propelling California into the uncharted reaches of the 21st century.

On a more prosaic level, Los Angeles is the unofficial capital of Southern California, a region that encompasses only seven of the state's 58 counties but which has what economists regard as the most diverse and dynamic economy of any region on Earth.

The economic output of the region is second only to that of the New York area in the United States and if Southern California were a separate nation, its gross national product would rank 13th in the world, slightly smaller than those of India and Spain but larger than Mexico's, Australia's or Poland's.

It contains a fourth of the Western states' population and accounts for half of California's employment, 60 percent of its manufacturing output and two-thirds of its international trade.

"Currently," said a 1980s planning report issued by the Southern California Association of Governments (SCAG), "the regional economy is undergoing one of its frequent (one might argue that it is perpetual) periods of change and transformation.

"No longer do we fit our traditional, prewar image as the land of orange groves, oil wells, motion pictures and sunny beaches. Similarly, the Southern California of the 1950s and 1960s—booming, low-cost housing development, sprawling aircraft plants, highly mechanized truck farms and freeway network expansion—has been altered over the past decade to create a 'new' economy."

The new economy of Southern California, centered in Los Angeles but evident throughout the region, is based on electronics, high-tech research and development—much of it defense-related—and what SCAG calls "an explosively expanding service base—particularly in finance, retail trade, medical and professional services and information technologies." The three largest private employers in the region are high-tech electronics and aerospace firms and there's been a marked upgrading of Los Angeles' standing as a center for art and industrial design. Japanese and American auto manufacturers have established design studios in Southern California even as the last auto production plant in the area shuts down.

Surprisingly, too, there's been an eruption of very low-tech manufacturing that uses immigrant labor, at least some of it illegal, to produce clothes, furniture and other products in hundreds of small factories. "In effect, Los Angeles is emerging as a garment manufacturing center, not because New

York has moved westward, but because Hong Kong and Singapore have moved eastward," a 1991 state Office of Planning and Research report noted. "The 'third world' is coming here and it is finding employment at corresponding skill levels."

During the last generation, the expansion of Southern California as a financial center has clearly downgraded the state's traditional financial capital, San Francisco, into second place, a shift symbolized by the southward movement of the Pacific Stock Exchange and physically represented by the high-rise financial towers along Wilshire Boulevard.

During the period that the Wilshire Corridor was becoming the financial capital of the Western United States and earning a reputation for fast dealing which sent some of its icons, such as Michael Milken, to prison, Los Angeles itself was undergoing still another chapter in its two-century history of cultural and socioeconomic change.

It is a history of migration, beginning with Spanish explorers and Catholic

Focus on Los Angeles

Area .... 4,079.3 sq. miles
Percentage of California 2.5%

Population
(with percentage of California total)

	1960	1970	1980	1990	2000	2005
Los Angeles Co.	6,071,900	7,055,800	7,490,400	8,863,164	9,9976,200	10,429,900
CALIFORNIA	38.3%	35.2%	31.2%	29.8%	27.5%	26.8%

Ethnic composition
(1990 Census)

	Anglo	Latino	Asian/Pacific	Black
Los Angeles Co.	40.8%	37.8%	10.2%	10.5%
CALIFORNIA	57.2%	25.8%	9.1%	7%

Economic Data

	Unemployment rate (Aug. 1991)	Taxable sales (1990 per capita)	Personal income (per capita) 1984	Personal income (per capita) 1989
Los Angeles Co.	8.5%	$10,718	$15,131	$19,600
CALIFORNIA	7.2%	$9,400	$14,593	$19,229

Political data

	1964	1972	1980	1984	1988
Voter registration (Democrat-Republican)	58-38%	57-35%	58-32%	57-34%	55-35%
Presidential vote (Democrat-Republican)	57-43%	43-57%	41-51%	45-55%	53-47%

Sources: State Department of Finance, 1990 Census, employment Development Department, Board of Equalization, Center for Continuing Study of the California Economy and the Secretary of State's office.

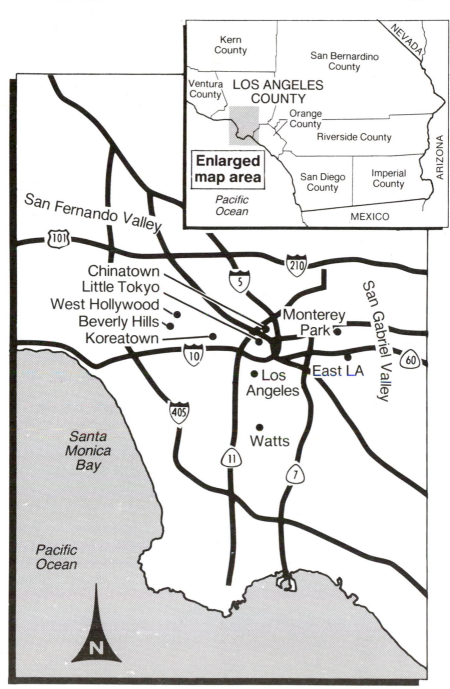

Graphic courtesy *The Sacramento Bee*

missionaries who founded a slow-moving agricultural society, through an invasion of Anglos in the late 19th century and the arrival of Asians to work the fields and blacks to work the factories to the waves of immigrants from Latin America, seeking refuge from political and economic upheaval.

It's also a history of dramatic events with far-reaching effects, such as the collective decision of mostly Jewish pioneers in the infant motion picture industry to relocate themselves from New York and New Jersey to the sunny weather of Southern California, a world war that created an aircraft industry almost overnight or the robber baron-like acquisition of water in the distant Owens Valley to support land development and population growth.

No one really planned Los Angeles. Indeed, arid, without a natural harbor and with few other resources, it is outwardly a poor site for a great city. It just happened to be where Spanish padres located another in their string of outposts to serve the local Indian population and promote agriculture, no less or more important than any other mission.

By the early 20th century, with California having become part of the United States, Los Angeles was a pleasant, medium-sized city with a distinctly conservative, Midwestern demeanor. Businessmen, many of them involved in land speculation, ran the city and they were interested only in public policies that served their economic interests, such as the development of distant water sources to supplement the scant local supplies. Minorities and the poor were discouraged from living in Los Angeles and treated harshly if they persisted.

No one objected in 1936, for example, when city officials dispatched police officers to create a "bum brigade" on the state's borders, physically turning back refugees from the Dust Bowl—a clearly unconstitutional practice. Nor were there many local objections when Japanese-Americans were uprooted from their homes for internment during World War II. Local businessmen rushed in to acquire the internees' properties for cents on the dollar.

Union membership was discouraged in the city's burgeoning industries— sometimes physically—leaving Los Angeles with one of the lowest unionization rates of any major city and the unions politically weak.

The evolution of Los Angeles into a polyglot of dozens of racial and ethnic groups is a fairly recent development. Its population expansion during the early- and mid-20th century had been fueled by migration, but mostly of white Americans from other states who maintained the city's conservative ambience.

Some of the immigration went into the city itself, the rest into suburban communities that eventually grew together into one uninterrupted, sprawling megalopolis, expanding into Orange and Ventura counties and, in more recent years, to San Bernardino and Riverside counties. They are, in effect, the buroughs of one continuous city that's nearly 100 miles long and 75 miles wide, even though their residents try to separate themselves from Los Angeles by postal designation or city limit lines.

Los Angeles was—and still mostly is—a low-rise city. Even public housing in the black ghettos and Hispanic barrios is only a few stories high. Los

Angeles grew out rather than up and transportation became the key to its ability to function. A once-extensive system of trolley cars was acquired and obliterated by bus manufacturers to create an instant market for their products, a momentous development, albeit one that was little-noticed at the time, and one that was fictionally chronicled nearly a half-century later in the animated motion picture "Who Killed Roger Rabbit?" Freeways—beginning in 1940 with the still-functioning Pasadena Freeway—were devised to meet the demand for personal transportation and eventually 1,700 miles of freeway were built in the region as tract after tract of weedy field was transformed into houses, factories and commercial centers.

The freeways and 13,500 miles of surface streets in Southern California are home to more than 7 million cars and 3,000 buses that travel more than 200 million miles each day. But there is more demand for transportation than the freeway system can manage, resulting in legendary, hours-long traffic jams that worsen by the minute and a serious air pollution problem. The Southern California Association of Governments has estimated that freeway congestion in the region will increase fivefold by 2010 from 1990 levels if current trends hold and the average freeway speed will drop from 35 miles per hour to 19 mph. Local leaders are trying to re-create the light rail system that once had 1,100 miles of track in the area, but it's expensive and faces resistance from motorists who would prefer to see highway improvements. Only one major highway project, the Century Freeway, has even been attempted in the past generation and it has become an sinkhole for hundreds of millions of dollars without, as yet, carrying a single car. Much of the money went not into concrete but into compensating thousands of mostly poor residents for the loss of their homes—an illustration of why freeway expansion in Los Angeles cannot even begin to keep up with transportation demand.

Although Anglos dominated Los Angeles and the surrounding region through most of the 20th century, significant pockets of minorities evolved.

Blacks, many of whom came to Los Angeles to work in war industries in the 1940s, settled in south-central Los Angeles, which became known as Watts. The descendants of farm laborers who migrated from Mexico re-established a strong Hispanic presence in East Los Angeles and there were small Asian enclaves in "Chinatown" and "Little Tokyo," both near a downtown that was noteworthy mostly for its complete lack of any distinguishing characteristics. There are tens of thousands of Angelenos who have been born, lived and died without ever once visiting downtown Los Angeles.

Somewhere along the line, Los Angeles changed from what it had been to what it became and many mark the beginning of change as Aug. 11, 1965, when Watts erupted in rioting after a black man was arrested by a white state Highway Patrol officer. During the five nights of rioting, a 50-square-mile section of the city became a combat zone in which National Guardsmen and police battled with rock- and bottle-throwing young blacks. It was the nation's first big urban riot of the 1960s and left 34 people dead and property damage estimated at $40 million.

Los Angeles has always had a reputation for toughness, one chronicled in countless private eye novels and movies and, until a 1950s reform movement, its police department was noted for both brutality and corruption. The corruption was repressed but the steely, occupation-army relationship of the police department and racial minorities continued. When a black man, Rodney King, was savagely beaten by police and the incident was captured on videotape, it shocked the nation, but to many Angelenos, it was just another in a long string of incidents that symbolized the city's racial polarization and the violence that had become an endemic part of its street life.

The wounds of the Watts riots are still evident, although there have been superficial efforts at civic betterment. And if anything, the underlying conditions of poverty have grown worse as employment opportunities have slipped away to the suburbs. The black population of Los Angeles actually declined in the 1980s, the census revealed, and remains largely confined to the south-central part of the city, and unemployment remains above 20 percent—three times that of the region as a whole.

A black man who was born in the area and left to become a college sports star and a policeman, Tom Bradley, rose to the mayor's office in the early 1970s as a direct result of the post-riot alliance of blacks and white liberals. But he faced the ironic fact that the wave of political reform that swept over California in the early 20th century made it difficult for him or any other political figure to change socioeconomic conditions by political organization. And he confronted a structural reality not faced by other major city mayors: the schools and most social services are not operated by the city, but by independent school districts and the powerful county government.

Indeed, Bradley's great achievements were not in Watts but in downtown Los Angeles, which has sprouted a skyline of high-rise hotels and office buildings. And while the black population of Los Angeles has remained relatively stagnant, that of Hispanics has increased dramatically, which has produced some competition between the city's two largest ethnic groups for political attention, housing and jobs. In recent years, even large parts of Watts have become Hispanic in flavor as immigration and high birth rates swelled populations that pushed outward from East Los Angeles. In the 1980s, the city's Latino population soared by nearly 71 percent to 1.4 million, nearly three times as great as Los Angeles' black population. Compton was a 75 percent black city in 1980 but blacks were only 55 percent of Compton's population by 1990 while Hispanics had increased from 23 to 44 percent.

Asians, too, are making their presence known outside of the traditional downtown enclaves with a population that jumped by more than 65 percent in the 1980s. An area west of downtown now is known as "Koreatown" for its large population of immigrants from that Asian peninsula. And to the east, what had been an Anglo suburb and then an Hispanic suburb, Monterey Park, has become a suburb of middle-class Asians fighting over whether business signs should be required to be printed in English.

The outflow of Anglos to the suburbs or out of the county altogether, the as-yet unexplained drop in the black population, the inflow of Hispanics and Asians and the continued presence of islands of incalculable wealth on the "west side"—Beverly Hills and environs—has produced a distinctly two-tier society.

There is a mostly white, affluent overclass and a mostly minority, relatively poor underclass, a trend that many futurists believe will become evident in the remainder of California during the 21st century.

The industrial middle class has faded away as the auto plants, tire factories and aircraft complexes have given way to paper-processing and high-tech manufacturing. The last major refuge of the Anglo middle class within the city limits is the San Fernando Valley and it is there that the sociological battles have been fought, mostly over peripheral issues such as busing of school children for integration. The wealthy enclaves avoid such battles by maintaining their own governments and school systems, Beverly Hills being the most obvious example.

The socioeconomic transformation of Los Angeles and its close-in suburbs is expected to continue into the 21st century, SCAG planners believe. Latino and Asian immigrants will continue to pack into the inner city, raising population densities in the absence of any major housing construction, while the older suburbs may lose population as their residents age and younger Anglos continue their exodus to the further-out suburbs in Los Angeles County and adjacent counties.

The 1990 census revealed that the urban core of Los Angeles County— 11 congressional districts inside and outside the city—experienced a million-person population gain in the 1980s with virtually no expansion of the housing stock. An analysis of the 1990 census by the state Office of Planning and Research referred to the phenomenon as a "fourth wave" of immigration, adding that "a single-family home in Watts that housed one black family in the 1970s...may now house two families recently arrived from Mexico."

The study concluded that "while population boomed in the inner cities, it busted in the inner suburbs" and wonders whether California may be "seeing in the 1980s the beginning of an urban California populated by crowded and growing inner cities surrounded by communities of declining population—the exact opposite of traditional urban-suburban development..."

The semi-desert suburbs in the north part of the county are expected to show the greatest population gain—5 percent to 6 percent a year—while the remainder of the county remains numerically stagnant. The deserty Antelope Valley on the county's northern edge has become a center for aircraft production and experimental aviation and freeway connections allow its residents to commute into Los Angeles, although there's been an on-again, off-again movement to split the northern fringes off into a new "Canyon County." Palmdale, one of the Antelope Valley's booming communities, saw its population grow by an astonishing 460 percent in the 1980s, with nearby Lancaster close behind.

Los Angeles County is expected to grow much slower than the state as a whole, about 1 percent a year for the remainder of this century and the first part of the 21st century. But because of its huge base population, even a slow growth rate means Los Angeles County will be adding an estimated 1.5 million people in the 15 years between 1990 and 2005, most of it outside the Los Angeles city limits in unincorporated territory or smaller suburban cities.

Since the remainder of California will be growing much faster, Los Angeles will lose a bit of its relative political clout. The post-1990 census reapportionment was expected to see a shift of legislative and congressional seats out of Los Angeles to the faster-growing suburban counties such as Riverside and San Bernardino and a conversion of some white-held seats to Latino control. The census revealed that Los Angeles County's Hispanic population had grown from 27.6 percent in 1980 to 37.8 percent, an increase of some 1.3 million persons. The Asian proportion nearly doubled and now stands at about 11 percent of the county population, the same as the black population.

The 1980 census documented that between 1970 and 1980, a half-million Anglos left the city, mostly to find new homes in the suburbs. They were replaced by Hispanics and Asians, many of them fleeing war-torn Southeast Asia, the overcrowded Philippines or Korea, while the black population remained fixed at about 13 percent.

The white flight continued in the 1980s and today, it's estimated that Hispanics make up at least 40 percent of the city's population and demographers believe it will top 60 percent by early in the 21st century, fed by high birth rates and high levels of immigration, much of illegal, from Latin America.

California State University, Northridge, geographer James Allen calculated that between 1985 and 1989, 310,000 legal and illegal immigrants moved into Los Angeles County but 403,000 persons moved out and there's little doubt that most of those leaving were middle-class Anglos.

"We're losing older people and middle-class families trying to escape the urban environment," Nancy Bolton, a University of California, Los Angeles, demographer, told The Los Angeles Times in 1990. "Many are the young elderly, people 55 and over who are retiring early."

These empty-nesters have been dubbed "equity refugees" because they may leave Los Angeles with several hundred thousand dollars in proceeds from selling their homes, which allow them to live extremely well in suburban or rural areas where housing costs are much lower. Throughout California, the transplanted Angelenos have made their presence felt and neighboring states, principally Nevada and Arizona, have reported large numbers of transplanted Californians.

A study by the state Department of Finance revealed that in one year—July 1, 1989, to June 30, 1990—88,000 persons moved out of Los Angeles County to other states and another 229,000 moved elsewhere in California.

Those who move out of Los Angeles—whites mostly—and those who move in—Asians and Hispanics mostly—roughly balance each other out. The county's continued population growth results largely from a high rate of births among recent immigrants.

With white job-holders heading for the suburbs, Los Angeles area freeways have felt even more pressure and congestion has increased far more than mere population growth. The state Employment Development Department has calculated that Los Angeles and Orange counties created 230,800 more jobs than their growth in resident workforce during the 1980s, meaning that many more workers were commuting into employment centers in the two counties from outlying areas. Not surprisingly, Riverside, San Bernardino and Ventura counties reported almost exactly that many more workers than new jobs. The intercounty commute load increased by nearly a quarter-million persons during the decade.

It was the expansion of the suburbs, said Mayor Bradley, that sparked his interest in revitalizing downtown—a program that has seen an explosion of high-rise buildings and redevelopment.

"A deteriorating core threatened the very life of the city," Bradley told an interviewer in his City Hall office. "The suburbs threatened the vitality of the inner city. All of the heart and guts would be drained out of downtown."

To Bradley the downtown renewal—"one of the most dramatic transformations that's ever taken place in a major city"—was a concrete symbol that despite its socioeconomic changes, Los Angeles was open to private investment and capable of dealing on a grand scale.

"The spirit is as important as the physical development," said Bradley.

Bradley forged an enduring alliance between business and labor for the downtown renewal and built on that alliance to successfully stage the Olympic Games in 1984 and quickly expand the city's airport to handle increasing demand for air travel. Los Angeles, Bradley believes, will enter the 21st century as "the gateway city to the Pacific Rim" in which its ethnic diversity is "recognized as one of the great resources."

What Bradley is saying is that Los Angeles, despite a development pattern that defies conventional wisdom and an increasingly complicated socioeconomic and ethnic structure, works—a belief shared by others in the Los Angeles leadership cadre.

To Mark Pisano, director of the Southern California Association of Governments, it not only works but may be the correct way for all cities to develop.

"We have a lot of individual communities...but we're beginning to understand how the pieces fit into a larger whole," said Pisano, who sees the 1984 Olympics as "a metaphor of how we fit into a larger wheel."

What is undesirable sprawl to classic urban planners is "a decentralized community" to Pisano.

"This is the way people want their community," he added—pointing to the fact that the rest of the state and the rest of the nation are becoming more like Los Angeles, with jobs dispersed to outlying communities and a multitude of economic centers rather than one downtown.

"The individual's mobility and freedom is where people want to go."

The spirit of community renewal that came out of the Olympics, however, soured later in the decade as Los Angeles was scarred by waves of inter-racial violence and saw its major industries begin to crumble because of cutbacks in Pentagon spending and/or competition from other states and nations.

By mid-1991, Los Angeles County was facing an unemployment rate approaching 10 percent and burying some 2,000 homicide victims each year.

This darker version of Los Angeles, one that approached the seedy degradation of the movie "Blade Runner," was symbolized by a series of highly publicized conflicts, most notably the televised beating of Rodney King. The incident tore apart what had been one of Los Angeles' most visible and steadfast institutions, its police department, and spilled over into the sheriff's office that polices large sections of Los Angeles outside the city limits.

A curious ambivalence developed: Angelenos, fearful of gang clashes and drive-by shootings, were demanding even tougher police tactics but they also were condemning violence by officers. It was only one paradox in a micro-society beset by such contradictions.

The "gated community" has evolved into a metaphor for Los Angeles' increasing ethnic and social stratification.

Rich people surround their homes and communities with fences and hire guards to monitor traffic in and out. But the Los Angeles police have blocked off entire neighborhoods of mostly black south-central Los Angeles and placed padlocked gates across streets to protect them from the random violence of submachinegun-toting gang members.

The obvious tradeoff is freedom for security and for many Angelenos of all economic classes and races, it's a good trade. But it's also an implicit concession that Los Angeles' ethnic and social conflicts have become too deep-seated to approach by conventional means. In addition to deflecting crime, the guarded gates also define enclaves by economic and racial group.

The conflicts are not always black and white. The expansion of Hispanics into formerly black neighborhoods of south-central Los Angeles has produced both physical and political friction. One south-central high school went from 80 percent black to 80 percent Latino in less than eight years and one black state legislator has a district that is more than 60 percent Hispanic. There have been sharp confrontations between blacks and Koreans who have become dominant shopkeepers in black ghettos, reminiscent of those between Jewish merchants and black ghetto dwellers in other major cities. Several of the conflicts have produced violent deaths, creating a permanent state of animosity between black and Korean communities.

They may becoming minorities in numerical terms, but Anglos remain in firm control of politics and government in Los Angeles.

Despite Bradley's presence as the city's mayor, Anglos continued to control the City Council because of high voting rates and council districts that minimized Latino and Asian influence. The council's first Asian, Michael Woo, and its first Hispanic in a generation, Richard Alatorre, were elected in 1985—the same year that the city was sued by federal authorities, alleging that Hispanics were being denied political rights.

The inner city, like all inner cities, is Democratic. White liberals have controlled the City Council and Bradley's long reign as mayor was predicated on de facto support from business interests and an alliance with white liberals from the west side, coupled with solid votes from black and Latino communities. That alliance offset competition from the city's only bastion of conservatism, the San Fernando Valley, but it's a coalition that seems to be breaking up.

The dominant white-liberal organization, headed by Congressmen Henry Waxman and Howard Berman, has extensively involved itself in both black and Hispanic politics and that activity has had the effect—and, some believe, the goal—of keeping minority communities politically divided.

Bradley's two-decade-old mayorship, which has included two unsuccessful bids for the governorship, may be ending. He's been damaged by personal scandals and won a weak re-election in 1989 to a fifth term. Many expect him to retire in 1993 although he officially still intends to run again. His alliance with the Waxman-Berman organization has been ruptured, a victim of both mutual ego and policy differences over environmental issues. The west-siders planned to run Councilman Zev Yaroslavsky against Bradley in 1989 but the campaign was scuttled when a memo detailing campaign strategy was leaked to the media. It characterized the conflict with Bradley in ethnic terms—black vs. Jew—and suggested that the mayor was stupid. With Yaroslavsky out, Bradley won re-election against another black candidate, Councilman Nate Holden.

Bradley is not only Los Angeles' first black mayor but most likely its last. The black population is stagnant and there's no other black political figure with the stature to replace him. The next mayor may be white—arising out of a de facto alliance between liberal whites on the west side and conservative whites from the San Fernando Valley. Assemblyman Richard Katz and ex-Assemblyman Michael Roos are among the Anglos angling for the mayorship. Or the next mayor may be Latino, possibly Councilman Alatorre or county Supervisor Gloria Molina, who are rivals. Alatorre has been a Bradley ally while Molina has support from liberal groups, including those allied with the Waxman-Berman organization.

The county Board of Supervisors, known as the "five little kings" for the vast political power they wield, meanwhile, seems to have settled into a pattern of membership: one black seat, one Latino seat and three white seats, two conservatives from the northern and southern suburbs and one liberal from the west side.

The board's black seat had been held for decades by a white man, Kenneth Hahn, one of the legendary figures of Los Angeles politics, but Hahn, suffering from age and ill health, announced that he would retire in 1992, thus allowing south-central Los Angeles to elect its first black supervisor. Local politicians spent much of 1991 positioning themselves to capture the prize.

Then-Gov. Jerry Brown appointed a black woman, former Congress-woman Yvonne Burke, to the board in the late 1970s from a southwest coastal district, but she was defeated at the next election by Republican Deane Dana, which allowed the conservatives to gain a majority. That didn't change for a decade, until another federal lawsuit forced the supervisors to stop dividing the Hispanic communities. Once Latinos were consolidated into one district, it elected Gloria Molina, a city councilwoman and former state assemblywoman, and control of the board shifted back to the Democrats.

The decade of conservative dominance of county government was a decade of political war. The majority slashed spending, at least in relative terms, for social and health programs that served the poor and inner city minorities as it beefed up spending for law enforcement and other programs favored by suburbanites. The conflict was exacerbated by the effects of Proposition 13, which reduced county revenues and local discretion over spending, by the presence in Sacramento of a conservative Republican state administration and by the influx of Asian and Latino immigrants into the county.

Liberals fumed about the cutbacks and tried to reverse them through state legislation. But those efforts largely failed and county-operated services deteriorated—most spectacularly hospital emergency services for an increasing number of victims from gang violence and auto accidents and the poor who lacked any other kind of medical care. The creation of the Latino seat changed the partisan and ideological makeup of the board, shifting control back to liberals. But it's uncertain that the new liberal majority can reverse fiscal priorities because the county is still dependant upon the state for financing and the state is facing fiscal crises of its own.

Political participation among blacks is relatively high, resulting in the election of several black City Council members, state legislators and members of Congress. But blacks are a declining portion of the city's population and if anything may lose ground politically in the 21st century. Hispanics are increasing rapidly in numbers but their level of political participation is very low due to language barriers, lack of citizenship in many cases and a seeming lack of organizational interest among political leaders. Assemblywoman Lucille Roybal-Allred's East Los Angeles district, for example, contains fewer than 60,000 registered voters, about a third of the statewide average for Assembly districts.

The low degree of political influence of Los Angeles Hispanics, most of them of Mexican extraction, stands in sharp contrast with what has occurred in the nation's other major concentrations of Latino population, San Antonio and

Miami. In both of those cities, Hispanics have become politically dominant.

State Sen. Art Torres, one of the area's and the state's leading Hispanic political figures, said low political participation stems largely from non-citizenship. And, as he points out, the underlying cultural conservatism of Hispanics makes them tend to vote conservatively as they move up the economic ladder and acquire voting rights.

"They move to the San Gabriel Valley and vote Republican," said Torres. "I've tried tell the Democrats that their image has to change to attract Hispanics. Both Hispanics and Asians are very conservative on law-and-order issues."

Asians, about equal to blacks in number, have distinctly higher educational and economic levels and have dispersed into the general population. There is, moreover, some friction among the various Asian nationalities, some of it a product of ancient national rivalries, such as the Chinese vs. the Vietnamese.

Councilman Woo was elected from a largely non-Asian district and acknowledges that Asians tend not to see themselves in political terms.

"There's a gradual trend toward more participation," he said. "There's more awareness on the part of Asians that government plays a part in their lives." But, he said, "there are many tensions, many divisions on issues. There is a tendency to be extremely dissimilar."

"You may need to develop a strategy of many specialized appeals," he said of future efforts to organize Asians for political purposes.

One ethnic group that does exercise political power in Los Angeles disproportionate to its numbers is the substantial Jewish community on the city's west side, much of it connected to the entertainment industry.

All but a few of the west side's state and federal legislators are Jewish and a political organization headed by Reps. Henry Waxman and Howard Berman not only controls politics on the west side but is influential throughout Southern California.

Another rising political star is the area's substantial homosexual community. West Hollywood, Beverly Hills' next door neighbor, was incorporated specifically as a gay-lesbian municipality and homosexuals are influential in local politics throughout the west side.

The politics of Los Angeles County cities outside of Los Angeles, meanwhile, tend to reflect their peculiar political and/or ethnic leanings— some very liberal, some very conservative, some very white and some very non-white. Asians and Latinos have their greatest bases of political power in the cities of the San Gabriel Valley on the county's southeastern side.

Because of its size—8.9 million persons in the 1990 census and headed for an estimated 10.4 million by 2005—Los Angeles could dominate state politics, but it doesn't. It leans slightly Democratic in top-of-the-ticket elections, but only slightly and that tendency is easily offset by the strong pro-Republican voting patterns in the rest of Southern California.

The county's large congressional and state legislative delegations reflect the extremes and contradictions of its population and rarely come to agreement on any major issue. More often, they are divided by personal rivalries.

As the 1980s ended and the last decade of the century began, Los Angeles began undergoing a period of public soul-searching.

The Los Angeles Times, the county's dominant news medium (especially so since Los Angeles television news is famous for its preoccupation with tabloid-style crime and show business coverage), has published an informal series of articles that probe the county's rapidly changing demographics and such quality-of-life issues as air pollution, traffic congestion, housing prices and racial conflicts.

The newspaper's periodic polls have revealed declining happiness among Angelenos with their lives. One, published in 1989, revealed that nearly half of Los Angeles' residents had considered moving out in the previous year. "Dreamland," as many had once described Los Angeles, had become a nightmare of crime, pollution and congestion. Six of 10 persons interviewed in the poll said their quality of life had deteriorated, even though they agreed that cultural amenities and some other factors had improved.

Geographer James Allen, who has studied the exodus of white, middle-class residents from Los Angeles, said that dissatisfaction with housing costs, crime, gangs and taxes are the often-mentioned reasons.

"Traditionally, bigger was better," he told American Demographics magazine, which reported his findings. "But for the last 40 years, social surveys have indicated that most Americans want to live in smaller places."

For the foreseeable future, Los Angeles County seems destined to continue down several perilous paths: increasing racial separation and conflict, more crime, more people and, at least in relative terms, fewer jobs as federal spending policies, competition and air quality concerns take their toll.

The 1984 Olympics demonstrated that when Los Angeles wants to do something, it has the initiative and resources to do it. But these days, the problem is figuring out what to do to when confronted by such a unique set of socioeconomic trends.

Orange County:
Squeezing out the oranges

For years, cartoon tycoon Walt Disney had yearned to build a different kind of amusement park, one that would appeal to both adults and children.

At first, he wanted to locate it near the Disney studios in the San Fernando Valley, but there wasn't enough land. He went south instead, into the orange groves of aptly named Orange County and there, in the sleepy little suburban city of Anaheim, he created Disneyland.

The rest, as they say, is history.

When Disneyland opened its doors in 1955, Anaheim contained about 35,000 souls and its prime industry was growing fruit.

In five years, the population tripled and dozens of motels and restaurants were built to accommodate the millions of tourists who wanted to visit a kingdom ruled by a fictional mouse.

Anaheim exploded, but so did the rest of Orange County, from an agricultural backwater to the state's second-most-populous county (it has since slipped to third), complete with major league sports and the other trappings of metropolitan status, but without the existence of a single dominating city to give it a cultural identity.

In 40 years, from 1950 to 1990, Orange County's population increased 12-fold to 2.4 million, but Anaheim, the largest city, still has only 11 percent of the popu-lation, leaving Orange County in the cultural and media shadow of Los Angeles.

The professional football team that plays in Anaheim Stadium, for example, still refers to itself as the "Los Angeles Rams" while the professional baseball team was named after Los Angeles and calls itself the "California Angels." Orange County even gets its television from Los Angeles—the largest urban area in the country without its own network affiliated television service.

What happened in Orange County in the space of a few decades—the conversion of farmland into homes, shopping centers and industries—is the quintessential story of postwar California.

"This is the culmination of the American dream," the British Broadcasting Corp. concluded in 1976 when it selected Orange County as one of three American regions to be explored to mark the nation's bicentennial.

And what has happened in the 1980s—a conversion of the economy from suburban shopping centers to tourism and high-tech industry, a slowing of population growth, an increase in racial minorities, even a loss of people and jobs to new growth areas—also mirrors the socioeconomic evolution of California in the latter part of the 20th century.

Irvine, a community created from raw ranchland enveloping a University of California campus, is seen by many urban planners to be the prototype California city for the 21st century. Its concepts of land use are so advanced that its master designer, the late William Pereira, landed on the cover of Time magazine.

But to critics, Orange County is an example of sterile suburban sprawl gone mad, of right-wing racial exclusivity and of affluent rootlessness.

The construction of Disneyland in the mid-1950s marked the end of Orange County's 65 years of slumber that began when the county was carved out of southern Los Angeles County in 1889. It spent the last years of the 19th century and the first half of the 20th century as a rural backwater, producing meat, milk, fruits and vegetables for nearby Los Angeles. World War II began to change Orange County as southern Los Angeles County became the site of massive, war-driven industrialization that continued after the war and produced incredible pressure on the Los Angeles housing market.

During the late 1950s, 1960s and 1970s, there was an invasion of newcomers—of young families searching for affordable homes and suburban schools, of Midwesterners yearning for agreeable weather, of Southeast Asian refugees from communism and of Mexicans seeking economic opportunities.

The orange groves were bulldozed—the acreage devoted to citrus shriveled from more than 75,000 acres in the 1940s to just over 3,000 acres by 1990—and the pastures were paved as mile after mile of Orange County was developed. What had been distinct small towns grew together, the city limits of one touching the other.

Along the Orange County coast, a California Riviera evolved as movie stars and business tycoons rubbed shoulders in such enclaves of wealth as Newport Beach. In the mid-1970s, one state legislator from Newport Beach carried what he con-sidered to be a prime piece of consumer protection legislation: licensing of yacht brokers.

The vast Spanish land grant ranches held by the Irvine and O'Neill families were subdivided into new cities.

The Irvine family had the presence of mind to provide for a University of California in the middle of its holdings, thereby providing an engine for both population growth and high-tech industry.

The O'Neills, whose holdings were so vast that the Marine Corps training center, Camp Pendleton, was once sliced off its edge, built Mission Viejo, another new city, and sold it to a conglomerate corporation for tens of millions of dollars before plunging into the development of more new cities.

Huge fortunes were made in real estate in Orange County, by those fortunate enough to inherit land or smart enough to acquire it before the prices went up. And, as often happens in areas with development pressure, there was political corruption.

By the late 1970s, more than 40 local political figures had been indicted for various embezzlement, bribery and other schemes. There was something about Orange County, perhaps the laissez faire attitude toward business or the lack of media attention from Los Angeles, that encouraged those in office to grab whatever they could.

Maybe it was simply that so much money was floating around Orange County during the period of intense growth that few could resist the temptation to cash in.

City councilmen, county supervisors and the county assessor were among those who wound up facing corruption charges. A political and financial organization headed by a local physician, Louis Cella, was described by one prosecutor as a "shadow government" that controlled the county.

Cella was eventually sent to federal prison for his role in a complex hospital embezzlement scheme—but not until he and his political and business partner, land baron Richard O'Neill, had financed a number of local politicians into office.

The regular scandals that wafted through the county, however, neither slowed nor seemingly affected the go-go conversion of raw land into valuable building sites.

As the O'Neills developed the south end of the county and the Irvines took care of the middle, the Segerstrom family was building shopping centers, hotels and office buildings at a breakneck pace, trying to keep pace with the insatiable demand for homes, offices and retail selling sites in the area. The Segerstrom family ranch became South Coast Plaza shopping center and the family branched out into other areas of the county.

Berry farmer Walter Knott, meanwhile, created another amusement park, Knott's Berry Farm, that is second only to Disneyland as a tourist attraction.

If Orange County lacks a dominating city, it does have a center—located appropriately along a freeway. On both sides of the San Diego Freeway

(Interstate 405) near the county's airport (named for movie hero and Orange County resident John Wayne), the land has sprouted high-rise office buildings and hotels.

It is there that the big accounting and law firms, banks and insurance companies locate their Orange County operations. In all of Southern California, only downtown Los Angeles has a greater concentration of office space than the airport area, located at the juncture of four of Orange County's cities. In 1991, American Demographics magazine said the Anaheim-Santa Ana area is expected to have the nation's largest growth of industrial payrolls during the 1990s. Already, the economic output of the county exceeds that of Austria.

"People don't yet understand what is happening in this area," said Donald Koll, chairman of The Koll Co., one of the county's major developers. "We are creating Southern California's most significant urban core."

Koll, with more than 6 million square feet of office space completed and millions more on the drawing board, pioneered development near the airport. Its Koll Center Newport and Koll Center Irvine are the two largest office complexes in the county.

What happened near the John Wayne Airport—which itself underwent a much-needed expansion in the late 1980s—has been termed an "edge city," the prototypical suburban development that evolves into a center of employment and commerce. A generation earlier, suburban commuters had lived in Orange County and driven northward over the then-new freeway system to jobs in Los Angeles County. But by the mid-1980s, more workers were commuting into Orange County each day—many of them from Riverside County to the east—than were leaving for jobs elsewhere. Although Orange County's population growth slowed markedly in the 1980s as housing prices soared, its economic development, both industrial and post-industrial, continued at a high clip. Between 1980 and 1989, the state Employment Development Department has calculated, Orange County's resident workforce increased by 302,400 while the number of jobs in the county rose by 365,800, thus drawing more commuters into the county each day.

The advent of in-commuting on a broad scale overburdened a transportation system designed for earlier and now-obsolete traffic patterns, and congestion sparked a backlash in the form of anti-growth ballot initiatives that pitted pro- and anti-development forces against one another in multimillion-dollar political struggles. Ultimately, after heavy campaigns financed largely by developers, the anti-growth measures were defeated, but there remained a political division that shattered Orange County's image as a political monoculture.

Development near the airport has shifted the focus of Orange County away from the older cities, such as Anaheim and Santa Ana, in the northern part and toward the southern end.

"The commercial and industrial development along the San Diego Freeway is causing the center of Orange County to shift south and we are gaining a better awareness that Orange County has to become more balanced in its use of land," said architect Stewart Woodard.

Orange County's major developers have learned that with anti-growth sentiment still running high, they must resist the temptation to fill the land with as much square-footage or as many homes as humanly possible.

That new attitude is most evident in the Irvine Co.'s plans to develop its vast acreages—more than 60,000 acres—in mid-Orange County, much of which overlooks the Pacific Ocean. It has included large tracts of open and publicly accessible space—nearly 20,000 acres, company officials say—in its development plans. As it fought off anti-growth campaigns, the Irvine company also promoted increased spending on transportation, especially new roads, that would open up its interior acreages to development. And when traditional sources of highway financing were not available, the company promoted legislation allowing toll roads to be built.

Orange County's economy evolved along with its physical appearance during the years of high growth.

From agriculture, it first shifted to land development and construction as homes, offices and shopping centers were built to accommodate the demand for housing and services. But within a few years, the jobs followed the people into the suburbs. High-tech manufacturing and office operations found the climate and topography equally attractive. Typical was the Fluor Corp., which in the mid-1970s found that most of its workers lived in Orange County and moved its operations south from Los Angeles, There are more than 700 high-tech firms in the county, by one count the fifth-largest such concentration in the nation.

The UC-Irvine campus became a center for research, much as Stanford University did to the north. In 1985, inventor-philanthropist Arnold Beckman, founder of Beckman Instruments, donated $20 million to help build a major think tank near UC-Irvine, aimed at establishing the area as a center for scientific and medical study—and of the ethical problems posed by technical advances.

Of the estimated 300 firms engaged in biotechnological development in the United States, 170 are located in Orange County.

"The best word to describe it is 'boomtown.' Orange County is racing to be the capital of biotechnology research and, given the available resources, it would have to work awful hard to screw things up," said G. Wesley Hatfield, director of genetic and biotechnology research at UC-Irvine.

The $150 million Beckman Research Institute is one sign of that leadership in a field whose products are expected to rise from $50 million in sales in 1984 to $6 billion by 1994. It's estimated that Orange County received 25 percent of all the venture capital invested in biotechnology in 1983. The job growth left the county with a low unemployment rate—just 4.7 percent in the recession year of 1991—and one of the state's lowest rates of welfare dependency, just 2.33 percent in 1991.

As Orange County evolved from a loose assemblage of bedroom communities whose residents commuted to jobs elsewhere, primarily in Los Angeles County, into an employment center of its own in the 1970s, it began to undergo still another socioeconomic change not unlike that which was occurring in Los Angeles—the creation of a two-tier society.

It's what one sociologist has called the "toothpaste syndrome"—rising real estate values force the working middle class out of the area and leave behind an affluent upper tier and a poor lower tier.

Those who worked at the jobs Orange County was creating in offices and high-tech industries often could not afford to live in the county, or at least could not afford to buy homes. As Orange County's median home prices climbed beyond $150,000 and then beyond $200,000, young working couples were compelled to look elsewhere—principally in adjacent Riverside County—for what real estate salespersons called "starter homes."

Subdivisions offering new homes in the under-$90,000 range mush-

Focus on Orange County

Area ....785.1 sq. miles
Percentage of California 0.4%

Population
(with percentage of California total)

	1960	1970	1980	1990	2000	2005
Orange Co.	719,500	1,431,900	1,942,200	2,410,556	2,877,900	3,047,300
CALIFORNIA	4.5%	7.1%	8.2%	8.1%	7.9%	7.8%

Ethnic composition
(1990 Census)

	Anglo	Latino	Asian/Pacific	Black
Orange Co.	64.5%	23.4%	10%	1.6%
CALIFORNIA	57.2%	25.8%	9.1%	7%

Economic Data

	Unemployment rate (Aug. 1991)	Taxable sales (1990 per capita)	Personal income (per capita) 1984	1989
Orange Co.	4.7%	$11,519	$16,098	$23,231
CALIFORNIA	7.2%	$9,400	$14,593	$19,229

Political data

	1964	1972	1980	1984	1988
Voter registration (Democrat-Republican)	47-50%	43-50%	42-46%	37-52%	35-55%
Presidential vote (Democrat-Republican)	44-56%	28-72%	23-70%	25-75%	31-69%

Sources: State Department of Finance, 1990 Census, employment Development Department, Board of Equalization, Center for Continuing Study of the California Economy and the Secretary of State's office.

roomed in Riverside County during the early 1980s and the freeway connecting Riverside and Orange became packed with commuters.

The migration to Riverside was a strictly middle-class phenomenon. The wealthy remained in Orange, especially in the coastal enclaves, and helped push the county's median family income well above the state average.

Middle-class residents who had acquired their homes before the quantum leap in prices in the mid- and late-1970s also stayed. Apartment houses, too, remained full of singles and young families unable or unwilling to acquire a piece of the Riverside County desert. But population growth slowed markedly. Although Orange had just under 2 million people in 1980, by 1985 that had

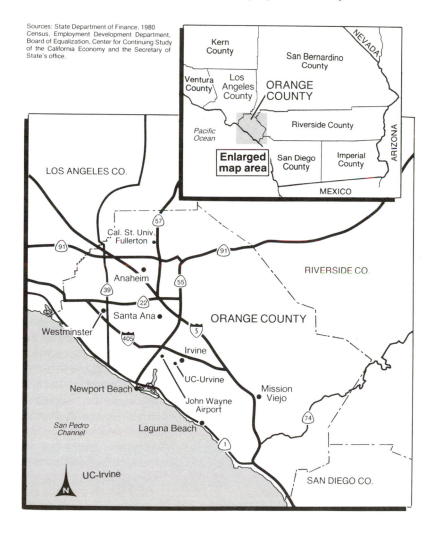

Sources: State Department of Finance, 1980 Census, Employment Development Department, Board of Equalization, Center for Continuing Study of the California Economy and the Secretary of State's office.

Graphic courtesy *The Sacramento Bee*

grown to only 2.1 million and by 1990 to just 2.4 million. Its growth rate was roughly that of the state as a whole and only a third of that in adjacent Riverside County during the 1980s. San Diego County, just to the south, replaced Orange as the state's second-most-populous county in 1985.

As white, middle-class families began looking elsewhere for their homes, Orange County's cultural face also began to undergo a marked change.

Orange County received more Southeast Asian refugees—an estimated 100,000—than any other urban area in the nation. Whole sections of Santa Ana, Garden Grove and Westminster became known as "Little Saigon" and "Little Cambodia." They are communities so distinct that freeway signs were erected to direct travelers to them and they were created from open fields and suburban housing tracts in less than a decade. By 1990, 10 percent of Orange County's residents were Asian.

"When we first came to this country, we had no shoes, our clothes were worn off and we couldn't speak English," physician Co Pham told The Sacramento Bee in 1990. "We took 15 years to build this town."

The cultural energy of these transplanted Asians quickly lifted many into middle- and upper-middle-class lifestyles as business persons, doctors, attorneys and accountants. By 1990, 47 percent of Garden Grove's Bolsa Grande High School was Asian and 18 of the school's top graduates were Asian as the dropout rate tumbled to a minuscule 3 percent.

A fifth of the undergraduates at UC-Irvine during the mid-1980s were Asian, and California State University, Fullerton, has reported similar numbers, reflecting the cultural drive to better one's parents.

Cal State Fullerton sociologist Myron Orleans, who studies Orange County's evolving culture, said Asians gravitate toward the marketable technical fields rather than sociology and education that would help their fellow Asians cope with the shock of migration.

"We need social workers and teachers who can relate to them (Asians) but their families are authoritarian in nature and they are pushed into technical fields," said Orleans.

Despite the astonishing level of affluence that Asians have achieved as a group in Orange County, there are pockets of poverty.

Minnie Street, in the middle of Santa Ana, is lined with scarred stucco apartment houses that contain thousands of Cambodians. As many as 16 may live in a two-bedroom apartment, fanning out to low-paying service and assembly-line jobs each morning and trying to get far enough ahead to move into better quarters.

The Vietnamese have assimilated rather quickly into Orange County's business and social structure but the Cambodians have lagged—a result, said social worker Phil Ehrman, of the special horrors that accompanied the Communist takeover of Cambodia. For Vietnamese and Cambodians alike, the Southeast Asian war that forced them to migrate to America remains a strong influence on community politics, much as Cuba dominates political life in

Miami. Southeast Asians who are viewed as being insufficiently anti-Communist find themselves shunned or even physically attacked and, as with Miami's Cubans, hopes of returning to the homeland burn brightly, even as Orange County's Asians seemingly become a more permanent part of the social and economic landscape.

As they moved into the Minnie Street apartments, the Cambodians began displacing Hispanics, many of them recent immigrants from Mexico, who had already given mid-Santa Ana a Latin flavor.

The cultural mix has not been without its frictions, most evident among the youngsters of both ethnic groups who roam in groups through the area.

"Something has to be done, especially for the teenagers," said Eherman. "They're stuck here with nothing else to do."

Despite the high visibility that Asians have achieved in Orange County, Hispanics remain the largest minority group and enlarged their presence from about 15 percent in 1980 to more than 23 percent in 1990, nearly that of the state as a whole.

Hispanics, like Asians, are concentrated in the older cities of Anaheim and Santa Ana but remain politically invisible. An effort to create "Hispanic seat" in the state Senate by Democratic leaders in Sacramento failed and the seat was taken, instead, by a conservative Anglo Republican. The one Orange County Latino with political power is a Republican, county Supervisor Gaddi Vasquez, a former aide to ex-Gov. George Deukmejian who is being touted by some GOP leaders as a future candidate for statewide office. But Vasquez does not mean that the county's nearly 600,000 Hispanics have anything more than token political presence. And Orange County's Hispanics, who are concentrated in low-wage service jobs, don't appear to be using education as a ladder. The proportions of Hispanic students at the area's two major colleges are relatively low and the Hispanic dropout rates in local high schools are high—mirroring trends in other areas of the state.

Orange County's poverty pockets are not only Asian and Hispanic.

Many of the small motels that popped up three decades ago to handle Orange County's influx of tourists have been converted into de-facto apartments. Inside live what are called "motel people"—those who can't afford the first- and last-month rent payments that would move them into apartment houses.

The Orange County Register, in a remarkable examination of the motel people, described them this way: "Mostly Anglo, they're the county's newest migrant workers: instead of picking grapes, they inspect semiconductors."

City officials have tried to discourage motel-living through various ordinances, but the motel people still exist—the working poor who are a few hundred bucks above the street and a few hundred below a more conventional life.

If, however, Orange County has become a two-tier society, the emphasis is definitely on the upper tier and expresses itself in a very high average income, very high consumption of goods and political conservatism. Orange County's "Gold Coast," stretching southward from Newport Bay, is a wonderland of yachts, mansions, first-class resort hotels and expensive shops. The southern end of the coastal strip is anchored by Laguna Beach, a one-time art colony that in more recent years has become a vacation haven—and the home of Orange County's gay community, which dominates local politics.

As a Los Angeles Times article on Laguna Beach's cultural evolution put it in 1988: "Rents have gone through the roof, sometimes tripling. Many of the small, family-run appliance stores, bakeries and even art galleries that gave the village its soul have disappeared. Many of the artists who thrived in Laguna's tolerance and progressiveness have found they can no longer afford the rent. They, too, are drifting away."

It's a change—from art colony to tourist draw—that mirrors what occurred 400 miles to the north in Carmel.

Laguna Beach politics have been traditionally liberal but generally, Orange County has long been considered a bastion of right-wing politics and religious fervor, a place where the John Birch Society is just another fraternal organization and the most architecturally impressive structure is the "Crystal Cathedral," the headquarters of a television evangelist.

A glance at political data seemingly confirms that observation. Except for a brief post-Watergate period in the mid-1970s, the county has had a solid Republican voter majority and the last remaining Democrat in the county's legislative delegation quit rather than face almost certain defeat in 1986, although four years later a Democrat did win an Assembly seat.

Ronald Reagan chose Orange County's Mile-Square Park to launch his 1984 re-election campaign and 50,000 of the faithful turned out to confirm that it was, as the billboards proclaimed, "Reagan Country." And on Election Day, Reagan beat rival Walter Mondale by a 3-1 margin in the county.

But the demonstrated political conservatism of Orange County has an interesting twist.

For several years, UC-Irvine professor Mark Baldassare has conducted an annual survey of attitudes among Orange County's residents and while those surveys do confirm the overall Republican orientation, there also are surprising levels of support for liberal positions.

During 1984, for example, Baldassare discovered that while more than 70 percent of the county's voters favored Reagan and a majority opposed gun controls and favored military intervention in Central America, more than 70 percent also favored ratification of the Equal Rights Amendment and free choice on abortions and a majority opposed more offshore oil drilling.

"These results and their comparison with national averages reveal Orange County to be more complex politically than the 'Republican-conservative' label it has been given," Baldassare said.

While Orange County remains safely in the Republican column, a newer generation of political leaders is markedly less conservative than those who emerged in the 1950s and 1960s, such as fast food tycoon Carl Karcher and amusement park operator Walter Knott. The most influential of these new leaders, and one who personifies the shift to moderation, is Donald Bren, owner of the Irvine Co. and once described as a "horizontal Donald Trump" because of his firm's vast holdings of vacant land.

Bren became an influential political figure in the 1980s as a financier of campaigns, both those of major state candidates and local politicians and causes. His company, for instance, was a major supporter of the drives against growth-control initiatives.

John Seymour, the moderate one-time mayor of Anaheim, became known as "the senator from Irvine" when he entered the state Senate because of his close connections to the company and those ties played no small role in Seymour's being named to the U.S. Senate by Pete Wilson in 1991 as the latter became governor. Wilson and Bren were Marine Corps buddies and Wilson's administration has drawn heavily on Irvine-connected figures.

The socioeconomic and political trends that emerged in the 1980s seem likely to prevail as Orange County nears the 21st century.

Jobs will grow faster than population, which will mean more commuters into Orange from Riverside and other areas, worsening traffic tieups and fueling local anti-growth sentiment. A 1989 countywide poll revealed that 51 percent of Orange County's residents wished they lived somewhere else. The working middle class will continue to be squeezed by high housing costs, furthering the two-tier society already evident and the county will continue to vote Republican. Even Hispanics and Asians, when they vote, tend toward the GOP.

All of this change and socioeconomic ferment means that Orange County will continue to be what the BBC said it was in 1976—the archetypical California society.

The Desert:
Blooming with people

ROSEMARY RENZEL WAS SELLING HOUSES IN A MORENO VALLEY DEVELOPMENT called Country Living, a short drive off Highway 60 east of Riverside, in 1985.

Each day, she saw dozens of would-be buyers troop through her models. And they were buying, attracted by prices in the $80,000-$90,000 range—only two-thirds of what the same house would cost nearer the coast.

They weren't buying much, judging by the home standards of a decade or two earlier. But it was a single-family detached home and it was several cuts above the crowded urban or suburban apartments from which they moved.

They would put up with long commutes. Renzel told a visitor that "90 percent of my buyers are from the Orange County-LA area and not one of the local communities" and were spending as much as four hours on the freeway daily to travel to and from jobs as far away as Long Beach.

They would put up with the smog that forms over the Riverside-San Bernardino area as pollution is blown eastward by ocean breezes.

They would put up with just about anything to get that first house.

What once was called the "Inland Empire"—hardly anyone uses that term anymore—of Riverside and San Bernardino counties exploded with people in the 1980s. Riverside was the state's fastest-growing county in the 1980s at 76 percent, nearly three times the overall state growth rate. And San Bernardino was second at 58 percent. Together, these two counties accounted for more than a million of California's 6-million-person population growth in the decade.

It was the region's turn to experience the relentless outward push of the Los

Angeles suburbs—a migration that began to change the California desert from a place of sandy solitude, dairy cows and orange groves into a place of houses, of kids and, if local boosters have their way, of light industrial and commercial development on an unprecedented scale.

It is, at least so far, an evolution that's confined to the desert communities closest to the Los Angeles-Orange megalopolis, fueled by the extension of freeways and the relentless Southern California search for the affordable home.

Further out, to the north and east, the desert and the mountains that poke out of the sandy valleys remain relatively untouched by the explosion of growth. And in Imperial County, an agricultural backwater, growth means a surge of population from nearby Mexico—without the jobs to support the newcomers.

The three desert counties—Imperial, Riverside and San Bernardino—contain more than 32,000 square miles, over a fifth of California. San Bernardino County, with its seemingly endless expanses of empty desert, is the largest county in the nation, as well as the state. But nearly 80 percent of San Bernardino's land is government-owned, as is more than 60 percent of the other two counties.

As late as 1960, the population of the three counties was less than a million. But since then, the area's population has been growing by 35-40 percent every decade, topped 2.5 million by 1990 and is expected to hit 3 million before the turn of the century. San Bernardino County's population will have tripled during the 45-year period between 1960 and 2005, according to the state Department of Finance, and Riverside's will have quadrupled.

Moreno Valley, a city formed by combining several unincorporated communities along Highway 60, is at the eye of the socioeconomic storm.

Country Living was just one of 42 subdivisions open for business in 1985 in a city with scarcely 43,000 people. Everywhere one looked, one saw the flags, billboards and directional signs of the developments like Country Living—all offering homes in the same sub-$100,000 price range.

In 1984, the two counties led the state in housing starts with 38,400 new units. In Moreno Valley alone, 400 new single-family homes and 400 apartments were built in 1984. By the end of the decade, the profusion of colorful subdivision banners had given way to more dignified, uniform signing, but the population had zoomed well past 100,000. The Census Bureau reported in 1991 that Moreno Valley was the nation's fastest-growing city over 100,000 population during the previous decade, a whopping 322 percent.

Each morning, the young suburbanites pull out of their driveways and point their cars westward, toward the jobs in Los Angeles and Orange. Their children spend as much as 12 hours a day in school and child care centers. One political consultant, puzzled by the low level of voting in Moreno Valley, concluded that its residents leave so early in the morning—as early as 4 a.m.—and get home so late that they are effectively precluded from voting because the polls are open only from 7 a.m. to 8 p.m.

One Moreno Valley commuter put it this way: "We figure it's a two- or three-year burnout on the freeways. You put up with it and then you either take your equity and buy a house closer in or you find a job out here."

So far, there are more people than jobs. Census data indicate that about a fifth of those who live in Riverside and San Bernardino counties work in Orange and Los Angeles counties—a fact underscored by the traffic jams that form on the east-west freeways every morning and afternoon, roadways originally designed for local traffic, not the crush of commuters. Population growth is expected to outstrip job growth for the remainder of the century.

"It is largely housing prices that drive this imbalance," a report by the state Office of Planning and Research concluded in 1991. "Housing prices are much lower in Riverside and San Bernardino than in the coastal counties, leading to the conclusion that housing prices do drive the choice to move to these Inland Empire counties. Obviously, these people are commuting to Orange and Los Angeles, which have almost a quarter-million more jobs than workers."

There is, however, a pattern to growth in Southern California—the commuters stretch out the urban limits and later the jobs come in behind them. That's what happened a generation ago in Orange County. "A lot of people hope there will be jobs coming out here, too," real estate saleswoman Renzel said.

It may be beginning to happen. Gordon's Cabinet Shop, for example, announced in 1985, that it was moving its manufacturing operations from Anaheim, in Orange County, to Riverside and would expand its payroll from 215 to 300 in the process. Company president Gordon Mullens said the availability of affordable housing in Riverside, in stark contrast to Orange, was the prime reason for the move. Since then, some other, relatively small payrolls have moved and American Demographics magazine in 1991 forecast that Riverside County would have the nation's 10th-fastest growth in manufacturing payrolls in the 1990s, but the "jobs-housing imbalance," as municipal planners call it, remains a worrisome issue for the area's civic leaders.

The same phenomenon has occurred, albeit on a less dramatic scale, in western San Bernardino County, which had an historic industrial base centered on the Kaiser Steel works at Fontana that closed in 1983.

The smokestacks of the Kaiser plant stand as silent sentinels along the cracked pavement of old Route 66. Once, more than 9,000 people were employed in the complex. A few years after the closure, fewer than 10 percent of that number worked in a small section of the plant taken over by a company that processed imported steel into finished products.

The closure of a plant of that magnitude could have had a devastating impact on a small community. And certainly it was a traumatic event for thousands of steelworkers. But the closure occurred just as western San Bernardino County was getting suburban-type development pressure, which filled the economic void with service and construction jobs.

"It may seem strange, but we're becoming an LA bedroom community," then-City Manager Jack Ratelle told a visitor as he presided over the growth in the 1980s. He saw Fontana's population jumping from 49,000 to 150,000 by the turn of the century.

The driving forces behind the suburbanization of Fontana and other nearby communities are the ones also working in Riverside County: cheap land and freeway access.

Dolly Stoner, who was peddling houses in a medium-priced subdivision called Northgate in Fontana, put it this way: "When Kaiser pulled out and the schools got better, developers got interested in Fontana."

"A lot of our buyers are commuters," Stoner told a visitor to her model home, "but we've had a lot of General Dynamics people buy, too."

As the smokestack industries pulled out of western San Bernardino, the warehousing and high-tech industries moved in—clustered around fast-growing Ontario International Airport.

Kaiser's closure also helped improve the air quality that is perhaps the most-mentioned negative factor in the area. Pollution from Los Angeles is pushed eastward by ocean breezes and is trapped by mountains that ring the San Bernardino-Riverside area, giving it the state's worst smog problem. Those who drive into the mountains on smoggy days often are unable to see through the blanket of noxious fumes that forms a few thousand feet above the ground; those on the ground, in turn, cannot see the sun through the yellowish canopy.

Oddly, the two major cities in the area, San Bernardino and Riverside, are not directly reflecting the heavy growth that both counties are seeing.

Although only 10 miles apart, and connected by a heavily developed freeway, there is a strong antipathy between the two county seats.

San Bernardino has the reputation of being a tough blue-collar city, the reputed birthplace of the Hell's Angels motorcycle gang and a city with a checkered record of race relations.

Riverside, meanwhile, was originally a resort town—the Palm Springs of its day—and has a genteel aura underscored by the historic Mission Inn in the downtown area and the presence of a University of California campus.

"They might as well be divided by the Berlin Wall," John Holmes, the city manager of the neutral community of Redlands once was quoted as saying.

San Bernardino has anxiously courted growth through such devices as a downtown redevelopment project, although it has been plagued with financial troubles. Riverside, on the other hand, has been somewhat resistant to growth. A strong liberal-environmentalist bloc centered around UC-Riverside has strongly influenced local development policies.

The anti-growth movement was captured in a 1979 Riverside ballot measure sponsored by a group called Riversiders for Reasonable Growth that created greenbelts in the city aimed at preserving its semi-rural character.

Voters not only approved the measure, which also required lower-density residential development, but elected a city council devoted to its implementation. The effect was to slow development within Riverside itself but not within the area. It gave rise to such fast-growing peripheral communities as Moreno Valley.

Walter Ingalls, who represented Riverside in the state Assembly and was closely allied with pro-development forces throughout his legal and political career before his death in 1991, was openly disdainful of the anti-growth movement in Riverside.

"They are effete intellectuals who have a disdain for economics," Ingalls said of the anti-growthers.

They appeal to a certain nostalgic desire to return to the time when

Focus on The Desert

Area .... 32,004 sq. miles
Percentage of California 20.2%

Population
(with percentage of California total)

	1960	1970	1980	1990	2000	2005
Imperial Co.	73,000	74,700	92,700	110,400	142,300	154,300
Riverside Co.	311,700	461,600	668,900	1,195,400	1,786,500	2,027,500
San Bernardino Co.	509,000	685,300	903,100	1,440,700	2,098,200	2,399,500
TOTAL	893,700	1,221,600	1,664,700	2,746,500	4,027,000	4,581,300
CALIFORNIA	5.6%	6.1%	7.0%	9.2%	11.1%	11.8%

Ethnic composition
(1990 Census)

	Anglo	Latino	Asian/Pacific	Black
Imperial Co.	29%	65.8%	1.5%	2.1%
Riverside Co.	64.4%	26.3%	3.3%	5.1%
San Bernardino Co.	60.8%	26.7%	3.9%	7.7%
CALIFORNIA	57.2%	25.8%	9.1%	7.0%

Economic Data

	Unemployment rate	Taxable sales	Personal income	
	(Aug. 1991)	(1990 per capita)	(per capita)	
			1984	1989
Imperial Co.	26.1%	$8,126	$10,929	$13,290
Riverside Co.	11%	$7,966	$12,275	$14,950
San Bernardino Co.	7.6%	$7,822	$11,232	$14,904
CALIFORNIA	7.2%	$9,400	$14,593	$19,229

Political data

	1964	1972	1980	1984	1988
Voter registration (Democrat-Republican)	56-40%	53-41%	50-39%	47-42%	45-46%
Presidential vote (Democrat-Republican)	43-57%	38-62%	32-61%	35-65%	40-60%

Sources: State Department of Finance, 1990 Census, employment Development Department, Board of Equalization, Center for Continuing Study of the California Economy and the Secretary of State's office.

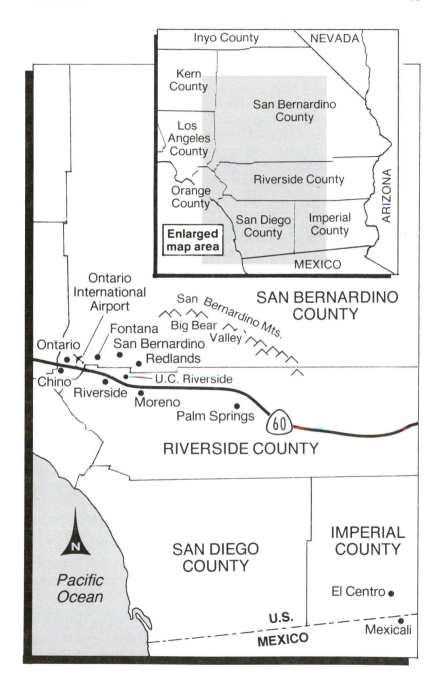

Inyo County NEVADA

Kern County

San Bernardino County

Los Angeles County

Orange County

Riverside County

Enlarged map area

San Diego County

Imperial County

ARIZONA

MEXICO

SAN BERNARDINO COUNTY

Ontario International Airport

San Bernardino Mts.

Big Bear Valley

Fontana

Ontario

San Bernardino

Redlands

Chino

U.C. Riverside

Riverside

Moreno

Palm Springs

60

RIVERSIDE COUNTY

Pacific Ocean

N

SAN DIEGO COUNTY

IMPERIAL COUNTY

El Centro

U.S. MEXICO

Mexicali

Graphic courtesy *The Sacramento Bee*

Riverside was a winter watering hole for wealthy Angelenos, rather than the center of a fast-developing suburban region, Ingalls told an interviewer. Redlands, too, has tried to preserve its agricultural character through slow-growth laws and the future of agriculture is one of the prime questions facing the entire region.

The citrus groves around Riverside and the dairy farms west of San Bernardino are threatened by the steady expansion of single-family subdivisions.

Creation of the citrus preservation zone in Riverside has allowed growers who wish to continue farming, but local environmentalists believe that the economic pressure to sell to developers will grow overwhelmingly intense unless local, state or federal governments step in to buy development rights.

Similarly, a 17,000-acre dairy preservation district has been created near Chino to isolate the odorous dairy farms from suburban encroachment. Many of the Chino dairy farmers have already moved once in the last generation, fleeing the suburbanization of southern Los Angeles County after World War II to the then-empty areas of San Bernardino County.

But developers are offering large sums for the dairy farms located enticingly close to east-west freeways and there are strong indications that some of the farmers are ready to sell, thus setting in motion, many believe, events that will lead to a complete wipeout of the industry in the area.

While growth in the Riverside-San Bernardino area spawned local anti-growth movements, developers staved off most of their impacts and as the 1980s evolved into the 1990s, the prospects for continued high levels of suburban-style growth remained strong.

East of Riverside and San Bernardino, out of the suburban commuter belt, the changes in the region are far less dramatic. Residents of the northern and eastern sections of San Bernardino County—much of it trackless desert—felt so alienated by the growth in the western portion that they sought to break off and form a new county, called Mohave, in 1988, but the split was rejected by voters. The alienation continues, however, and has been exacerbated by plans to use desert sites as dumping grounds for Southern California urban waste and by a protracted political battle in Washington over a desert protection bill that would restrict, if not eliminate, mineral extraction and other underpinnings of the desert economy.

Looming above the smoggy valleys are the San Bernardino Mountains, mostly in federal ownership but with substantial year-round communities at Big Bear Lake, 7,000 feet above sea level, and nearby Lake Arrowhead. Their presence within a few hours' driving time of 10 million people—an alpine respite from the heat of the desert and the smog of the city—creates traffic jams of monumental proportions on summer weekends.

Each year, about 5 million visitors flow into Big Bear Valley. That's expect to hit 6 million by 2000 and the year-round population of the area, now about 15,000, is expected to approach 20,000.

The insatiable demand of urban dwellers for recreation has produced ambitious plans for expansion of visitor facilities, including winter ski areas. But it also has produced a backlash among some local residents who see their alpine aerie acquiring the social problems of the cities below. Nevertheless, the Big Bear Lake civic leadership, tied closely to the tourist-related economy, is so gung-ho for development that it seems inevitable.

Palm Springs and other communities of the Coachella Valley remain what they became in the postwar era, bastions of often wealthy and mostly elderly sun- and golf-worshipers who spend their pensions, trust funds and other forms of imported money.

The resort towns are almost deserted in the blindingly hot summers, but during the fall, the grassy expanses, watered from an underground aquifer, are reseeded and fertilized into an unreal greenness and the condos and homes are opened up for the real season, the winter. Even then, however, the Palm Springs area retains its quietude, rolling up its sidewalks at dusk and seemingly coming alive only during championship golf tournaments and the annual Easter Week invasion by beer-swilling, semi-naked college students. Local residents bitterly resent the arrival of the young as an intrusion on their purposely uneventful lifestyle and often advance their vernal departures to avoid the hordes.

The ostentatious, if transient, wealth of the Palm Springs region—the fancy cars, expensive restaurants, exclusive shops and walled-in and security-guarded country clubs and residential areas—masks an invisible subculture of poor, mostly Latino workers who tend the vineyards and date orchards, clip the lawns and fairways, perform the household chores and wash the dishes. They struggle, and often fail, to find decent and affordable housing and medical care and do their shopping in flea markets. Indian Wells, one of the area's richest enclaves, sought special state legislation in the late 1980s to exempt it from the requirement to build low-income housing within its borders as it used redevelopment powers to subsidize a new resort hotel development. City officials contended that such housing would be incompatible with the ambience of Indian Wells. With such contrasts, the Coachella Valley may be the starkest example of California's increasingly stratified culture.

Hemet, in southern Riverside County, has become the linchpin of what some are calling the "Golden Triangle" of retirement complexes stretching from the southern Orange County coast to northern San Diego County and then to Palm Springs. By one account, Hemet has the highest concentration of banks of any city in the state—a testament to the wealth of retirees and the competition of financial institutions to serve them.

The stepchild of the interior desert counties is Imperial, located in the southeastern corner of the state, bordering on Arizona and Mexico.

Of all the Southern California counties, it is the newest, having split off from San Diego in 1907, the least populous at just over 100,000 population, the slowest-growing (19 percent in the 1980s), the only one with a Latino majority and the poorest, with double-digit unemployment and large welfare rolls the norm.

Farmers were first attracted to the Imperial Valley in the late 19th century by weather—blazingly hot in the summer, mild in the winter—that promised year-round harvests. They brought water to the valley, much of it below sea level, from the Colorado River, leached the crop-destroying minerals from the valley's soil and saw it bloom with an astonishing variety of foods and fibers.

Agribusiness is still king, but in recent years, Imperial Valley farmers have suffered along with their brethren elsewhere in the state from crushing debt loads, infestations of pests and low crop prices. And a kind of permanent recession has developed, thanks in part to economic developments across the border in Mexico.

There are scarcely 100,000 people in Imperial County and the largest city, El Centro, has fewer than 25,000. But just across the international line, Mexicali, the capital of Baja California-Norte, has experienced a huge population boom in the last quarter-century.

There are an estimated 750,000 persons in and around Mexicali and the city's pulsating presence is felt on the California side of the line.

Historically, there has been a symbiotic economic relationship between Mexico and California in the area. Mexico supplied the labor for the Imperial Valley farms and the wages kept Baja California relatively prosperous.

Calexico, the border town on the California side, "was the shopping center for Mexicali," Fred Knechel, manager of the city's Chamber of Commerce, recalled for a visitor in 1985 as the pinch began to make itself felt.

As long as dollar-peso exchange rates remained relatively stable, it was a mutually beneficial arrangement. But when Mexico began to undergo its series of economic and natural upheavals, topped by the Mexico City earthquake in 1985, the local economy got caught in the backlash.

A strong dollar meant a weak peso and by the 1990s, the Mexican currency had been devalued to nearly 3,000 to the dollar, which made goods on the American side prohibitively expensive for many Mexicans.

"Several of the merchants are talking about being off 40 percent for this time of the year," Knechel said.

The decline of retail sales meant layoffs of bilingual retail workers, most of them Hispanic, which contributed to the overall malaise in the economy. The chronically depressed local economy has spurred efforts, in turn, to attract payrolls not tied to either agricultural or international trade. Those new jobs are sorely needed. Imperial had California's highest unemployment rate in August, 1991, at 26.1 percent and more than 10 percent of its residents were on the welfare rolls. But the remoteness of the area from markets and its fierce summer climate have inhibited economic development efforts.

Bob Liggett, who edits the daily newspaper in El Centro and has been active in the economic development program, acknowledge the uphill struggle to acquire non-agricultural payrolls.

"Maybe we can get the snowbirds," he said, referring to the refugees from winter weather who flock to the California desert annually—the more affluent to hotels, second homes and condos in the Palm Springs and Hemet areas, the less affluent to trailer parks along the Salton Sea and the Colorado River. One informal community of winter dwellers near the Salton Sea—formed early in this century when the Colorado River flooded into an old marine basin—is called "Slab City" because its motorhomes and trailers sit on the concrete slabs left from a long-gone government installation.

The only substantial non-farm economic development came to Imperial County in the late 1980s when the state Department of Corrections announced plans to build two state prisons in the county, one near Calipatria, the other closer to El Centro. It was a continuation of the state's reliance on depressed rural communities as sites for its new prisons—the only real rural economic development program the state has undertaken. But it promised more than 2,000 jobs in Imperial County, a welcome surge in an otherwise chronically depressed area.

Imperial's proximity to Baja California will continue to shape its future through at least the remainder of this century.

As relatively poor as it may be by California standards, Imperial is affluent by Mexican standards and continues to attract thousands who seep across the border, legally and illegally.

The Hispanic population of Imperial already is large—over 65 percent in the 1990 census—and is growing much faster than the Anglo population, which remains firmly in control of the local agribusiness and commercial infrastructure. It's large enough that Imperial is the only county in California to have a major Latino political presence; at one time, two Hispanics sat on the five-member county Board of Supervisors.

Politically, California's inland desert region has historically been a mixed bag—rigidly conservative in the Imperial Valley and the outer deserts, blue-collar Democratic in the San Bernardino area and liberal in the Riverside area.

There are, however, signs of change in both directions.

The rapidly developing suburban areas are moving to the right politically, not unlike what happened in Orange County a quarter-century ago when it evolved from orange groves to homes. Although most of the state and federal legislators are Democrats, Republicans look at Riverside and San Bernardino as areas of potential long-term gain and Democratic leaders must struggle constantly to hold their seats.

The Senate district represented by conservative Democrat Robert Presley of Riverside, for example, slipped to under 50 percent Democratic registration in the 1980s. Both Riverside and San Bernardino counties now have Republican voter pluralities and their rapid growth forced the creation of new legislative and congressional seats that are likely to go to Republicans.

At the other end of the region, in the Imperial Valley, the rapidly increasing Hispanic population is the key to its political future. If Hispanics can translate their numbers into votes, they will take control of local government away from the Anglo power structure and have greater impact on state and federal legislative elections as well. But given low levels of Latino voting, that's a problematic scenario.

San Diego:
Cul-de-sac culture

DURING THE 1984 NATIONAL LEAGUE PLAYOFFS BETWEEN THE SAN DIEGO Padres and the Chicago Cubs, Chicago newspaper columnist Mike Royko cast his jaundiced eye on the competing city.

While Chicagoans took their city and their baseball seriously, Royko observed, San Diegans were a bunch of "quiche-eating wimps" so laid-back that a baseball pennant race was "just another pleasant recreational diversion."

The hyperbole aside, there was a grain of truth in the observation. Relaxation does at times appear to be San Diego's chief pastime, from strolls along the city's spectacular waterfront to an annual orgy of beer and bare-breasted bathing beauties called the "Over the Line Tournament."

San Diegans like to live the good life and their chief worry is that so many others will want to share it that San Diego will become too much like the much-hated big city to the north, Los Angeles. It may be a well-founded fear; San Diego County zoomed past Orange County to become the state's second-most-populous county and the City of San Diego was already second only to Los Angeles among the state's cities. San Diego was easily the fastest growing major county in the 1980s, with its population increasing by more than one-third to 2.5 million, and it began experiencing some of the interracial friction that had already hit Los Angeles. Gangs and drugs, moreover, have found their way to what local boosters call "America's Finest City."

"The problem with San Diego is that it has big-city problems but a small-town mentality," University of San Diego professor Dennis Rohatyn was

quoted in The Los Angeles Times. "It prefers to think of itself as this idyllic little
seaside village, where we wink our eye and pretend that typical urban problems
don't exist."

San Diegans' anti-LA paranoia reached its zenith in 1985 when zealous
protectors of the local lifestyle, worried about an influx of newcomers that had
made San Diego the state's fastest-growing major urban area, persuaded voters
to adopt a stringent anti-growth law.

The campaign over Proposition A, as the measure was called, evolved into
a debate over what kind of city San Diego had become and where it was going
in the future.

To its environmentalist supporters, Proposition A was a popular revolt
aimed at protecting the city's green canyons and other open space from the
rapacious greed of developers who had come to dominate local politics and
already paved over much of the landscape.

Over a $3\frac{1}{2}$-year period, at the behest of developers, the City Council had
opened up nearly 35 percent of the 19,000-acre urban reserve to development,
including 5,100 acres of La Jolla Valley that could become the site of up to
25,000 new homes.

That action created the backlash that placed Proposition A on the ballot.

"All you've got to do is get five votes (on the City Council) and you can
damn well do what you want in this city..." pro-Proposition A activist Jay
Powell, a Sierra Club coordinator, said during the campaign preceding the
November 1985 vote.

"All you have to do is look at the campaign contribution lists and you'll
see who is fueling these campaigns. So what choice does a fellow have?"

But to critics, Proposition A—which required citywide votes on any plans
to develop in the reserve areas—was overkill that threatened to throttle
reasonable development aimed at handling the huge influx of newcomers into
the area.

"It's vigilante politics," one critic, University of California-San Diego
political science professor Sam Popkin, said prior to the vote. "They are going
to tar and feather the City Council because these people (council members) had
to balance the interests of lots of groups and lots of voters..."

Opponents of the measure said it would hurt, rather than improve San
Diego's quality of life by compelling denser development in existing areas,
rather than opening up new sites. It's foolish, they said, to think that population
pressure can be controlled by laws.

Despite the efforts of developers to defeat the measure, it passed handily—
with especially heavy votes coming in areas immediately adjacent to the urban
reserve areas under development pressure, such as La Jolla Valley.

It was, however, only the latest in a long string of debates between pro- and
anti-development forces in the city in a kind of slow-motion war over San
Diego's future, even though a strong argument can be mounted that San Diego
has made a more peaceful transition into major metropolitan status than any

other California city.

To those who lived there, San Diego always was a special place where early California history merged with the 20th century in a spectacularly beautiful natural setting, blessed with perhaps the most perfect climate of any city in the world.

For most of the 20th Century, San Diego existed in a kind of cul de sac of consciousness, separated from the rest of the world by an ocean, an international border, a forbidding desert and a huge Marine Corps training base.

If anything, Americans thought of San Diego as a Navy town, the headquarters for much of the Pacific Fleet, the place that generations of young Navy and Marine Corps recruits called "Dago" as they experienced the rites of passage in the city's notorious red light district or across the border in Tijuana.

San Diego was an early center for aircraft production and that, plus its role as a naval port, led to the first great influx of newcomers during World War II.

That growth jerked San Diego into the category of a medium-large city but the downtown remained low-rise and rather tawdry and the heart of the city during the 1950s and 1960s was to be found in the residential suburbs and the city's magnificent Balboa Park and zoo.

In 1963, however, the first major new building in 40 years was erected in the downtown area, signaling the onset of a population boom that is continuing strongly, not only in the city but in the outlying suburbs as well, especially in the previously rural northern part of San Diego County.

San Diego County had just topped the 1 million mark in population by the 1960 census with perhaps half that in the city.

By 1970, it had reached 1.4 million, by 1980 1.9 million, by 1990 2.5 million and by the end of the century, the county is projected to have more than 3 million residents.

Its projected annual average growth rate of 2.2 percent during the remainder of the century is tops for any major urban area in the state.

"The population growth estimates are staggering as we prepare to deal with the consequences of rapid growth," said Steven Erie, a UC-San Diego political scientist who specializes in urban problems.

"We know now that we can't stop growth unless we build a wall. We can disperse the population, delay the impact by slowing the process of growth, thus making it a little more orderly. But we won't stop it."

The strong anti-growth sentiment in the city is forcing development into the suburbs, especially to the fast-growing interior communities of northern San Diego County, which are now connected to the city via the Interstate 15 freeway.

In that sense, San Diego typifies what is happening in other areas of the state—a dispersal of population and the economy to inland areas on the suburban fringes.

What is happening to San Diego socioeconomically, too, is almost a microcosm of what is happening to California as a whole—the evolution into

a two-tiered society of affluent, mostly Anglo managerial-technical-profes-
sional workers at the top and a largely minority second tier of relatively low-
paid service and industrial workers.

The traditional industrial class—the people who used to work in San
Diego's aircraft factories and other industries—is shrinking.

As San Diego County grows by 45 percent between the mid-1980s and
2020, racial/ethnic minorities, mostly Asian and Hispanic, will account for
almost 40 percent of the expansion. By 2000, Asians are expected to be San
Diego's largest minority group, many of them from Southeast Asia. There also
is a very large Filipino community centered on retired sailors.

As California experienced a wave of immigration, much of it illegal, from
Mexico and other Latin American countries during the 1980s, the border
between San Diego County and Mexico was the major point of entry. Daily and
nightly, Border Patrol agents played cat-and-mouse games with the border-
crossers and their guides. A rabbit's warren of dirt bluffs and arroyos known

Focus on San Diego County

Area .... 4,280.6 sq. miles
Percentage of California 2.7%

Population
(with percentage of California total)

	1960	1970	1980	1990	2000	2005
San Diego Co.	1,049,000	1,367,200	1,874,800	2,520,500	3,262,700	3,598,000
CALIFORNIA	6.6%	6.8%	7.9%	8.4%	9%	9.2%

Ethnic composition
(1990 Census)

	Anglo	Latino	Asian/Pacific	Black
San Diego Co.	65.4%	20.4%	7.4%	6.0%
CALIFORNIA	57.2%	25.8%	9.1%	7.0%

Economic Data

	Unemployment rate (Aug. 1991)	Taxable sales (1990 per capita)	Personal income (per capita) 1984	Personal income (per capita) 1989
San Diego Co.	6.1%	$8,630	$13,444	$18,198
CALIFORNIA	7.2%	$9,400	$14,593	$19,229

Political data

	1964	1972	1980	1984	1988
Voter registration (Democrat-Republican)	51-46%	48-43%	44-40%	42-44%	40-47%
Presidential vote (Democrat-Republican)	50-50%	36-64%	28-62%	34-60%	39-61%

Sources: State Department of Finance, 1990 Census, employment Development Department, Board of Equalization, Center
for Continuing Study of the California Economy and the Secretary of State's office.

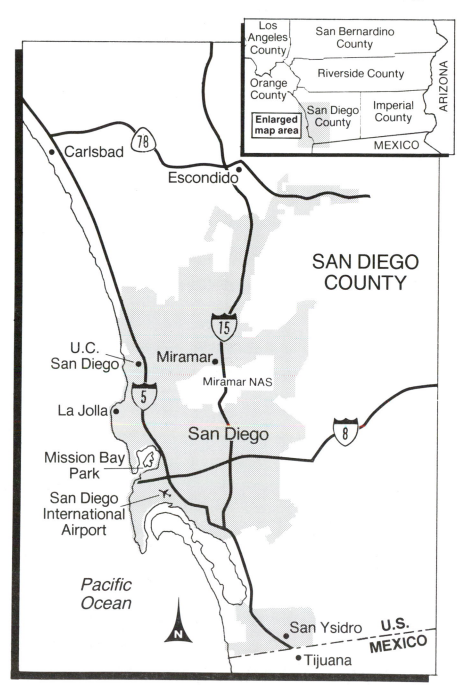

Graphic courtesy *The Sacramento Bee*

as Otay Mesa became the arena for the game, which included a third set of players: bandits who preyed upon the illegals, leaving them ravaged and robbed. And dozens of the Mexicans who made their way across the border were run down by cars as they attempted to scamper across Interstate 5 and other local freeways.

"Most of these people trying to cross have no conception of high-speed traffic and don't know what freeways are," Highway Patrol spokesman Jerry Bohrer said in 1991 as the patrol reported that 127 immigrants had been killed in the previous four years on local freeways. The slaughter became so severe that advocates for immigrant rights began distributing little yellow cards in Tijuana and other border towns warning of the danger.

Initially, San Diego County was merely a waystation as the immigrants attempted to find their way past the checkpoints and patrols to Los Angeles, where they could be absorbed into that city's huge Latino population and find work in its low-skill, low-wage industries. But during the latter years of the decade, increasing numbers of immigrants remained in San Diego County, seeking work in the fast-growing northern part of the county as day laborers or household workers. They established makeshift camps in the brushy canyons of the region and certain street corners of upscale north county communities became informal gathering points, called "el moscas," where employers would come each morning to find black market labor for construction, flower-growing operations and thoroughbred horse farms—labor that didn't demand fringe benefits, labor paid in cash, off the books.

That phenomenon, in turn, sparked a backlash. Roger Hedgecock, a one-time mayor of San Diego who had been driven out of office by scandal, used his popular radio talk show to agitate for tighter controls on the border, often personally leading "light up the border" protests in which San Diegans would park their cars, many of them carrying "We Want Order on Our Border" bumper stickers, on Otay Mesa at night and leave their headlights burning.

The confrontation is even more severe in the north county, long a center of activities for white supremacist groups. One town, Encinitas, declared the illegals to be a public nuisance and tried to legislate them from seeking work on its streets and there have been several racially tinged deaths and assaults. In 1990, a Mexican farm worker was found in a field, his hands and feet tied, a paper bag over his head, emblazoned with the Spanish words "no mas aqui" or "no more here." The owner of a grocery store frequented by Mexican workers was found guilty of the assault.

A 1987 study conducted for the Encinitas City Council gave some indication of how permanent the culture clash between upscale Anglos and poor, undocumented alien workers may become.

"Population growth and poverty will continue to drive Mexican workers northward for at least the next decade," the study concluded, "even in the face of constricted opportunities.... It is, therefore, not likely that undocumented workers will disappear from the Encinitas landscape."

Despite its proximity to Mexico, San Diego County's overall Latino population has lagged behind those of other major metropolitan areas as immigrants quickly passed through to Los Angeles. But with the new phenomenon of immigrants remaining in San Diego, its Hispanic population is growing rapidly; it reached 20 percent in the 1980s and is expected to hit 25 percent by the end of the 1990s. It's a trend exacerbated by another demographic fact about San Diego: its Anglo population is aging rapidly, in part because its mild climate and other attractions make it a highly desirable retirement site.

For decades, retired Navy and other military personnel had settled in San Diego in large numbers. The availability of medical care and other military-provided perks, as well as the weather, created one of the nation's largest concentrations of military retirees. In more recent years, non-military retirees have flocked to San Diego County, many into large retirement complexes (one of them founded by and named after bandleader Lawrence Welk) in the northern part of the county.

The immigrants to San Diego, whether they be from Asia, Mexico or Snow Belt states, are the major factor in the area's projected growth.

"San Diego's attractive power for foreign immigrants can be easily understood," said Rand Corp. demographer Kevin McCarthy. "A rich economy, proximity to the border and a history along with the rest of the state, as a center for non-European immigration."

The large numbers of immigrants and the large numbers of retirees on fixed incomes means that San Diego County's economy will suffer from a general low level of income as it moves into the 21st century. Demographers project that San Diego will not even be in the top 10 urban areas in terms of median personal income by the turn of the century despite its status as the state's second-largest city.

As San Diego has grown dramatically over the past quarter-century, so has its ambiance—from a sleepy Navy town into a bustling major city with big league sports.

Mission Valley, a weedy slough on what had been the northern edge of the city, has been completely transformed into a complex of hotels, shopping centers and office buildings, including the headquarters of the very influential Copley newspapers.

Mira Mesa, once just the site of another Navy air base, has become honeycombed with homes. Mission Bay, a man-made creation, sprouted hotels and tourist attractions and nearby Mission Beach became a swinging singles hangout.

The erection of that first modern new office building in San Diego in 1963 set the tone for an explosion of downtown construction. One after another, towering boxes with black glass skins and the names of banks affixed to their tops arose in the downtown, giving Sam Diego the feel of a major city. But the corporate merger mania that swept the country in the 1980s claimed at least a dozen local companies and their headquarters operations, creating what one local observer called a "stepchild mentality."

When San Diego Gas and Electric agreed to merge with Southern California Edison in the late 1980s, the anti-Los Angeles fervor and the stepchild mentality joined to create a monumental civic backlash. San Diego's leaders arose like one to battle the merger and won their battle when the state Public Utilities Commission, after years of hearings and debate, rejected the deal in 1991.

The old red light district that once catered to the carnal desires of sailors evolved into a trendy "Gaslight District" replete with brick sidewalks, ornate light fixtures, boutiques and restaurants that feature brie on their menus. And nearby, a unique urban shopping center, Horton Plaza, lured shoppers from the suburbs with its eclectic, high-rise architecture and abundance of specialty shops.

The housing developments have spread northward and southward, nearly to the Mexican border. Eastward expansion, into the mountains that separate the city from the desert, has been less intense.

But perhaps the most impressive transformation has occurred in the communities scattered along San Diego County's northern edge, from Carlsbad to Escondido.

Construction of freeways along Interstate 5 and Interstate 15 made the north county attractive to commuters, one of the ways in which San Diego has emulated its larger municipal cousin to the north while angrily rejecting any comparison.

Developers, stifled by the anti-growth attitudes in San Diego itself, have eagerly moved into the outlying areas.

The San Diego Association of Governments has estimated that between 1980 and 2000, central San Diego will grow by only 12 percent but the populations of outlying suburbs, especially those in the north county, will grow by 100 percent or more. There is, however, a downside to that—not unlike that seen in Los Angeles. Eventually, the city could become a core of mostly poor minorities encased by affluent suburbs.

As it has grown, San Diego has seen a sharp evolution in its economy.

From its Navy and airplane days, the San Diego economy has matured into high-tech manufacturing, plus the strong growth in retail, tourism and service sectors seen elsewhere in California.

The area surrounding the University of California campus has evolved into a high-tech research center, what local officials are fond of calling "Silicon Beach," and San Diego now is home to more than 200 biotechnical companies that have spun off the region's medical and biological research facilities. The 1985 opening of the San Diego Supercomputer Center was aimed at luring more research operations to the area. It's one of four being established in the country by the National Science Foundation and the only in California.

San Diego, meanwhile, has become a prime tourist draw. Its sparkling waterfront has sprouted hotels and other tourism-related facilities and the city's new waterfront convention center puts it into the hunt for the big national conventions with their multimillion-dollar impacts. And northern San Diego County has seen the development of a number of golf and tennis resort hotels. During the summer months, countless thousands of trailers and motor homes carrying Arizona license plates show up in San Diego and a certain hostility has developed between local residents and "Zoners," as they are derisively termed.

Another unique economic development is the establishment of a series of factories along San Diego's border with Mexico using capital from the north and labor from the south. But it's scarcely made a dent in perhaps the most important factor affecting San Diego's future, the existence only a few miles and a flimsy fence away of a Third World city containing more than a million persons.

The contrast of lifestyle between San Diego and Tijuana is startling, but only in recent years has there been any serious effort to deal with issues, ranging from illegal immigration to the flow of sewage, on an international basis.

Tijuana has experienced its own population explosion as hundreds of thousands of Mexicans have come to the border in hopes of overcoming the economic decay of the interior cities.

But despite its distance from Mexico City and the rest of the nation, Tijuana is not immune to Mexico's economic ills. The earthquake that flatted much of Mexico City in 1985, for example, led to a further devaluation of the peso that affected the buying power of those living in Tijuana.

"The history of Tijuana is of anarchic growth," Tijuana's mayor of the mid-1980s, economist Rene Trevio Arredondo, said. "The population arrived and didn't find public or private housing. There wasn't sufficient construction, so people put themselves on land wherever they could. They'd live in canyons, find a space for their car, another for a house. Tijuana then exploded demographically and created many problems for us in offering adequate services."

Trevio and other Mexican border leaders have tried to establish order out of economic chaos and deal realistically with their counterparts across the border on joint problems.

There are plans afoot for a trolley system on the Mexican side of the border to link up with the new San Diego trolley and efforts to disperse the population into new cities further east, linked to bi-national economic development. Otay Mesa, the informal border crossing center, also has become a complex of warehouses and other businesses that thrive on cross-border commerce. Tijuana's international airport abuts the border at Otay Mesa and a new official border crossing has relieved some of the pressure on the older checkpoints at Tijuana.

The presence of Tijuana's impoverished millions looms over the San Diego suburbs closest to the border, which must contend with the flow of illegal immigrants, the presence of bandits that prey upon the immigrants and other problems unique to the border.

"This problem at the border now is just a drop in the bucket of what we're going to have in the 21st century," National City Mayor Kile Morgan predicted in the mid-1980s.

Rapid growth throughout San Diego County and neighboring Baja California has put a severe strain on the infrastructure of water mains, streets and sewage treatment facilities and bringing those support services up to date is expected to be one of the major challenges facing San Diego as it approaches the 21st century and its population continues to grow.

The state has sliced freeways throughout San Diego, a la Los Angeles, but during rush hours they are packed and there is a strong local movement away from freeways and toward some form of mass transit. San Diego made history when it built a new trolley system linking the downtown area with the Mexican border and there are plans not only to extend the trolley into Mexico but to lay track eastward into residential suburbs.

The popularity of the trolley system notwithstanding, it has not yet had a major effect on the auto congestion in the urban area and the San Diego Association of Governments predicts that auto traffic will more than double by 2005, bringing the city even closer to the Los Angeles-like conditions that San Diegans abhor.

Still another pressing transportation issue is San Diego's airport, which is virtually at the edge of the downtown area. That makes it convenient for business travelers but having airliners dodge through high-rise downtown buildings is scarcely the safest approach and a major airliner collision over the city in the late 1970s has made everyone nervous about the location.

Several alternatives have been proposed but level land in San Diego is hard to find and the military already has the most attractive sites. The Navy has refused to consider turning over Miramar NAS on the northern edge of the city, perhaps the best site for a new airport. The other site most often proposed is on Otay Mesa, just north of the Mexico-U.S. border near Tijuana's new international airport. Some visionaries see expansion of the Tijuana airport to serve both cities as the most rational international approach.

The dynamics of rapid growth have created a political structure in San Diego that tends to focus on local issues rather than statewide or national ones, part of the "San Diego cul-de-sac" syndrome often cited by observers.

Historically, the area has voted conservatively, accurately reflecting the Copley press, the large military presence and the local power structure of developers and bankers. San Diego County is one of the few in the state with an absolute majority of registered Republicans and voted 2-1 for Ronald Reagan over Walter Mondale in 1984. But there is a libertarian tinge to the area's Republicanism when it comes to such lifestyle issues as abortion and environmental protection and there are pockets of liberalism in the mid-town area. Democrats have been mildly successful in winning legislative and local offices when they stress their environmentalist credentials. One notable battle occurred in 1990 when two state assemblywomen, Democrat Lucy Killea and Republican Carol Bentley. squared off over a vacant state Senate seat. It became a national story when the local Catholic bishop denounced Killea, a Catholic, for supporting abortion rights and the notoriety helped her win in what had been a Republican stronghold.

The Republican Party leadership that emerged in the area during the 1970s took the quality-of-life movement seriously. Pete Wilson, the city's mayor during the 1970s, personified that trend, strenuously promoting slow- and planned-growth policies that won favor with the city's power structure, staved off more radical anti-development movements and, by common consent, eased San Diego's transition from medium to large city, although critics say that he began cozying up to developers later in his mayorship, when he wanted to seek statewide office and needed campaign funds.

Wilson ran for governor unsuccessfully in 1978, having antagonized conservative Republican Party leaders with his centrist pronouncements and refusal to endorse Reagan's 1976 presidential bid. Four years later, in 1982, Wilson moved up to the U.S. Senate (and was elected governor in 1990). His Republican successor in the mayor's office, Roger Hedgecock, seemed to be cut from the same proactive, moderate mold and vowed to continue Wilson's policies vis-a-vis development. But Hedgecock also became ensnarled in one of the scandals that waft through San Diego's tight financial-political community periodically and was forced to resign after being convicted on political corruption charges.

The influx of immigrants from Mexico and Asia creates the potential for a political change in the county—if the newcomers can be organized into an effective political force. So far they haven't been and political participation by the Hispanic community is as low here as in other centers of Hispanic population. Only one Latino, backbench Assemblyman Peter Chacon, serves in San Diego's legislative and congressional delegations and there is very little Hispanic political leadership evident. San Diego has a highly concentrated black population, but it is too small to have more than tangential political impact. Black leaders protested in vain when the city's first black city manager was fired and there was another clash when the Port Commission refused to name the city's new convention center for Martin Luther King Jr.

The fast-growing suburbs in the north county, meanwhile, are as politically conservative as their counterpart areas around Los Angeles, and as they expand, the overall political prognosis is for a continued rightward tilt in local politics.

Ideology aside, San Diego's civic and political life has another distinguishing characteristic: the unusually powerful roles played by women, one which prompted television personality Jane Pauley to comment during a "Today" show episode broadcast from San Diego that "The power brokers in this town are all women."

At the time of that show, May 1989, the mayor of San Diego, Maureen O'Connor, was a woman, as was the publisher of the Copley newspapers, Helen Copley, the owner of the San Diego Padres baseball team, Joan Kroc, the

chairperson of the county board of supervisors, Susan Golding, and the head
of the city school board, Susan Davis. Women hold several other powerful
positions in the area as well, including one of the county's state Senate seats
(Killea) and three of its state Assembly seats.

Some of the seeming dominance of women in local civic and political life
is a matter of happenstance. Both Copley and Kroc inherited their positions
when their husbands died. Copley had been newspaper tycoon Jim Copley's
secretary before she married him and Kroc's husband, Ray, founded the
McDonald's fast food empire.

O'Connor, who was elected mayor after Hedgecock was driven from
office by scandal, is married to another fast food mogul, Jack-in-the-Box co-
founder Robert Peterson, while Golding was married to Peterson's erstwhile
partner, politician and financier Dick Silberman, who became enmeshed
himself in a drug money laundering scandal and was sent to federal prison while
his wife was on the Board of Supervisors.

Nevertheless, even those with inherited clout are accepted among San
Diegans as effective power brokers and many of the San Diego women who
are prominent earned their positions strictly on their own, such as Killea.

What some call the "San Diego matriarchy" does not seem destined to
endure. Copley and Kroc have gone into semi-retirement, O'Connor announced in 1990 that she wouldn't seek another term in 1992, even though she
was being touted as a future Democratic candidate for statewide office, and
Golding's career was severely damaged by the scandal revolving about her
husband.

Such scandals—the intertwining of money and politics—have become
common fixtures in San Diego politics. Despite its size and its aspirations
toward world-class civic status, San Diego's civic and political subculture is a
tight and relatively small structure, one in which it is difficult to maintain the
kind of compartmentalization that makes for scandal-free government, and
there's a lot of money to be made in such a fast-growing area.

San Francisco:
Panache, plastic and procrastination

SAN FRANCISCO USED TO BE A REAL CITY, WHERE FISHERMEN LANDED THEIR CATCHES, where stevedores unloaded ships, where workers made things in factories, where people rode cable cars and lived in turn-of-the-century buildings.

San Francisco was a city whose rich ethnic diversity reflected the succeeding waves of immigrants who had been lured by the promise of better lives—the descendants of Chinese railroad builders, Italian and Portuguese fishermen, Russian and Jewish merchants, blacks from the Deep South and Mexican farm workers.

It was a delightful city, full of color and excitement and honest emotion. There was political and intellectual ferment, a sense of great things happening. It was a favorite destination for tourists but tourism was only an incidental economic activity.

Somewhere, somehow, it turned sour. San Francisco sold out.

It sold its funky downtown financial district to the erectors of glass-and-concrete boxes that masked the hills and blotted out the sun.

It drove the fishermen, the longshoremen and the factory workers from their workplaces to make room for tacky tourist traps.

It converted its cable cars, once a means to traverse the city's hills, into a tourist experience more suitable to an amusement park than a great metropolis.

It allowed its politics to become so fragmented that only those with pull could navigate the city hall thicket and public policy decisions on such matters as an athletic arena, an unfinished freeway or a housing project would be left hanging for years.

It made rents and homes so expensive that the middle-class and poor residents were driven from the city in despair, leaving few but the affluent and the down-and-out to call it home. And as it closed its doors to all but the wealthy, it allowed Los Angeles to become the new melting pot of the West, where immigrants flocked to seek their fortunes in a dynamic economy.

Slowly, but inexorably—and still claiming that it was "the city that knows how"—San Francisco became a caricature of the city that had once been the jewel of California and the envy of millions. Even San Francisco's most ardent fans, such as newspaper columnist Herb Caen, became apologetic for what it had become and nostalgic for what it had been.

And while San Francisco was being converted into Disneyland-north—the world's most popular tourist destination, according to a 1991 survey by Conde Nast Traveler magazine—its once preeminent position in finance and trade was being usurped by communities more interested in the real world.

The new manufacturing jobs were being created in the Santa Clara Valley and San Jose was growing so fast that it surpassed San Francisco in size by the late 1980s.

The shipping lines gave up on San Francisco and began using the more modern facilities in Oakland.

The Pacific Stock Exchange moved to Los Angeles and the much-hated rival to the south became the West's banking center—especially so after giant Bank of America, founded by an Italian immigrant to serve hard-working fishermen and farmers, fell on hard times by ignoring its roots.

Even the office jobs—the supposed reason for the conversion of downtown into forest of boxy high-rises—began moving out, to places, such as Walnut Creek and Concord, lower in cost and closer to transportation access and affordable housing.

San Francisco's employment base, data from the Association of Bay Area Counties (ABAG) indicate, is growing in two directions _ high-paying managerial and professional positions and low-paying service jobs.

Middle-income manufacturing, utility and transportation jobs are stagnant or declining. San Francisco, therefore, is developing a two-tier economy of the affluent and non-affluent, the served and the servers, the haves and the have-nots. While tourism became the city's largest industry with a value of more than $1 billion a year, the hotels, restaurants and other tourist-related businesses offered few middle-class jobs. Indeed, the 1980s saw San Francisco add more workers—many of them poor immigrants—to its population than jobs and the gap, some 28,000, means that significant numbers of San Franciscans are now commuting to other communities to work, a reversal of historic trends.

It is as if the city has consciously made its amenities accessible only to the residents and visitors who can afford the price of admission and deliberately shunned those who cannot. And it has done so under a succession of city governments that have professed to be liberal and humanistic in their policies but which have been seduced by the blandishments of those who hoped to turn a buck off the city's image.

The physical signs of the conversion are evident wherever one looks in San Francisco.

Take, for example, the waterfront, the city's doorway to the great harbor that was its original reason for being. At last count, slightly more than a dozen fishing boats still were berthed at what the garish neon signs proclaim to be Fisherman's Wharf. The boats and their masters have disappeared, one by one, to retirement, death or other ports where fishing is still more important than catering to the tourist dollars.

"They are turning Fisherman's Wharf into a carnival," one of the few remaining fishermen, Peter Bentivegna, complained at a 1985 Port Commission meeting.

"They got a man who dresses like a pirate and has parrots. There is a guy who wears a gorilla suit. They got guys driving rickshaws. There's horse-and-buggy rides. What's that got to do with fishing?" Nothing. The restaurants that the fish companies built to accommodate visitors—as a sideline—now must bring in fish from other ports to serve visitors who don't know the difference but want, in the words of one tourist attraction, a "San Francisco experience." The T-shirt and coffee mug shops, meanwhile, continue to proliferate.

The city professes to have plans to revive the fishing trade and officials have unveiled a grandiose plan to build new berths for fishing boats and otherwise make life easier for fishermen, who must now compete with tourists even for parking places. But city officials also don't want to do anything that interferes with tourism, which has become San Francisco's number one industry, and both fishermen and tourists are uneasy with the situation.

"We've received so many promises that we don't believe anymore," Fisherman's Wharf activist Al Baccari said in a newspaper interview as the renewal plans were unveiled in 1990. "There are enough blueprints to paper walls, but it's all recycled reports from Day 1."

Even the plans to restore fishing have had a tourist angle. "I want to bring back the fishing industry, make it more visible again," Christopher Martin, president of the Fisherman's Wharf Merchants Association, told an interviewer when the plans were first being formulated. "It provides what people want to see. They want to see fish being unloaded. They want to see all the old fishermen with leathered faces. It's something they can't see in the Midwest and it's what draws in tourists."

One senses that an animated robot from the Disney studios would suffice.

Martin is an executive at The Cannery, one of the many waterfront structures that have been converted into tourist draws.

Nearby, the old Ghirardelli chocolate works is another rabbit's warren of tourist-oriented shops and south along the waterfront, Pier 39 is still another—a sad, plastic reminder of the great maritime industry that once thrived here.

"There's so many tourists down here that they're all stepping on each other's toes," Jim Phelan, a charter boat captain, mused. "The fishermen originally were the people who mattered at the wharf. Now, it's just tourists, that's all."

The San Francisco Examiner's urban planning writer, Gerald Adams, said much the same thing in a critical, 1987 examination of what had happened to Fisherman's Wharf.

"Once a vibrant fishing center with charming marine scenery, steaming crab pots and colorful boats," Adams wrote, "the wharf is now dominated by a glitzy hodgepodge of souvenir stands and stores that have nothing to do with its fishing heritage."

The evolution of the waterfront from a place of fishing boats and freight-laden ships into a tourist trap symbolizes the evolution of San Francisco itself, one that has sparked much soul-searching.

The election of Art Agnos as mayor in 1987 was, in effect, a popular uprising against business as usual. Agnos, a transplanted New Englander who rose through the staff ranks of the state Legislature to become a state assemblyman before challenging the business establishment for the mayorship, promised to restore authenticity to San Francisco and broaden access to decision-making power. Agnos' first term, however, was a mixed bag of brilliance—taking command during a devastating, 1989 earthquake, for example—and petty, vindictive politics that dismayed some of his strongest supporters, and Agnos went into a 1991 re-election campaign with only a so-so chance of winning. He ran second in a multi-candidate field and was forced into a runoff with the front-runner, former Police Chief Frank Jordan, who gave voice to middle-class frustration at the hassles of life in San Francisco, especially the army of homeless that occupies the civic center area.

Jordan coasted to what turned out to be a remarkably east victory over Agnos in the runoff election, even though the normally abrasive mayor adopted a much-humbler, apologetic attitude during the closing days of the campaign.

Post-election analyses indicated that while traditionally liberal neighborhoods voted for Agnos and middle-class areas favored Jordan, swing voters turned away from the incumbent. That was especially evident among Asian voters, who favored Jordan over Agnos by a large margin and may have been decisive.

Being mayor of San Francisco may be the toughest political job in California because of the city's disparate and often contradictory political streams. No matter what a mayor does on any issue, approximately half of his or her constituents are going to be unhappy.

And because of its complex and interlocking politics, San Francisco has a difficult time making any major public decision, even a wrong decision.

Historian Kevin Starr called it an "environment of Balkanized infighting, the vetoing of public activity by absurd groups" and added, "What is missing is the civic energy and vision that bring those disparate energies together behind bold city projects. San Francisco used to be a city that always said 'yes'; now it seems to only say 'no'."

That chronic lack of civic direction is why, for instance, none of the three major freeways that were designed to carry traffic through the city was ever completed. They were partly built but left unfinished because of changing political tides. One of them, along the waterfront, was severely damaged by the 1989 earthquake and demolished afterwards, but had nature not interceded, it's likely that the Embarcadero Freeway would have remained hanging in midair, a physical metaphor for the city, for another generation.

San Francisco's endemic inability to decide whether to build a new baseball park is another example of this civic procrastination, as is the years-long political struggle over the city's largest parcel of developable land, the so-called Mission Bay area that had been Southern Pacific Railroad's complex of shops and yards south of Market Street and later fell to the Santa Fe Railroad during the two corporations' brief merger. At one point, the Mission Bay and baseball park controversies were even intertwined.

Southern Pacific, and then Santa Fe, wanted to develop Mission Bay into 313 acres of offices, shopping centers and housing but the precise mix has been a hot political issue that has enmeshed San Francisco politicians since 1979. "This is not a political issue. This is the future of the city at stake," one high city official, Rudy Nothenberg, said.

When it was Southern Pacific's project, the railroad hired Willie Brown, the speaker of the state Assembly who has made a profitable career out of helping development interests with their city hall problems. And later, John Burton, former congressman and future assemblyman, was added to the railroad's lobbying crew.

Agnos had been a sharp critic of Mission Bay as an assemblyman, saying it would make big profits for its owners but do little to solve the city's chronic lack of affordable housing. The development plans also violated a 1986 anti-development law passed by voters.

As mayor, however, Agnos finally negotiated a settlement with Santa Fe Railroad (its real estate arm is called Catellus Development Co.) that allowed the office and retail development at a reduced level and also required that 38 percent of the 8,500 housing units to be affordable to middle-income tenants, thus making a dent in one of the city's most persistent problems and powerful social factors. San Franscisco voters implicitly rejected the deal by denying the project an exemption from the development control law, but the first phase is being built anyway and company officials hope to gain their exemption in a subsequent election.

Mission Bay is just one of San Francisco's hot spots, however. The city is really a collection of small towns, enclaves that are differentiated by ethnicity, lifestyle or income. And each has its own story.

A few blocks from the waterfront is North Beach, once a colorful Italian-American enclave filled with cafes and coffee shops, later the home to artists and writers of the 1950s beatnik area and in recent years the site of a sleazy row of sex shows and strip joints catering to tourists.

The few local businesses that remain are being squeezed by sharp increases in rent, imposed by landlords who have tourist-oriented businesses waiting to take the storefronts.

"There's nothing left of North Beach anymore," delicatessen operator Alda Maggiora complained in a 1985 newspaper interview. "Everything's become a problem. I don't want anymore of this. I want out."

Her landlord wanted to double her rent.

Broadway, where the sex shows flourished for years, has become what one longtime resident calls "a war zone," filled with drunks who frighten pedestrians.

Sal Romano uttered that description at a police department hearing into expanding problems with vandalism and public drunkenness along the famous night club strip. Local residents blame the clubs for the problems.

Their complaints reverberate throughout the city—middle-class residents saying they are being forced out of their homes and businesses by skyrocketing rents, street crime and a lack of facilities for all but the poor and the rich.

Many of the neighborhoods have evolved from middle-class workers to gay couples whose combined incomes are sufficient to buy the homes (average cost, $250,000-plus) and rent the apartments ($700 a month and up.)

The gays who first came to San Francisco to find a tolerant atmosphere have become one of the city's most important economic and political blocs.

The Haight-Ashbury district near Golden Gate Park, for instance, was a working class neighborhood whose low rents made it the home of the "hippies" during the late 1960s and early 1970s—just as North Beach had been home to the beatniks—and in more recent years has blossomed with trendy shops catering to the neighborhood's newest residents, affluent professionals of both heterosexual and homosexual persuasion.

In Haight-Ashbury, the average value of a home increased by 439 percent between 1970 and 1980.

It's part of another trend in San Francisco—the so-called "gentrification" of older neighborhoods that draws in the affluent and drives out the poor.

It's a trend, moreover, that runs against the grain of most urban areas, where the affluent move to the suburbs and leave the poor in the central city. That's what is happening in Los Angeles, for example. An estimated half-million Anglos left Los Angeles between 1970 and 1980, moving to the suburbs and leaving behind a city that is increasingly Hispanic and Asian.

The poor and the middle-class San Franciscans who leave the city are moving to other Bay Area counties where housing is more affordable, census records indicate. A third move south into the working-class neighborhoods of northern San Mateo County and a quarter move across San Francisco Bay to Alameda County. They are replaced, the census records indicate, by well-educated, highly paid professionals, mostly Anglo and Asian, who can afford the housing costs and want the cultural amenities of the city, although Anglos, the 1990 census revealed, are now less than half of the city's population with Asians comprising another 26 percent.

Gentrification is evident throughout San Francisco but startlingly so in the Western Addition, the city's traditional black area.

Blacks came to San Francisco, like the gays a generation later, looking for economic opportunity and tolerance. Tens of thousands of blacks moved into San Francisco from the South during World War II, finding jobs in the shipyards and other defense industries that sprouted overnight around the Bay Area.

Blacks moved into the Western Addition—often taking homes hastily vacated by Japanese-Americans, who were being shipped off to internment camps after Pearl Harbor—and for three decades thereafter, it was San Francisco's Harlem with clubs, theaters and stores that preserved an ethnic culture.

But postwar poverty and the strategic location of the district made change inevitable. To real estate speculators and redevelopment authorities, the land simply was too valuable to be occupied by poor people—especially poor people who lacked clout at city hall.

Authorities promised to set aside housing units for the longtime residents, but with every wave of redevelopment, the black population got a little smaller. Between 1970 and 1980, the city's black population dropped by 10,000 and most of those who moved out went to Oakland, which became a predominantly black city. There was another 10,000-person drop in San Francisco's black population in the 1980s. And now, the Western Addition is the latest San Francisco neighborhood to be converted into development oriented toward the yuppies.

Sausalito developer Donald Tishman acquired four square blocs of the area from the city's Redevelopment Agency and laid plans for a complex of apartment towers and townhouses. Some units were set aside for low-income residents and Tishman brought some blacks into the project as minority partners, but the overall effect of the project is to further San Francisco's transformation into a two-tier city.

Gentrification is even striking the city's other black ghetto, Hunter's Point. The city's famed Chinatown, meanwhile, has become packed with refugees from the political and economic turmoil of China and Hong Kong and despite the shining face shown to tourists, much of Chinatown is a ghetto in which low-income Chinese, many of them elderly, are packed into substandard and potentially dangerous housing.

"Chinatown's housing is still some of the worst in the city, if not the country," said Gordon Chin, executive director of the Chinatown Resource Center. "The continuing aging of the housing stock and the lack of alternatives all combine to make this a difficult situation."

The city's large Asian population—nearly 30 percent according to the 1990 census and dispersed from Chinatown into many neighborhoods, most notably the Richmond district—is economically important but has only begun to flex political muscle. In terms of political activism, even voting, Asians remain the least influential group in the city. Despite having nearly a third of the city's population, for instance, Asians can claim just one of the city's 15 Board of Supervisors seats.

Nowhere is the drastic change in San Francisco of the last generation more evident than in the downtown business district.

A quarter-century ago, San Francisco's skyline meandered with its hills. The old-line corporations such as Bank of America and Standard Oil had their impressive headquarters buildings, but San Francisco was essentially a low-rise city.

Over a phenomenal two-decade period, beginning in the mid-1960s, dozens of skyscrapers were erected in the city's financial district, doubling the amount of downtown office space, blocking the sun and creating dark concrete canyons

Focus on San Francisco

Area .... 91.1 sq. miles
Percentage of California .... .05%

Population
(with percentage of California total)

	1960	1970	1980	1990	2000	2005
San Francisco Co.	741,500	713,200	680,800	723,900	680,500	632,300
CALIFORNIA	4.7%	3.6%	2.9%	2.4%	1.9%	1.6%

Ethnic composition
(1990 Census)

	Anglo	Latino	Asian/Pacific	Black
San Francisco Co.	46.6%	13.9%	28.4%	10.5%
CALIFORNIA	57.2%	25.8%	9.1%	7.0%

Economic Data

	Unemployment rate (Aug. 1991)	Taxable sales (1990 per capita)	Personal income (per capita)	
			1984	1989
San Francisco Co.	5.3%	$11,875	$18,624	$26,797
CALIFORNIA	7.2%	$9,400	$14,593	$19,229

Political data

	1964	1972	1980	1984	1988
Voter registration (Democrat-Republican)	64-32%	67-25%	60-21%	65-19%	65-18%
Presidential vote (Democrat-Republican)	71-29%	57-43%	55-33%	68-32%	74-26%

Sources: State Department of Finance, 1990 Census, employment Development Department, Board of Equalization, Center for Continuing Study of the California Economy and the Secretary of State's office.

through which the wind whistled.

Critics lamented the "Manhattanization" of downtown San Francisco but developers pulled the right strings at city hall and building after building rose, shielding the hills from view and dwarfing what had been the city's landmarks, such as Coit Tower.

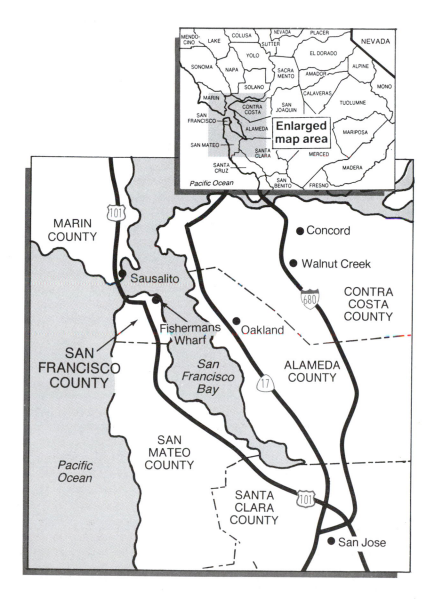

Graphic courtesy *The Sacramento Bee*

Dianne Feinstein, the city's mayor during the late 1970s and early 1980s, called them "ice cube trays" for their rectangular similarity _ except for the striking Transamerica Pyramid—but did little to stop their proliferation.

The critics finally rebelled and collected enough signatures to place on the 1985 ballot a measure that would have banned all new high-rise office construction for three years.

It scared downtown business interests and city hall enough that two months before the election, the Board of Supervisors—San Francisco's city council—adopted a so-called "downtown plan" that limits high-rise construction to 950,000 square feet a year, imposes a high limitation of 550 feet (about 42 stories) on new buildings, preserves historic buildings and requires developers to contribute for child care, transit, open space and public artworks.

Feinstein, who advocated the plan as a more moderate alternative to the ban proposed in the initiative, hailed it as "a milestone moment in San Francisco and a giant step for city planning everywhere."

"We really are trying to move the architectural community beyond the boxy international style buildings," George Williams, a city planner and principal author of the downtown plan, said. "We want to see a lot more visual interest in the buildings... We're challenging the architects to come up with different styles."

With the downtown plan in place, developers then financed a massive campaign against the moratorium initiative, focusing on more conservative voters and blacks in low-income areas, telling both that a high-rise ban would mean a loss of jobs.

The pro-moratorium forces had almost no campaign money and the measure was defeated in a low turnout election.

Feinstein hailed it as an endorsement of her plan. "We now have curbs on downtown...and this vote shows people realize that," she said after the election.

Even a moratorium, however, would have done nothing about the forest of buildings already in place. Nor can it alter the economic facts of life: despite the high-rise blizzard, San Francisco is losing its dominant role in the Bay Area economy.

Its population (just over 700,000) and workforce are stagnant while those of other areas, such as Contra Costa, Santa Clara and Sonoma counties, are growing. San Jose's former mayor, Tom McEnery, often talked about San Francisco as being a "dying city" as he watched San Jose zoom past the older rival in population.

It's not dying, but it is changing into a bedroom town for the affluent who can afford homes that cost an average of $250,000 each and a draw for tourists.

If present trends continue, demographers say, the 21st century San Francisco will have completed the transition from a city of great diversity to one of great sameness: well-to-do, white and Asian residents with first-rate amenities that only they can afford but with almost no poor and relatively few middle-class families.

Richard LeGates, who directed an urban studies program at San Francisco State University, said the city "may be pricing out its janitors, its teachers, its nurses and its gas station attendants like Marin County already has."

"Aside from humanitarian concern for people, there's a tremendous social cost of pricing them out. On a more mundane level, there's just the texture, quality of life, being made more interesting by a mix of ages and incomes and backgrounds."

San Francisco remains, however, a major city, not only in California terms but in global ones, and the center of a region that continues to undergo wrenching social and economic change.

The nine counties of the Bay Area have created some regional organizations, both voluntary and governmental, and are likely to embrace California's first true regional government that would deal with water, transportation, air quality, solid waste disposal and other regional issues.

Bay Vision 2020, a blue-ribbon commission, concluded in 1991 that chaos will overtake the area unless regional government is established. Raising that most frightening of specters, Los Angeles, the commission said, "We fear that present development trends, unless otherwise channeled, will result in a region that emulates Los Angeles rather than insures the character long associated with the Bay Area."

Regional government, however, will be difficult to create because of decades of competitive pressures and mutual suspicions. When, for example, it was proposed to create a comprehensive port district for San Francisco Bay, Oakland officials bitterly opposed it. They feared that a single port district would be a vehicle by which San Francisco would drain resources from the more modern and busier Oakland port facilities. The fast-growing suburbs, meanwhile, fear that San Francisco will exercise its political muscle to dump unwanted problems—trash disposal facilities, for instance—on them.

A 1991 poll by The San Francisco Chronicle found that support for regional government was soaring among Bay Area residents because of traffic congestion, but opposition among local officials, especially those of suburban cities, remains strong.

What of the future?

San Francisco will continue to decline in economic importance vis-a-vis other cities, even other cities, such as San Jose and Sacramento, in Northern California. But it will remain the region's cultural center and the tourist industry will strengthen its grip on the city's economy. If regional government does come to pass, San Francisco will be its center and may gain more influence over land use, transportation and other decisions now made in suburban communities that affect its future.

What's most critical, many San Franciscans believe, is for their city to regain the spirit of cooperative tolerance that once was its hallmark—the communal effort to rebuild after the 1906 earthquake and fire being its finest flowering—and subdue the single-interest, slash-and-burn politics that have become its more recent public motif.

As historian Starr put it: "For the time being, only the 49ers or the Giants have been able to bring about such a collective identity. In the meanwhile, the San Francisco we all have in common awaits our repossession. It is, after all, the actual and symbolic center of the fifth-largest urban population in these United States. It is inconceivable that this internationally known American city should deliberately disestablish its public identity. It is inconceivable that a world city should devolve into warring factions and repudiate its soul. On the other hand, there is always the example of Beirut."

East Bay:
A study in contrasts

As the crow flies, it's about 10 miles from downtown Oakland to downtown Walnut Creek.

The crow would have to fly over some hills. A motorist might make the trip in 15 minutes if he didn't try it at rush hour when the Caldecott Tunnel is packed with commuters.

It isn't very far in miles, but the East Bay area—Alameda, Contra Costa and Solano counties—represents a socioeconomic dichotomy without parallel in California.

Walnut Creek, a once-sleepy if affluent suburb, is at the center of an explosion of population growth and economic development that is creating a new megalopolis along Interstate 680 in the shadow of Mount Diablo.

Companies have moved, are moving and will move tens of thousands of jobs into Contra Costa County, creating traffic jams, driving up housing prices and causing other impacts that are sparking a political backlash.

But if Walnut Creek, Concord, Pleasant Hill, San Ramon and the other communities of what is called "ContraCostapolis" have too much development pressure, only a few miles away there is Oakland, trying desperately to stay alive as a city, begging employers and developers to invest and sometimes teetering on the brink of municipal collapse as it copes with an unprecedented series of natural and manmade calamities.

It's a city that has undergone an astonishing change of power structure in a single generation. It had been identified with Republican conservatism for generations, personified by the Knowland newspaper publishing family. The "black power" movement of the 1960s—especially the emergence of the Black Panther Party—frightened the power structure. The city's black population had expanded dramatically during World War II and the postwar era as Oakland's factories and shipyards clanged with activity, reaching nearly 50 percent by the 1980 census.

What emerged from the sometimes violent racial confrontations of the era, however, was relatively moderate black leadership that today struggles with a continued flight of whites and jobs to the suburbs.

The city was unofficialy adopted by Gov. Jerry Brown's administration in the 1970s and early 1980s and the state poured millions of dollars into civic renewal. The city responded with an ambitious but financially shaky makeover of its downtown area, complete with world-class hotel and convention center, and tried to develop a major downtown shopping center in an effort to attract business back to the city. It even sold the city hall and other public facilities on leaseback contracts to raise capital for civic improvements.

The deals enriched attorneys and financiers with connections at city hall, but so far they have resulted in only a modest gain in jobs and some of the bills are coming due. In 1985, Oakland was forced to restructure the debt backing the hotel-convention center complex because of a lack of business, and the city had the dubious distinction in early 1986 of having the nation's highest office vacancy rate, more than 27 percent.

Lionel Wilson, a former judge, became Oakland's moderate black mayor in 1977 and found himself simultaneously battling more militant black rivals and the continued reluctance of major employers to relocate into a city renowned for its crime problems. He watched, instead, as big, job-heavy developments bypassed Oakland and went to the new office complexes in ContraCostapolis.

"The bottom line was the crime fears those people who make those decisions have about the city," Wilson told a visitor to his ornate city hall office before placing third in the 1990 mayoral election.

"What Oakland does is to continue to try to develop itself and build insofar as it can. Basically it's a waiting game. But already we're seeing positive signs that people are moving back into the city from those outlying areas." Residents of some poor neighborhoods, Wilson said, are complaining about white gentrification that is driving up housing costs.

"The boom you see out there (along Interstate 680) is going to stop," Wilson said hopefully—a prediction that did not become a fact during his mayorship.

A study by University of California Professor John Landis concluded that Oakland lost thousands of jobs in the early 1980s—especially in manufacturing and the transportation, communications and public utilities sectors—but staged something of a comeback in the latter half of the decade and wound up about even, largely because government agencies were consciously shifted into the city as a means of propping up its economy, most notably those in a new federal government office complex and in a University of California system headquarters that was moved from nearby Berkeley. Bureaucratic commuters who come into downtown Oakland to work, eat their lunch in a building cafeteria and return home to the suburbs, however, don't do much for Oakland's economy.

Pro-Oakland commentators have called it a "quiet boom," although the boarded-up storefronts and empty lots in downtown Oakland don't offer much physical evidence of change. The Port of Oakland's political and financial problems, financial scandals in local school systems and the near-demise of Oakland's black-owned newspaper, The Tribune, contribute to the widespread feeling that Oakland may be just one bad recession away from collapse.

"Some of the doom and gloom about Oakland is misleading," urban economist Linda Hausrath told The San Francisco Chronicle in 1991, adding that the city's central Bay Area location should make it a strong prospect for growth in the 1990s.

Even Oakland's most ardent advocates, however, acknowledge that it has a huge image problem—a reputation for violent and persistent crime—that makes employers reluctant to relocate. Bay Area media, centered in San Francisco, exacerbate the city's image problem by dwelling on crime in Oakland, even though statistically San Francisco's crime problems are just as bad. It's an illustration of how Oakland has existed in San Francisco's cultural shadow.

Regardless of their ideological orientation, Oakland's leaders always have resented that and tried to establish the city's separate identity through such things as enticing major league sports. but, ironically, it was Oakland's expensive and unsuccessful bid to entice the Raiders professional football team back to the city of its birth (the team had moved to Los Angeles in the early 1980s) that was Wilson's undoing. His rivals jumped on the failure and when the dust had settled, Elihu Harris, a young state assemblyman, had become Oakland's new mayor on a pledge to restore the city's lost luster.

Harris' task has been made immeasurably more difficult by disasters that have clobbered Oakland with depressing regularity. More than 40 persons died when the 1989 Bay Area earthquake flattened an Oakland freeway choked with rush hour traffic and exactly two years later, a wind-shipped firestorm swept through the city's most expensive hillside neighborhoods, destroying thousands of homes and apartments, leaving dozens dead and causing damage estimated at between $1 billion and $2 billion. Contributing to the fire's rapid spread was Oakland's less-than-sterling ability to respond because of manpower cuts and antiquated equipment in its fire department. And the disasters have imposed a huge financial burden on the city and sucked civic energy from economic and social reconstruction.

Berkeley, Oakland's municipal neighbor, also has undergone a dramatic change of image in the last quarter-century.

It's difficult to believe now, but Berkeley, like Oakland, was once a stronghold of conservative politics, despite its dominance by the University of California's original campus.

During the 1960s, however, it acquired a different image as both city and campus underwent civic upheavals that pitted the establishment against New Left militants on issues ranging from "free speech" to America's involvement in Vietnam.

Eventually, and after more than one armed clash, the more visible signs of confrontation faded. But students and non-students in the college community gradually took over city government and embarked on an experiment in

Focus on East Bay

Area .... 2,495.5 sq. miles
Percentage of California 1.6%

Population
(with percentage of California total)

	1960	1970	1980	1990	2000	2005
Alameda Co.	912,600	1,073,000	1,109,100	1,282,400	1,420,000	1,475,500
Contra Costa Co.	413,200	557,500	658,200	810,300	978,200	1,047,900
Solano Co.	137,100	172,500	237,300	345,700	471,900	529,200
TOTAL	1,462,900	1,803,000	2,004,600	2,438,400	2,870,100	3,052,600
CALIFORNIA	9.3%	9.0%	8.4%	8.1%	7.9%	7.8%

Ethnic composition
(1990 Census)

	Anglo	Latino	Asian/Pacific	Black
Alameda Co.	53.2%	14.2%	14.4%	17.4%
Contra Costa Co.	69.7%	11.4%	9.2%	9.1%
Solano Co.	60.9%	13.4%	11.9%	12.9%
CALIFORNIA	57.2%	25.8%	9.1%	7%

Economic Data

	Unemployment rate (Aug. 1991)	Taxable sales (1990 per capita)	Personal income (per capita)	
			1984	1989
Alameda Co.	5.4%	$10,210	$15,324	$20,581
Contra Costa Co.	5.4%	$9,213	$16,712	$23,514
Solano Co.	6.3%	$7,237	$12,444	$15,374
CALIFORNIA	7.2%	$9,400	$14,593	$19,229

Political data

	1964	1972	1980	1984	1988
Voter registration (Democrat-Republican)	62-34%	63-31%	59-29%	59-28%	58-30%
Presidential vote (Democrat-Republican)	66-34%	52-48%	39-55%	53-47%	59-41%

Sources: State Department of Finance, 1990 Census, employment Development Department, Board of Equalization, Center for Continuing Study of the California Economy and the Secretary of State's office.

municipal radicalism.

A stringent rent control law and a decidedly left-wing foreign policy are only two manifestations of a city government that is an exercise in political theater.

As the 1970s evolved into the 1980s, the UC student body moved a few notches to the right. Social conflict gave way to employment opportunities in the list of undergraduate priorities. But the city government went the other way,

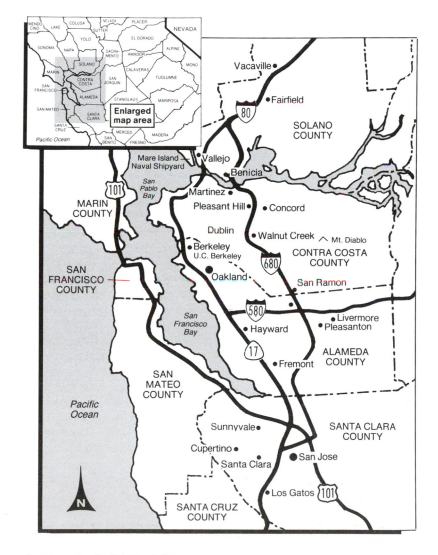

Graphic courtesy *The Sacramento Bee*

edging even further leftward in the 1984 elections as voters eliminated liberals and replaced them with a majority of "progressives" led by Mayor Eugene Newport, who was later succeeded by similarly left-leaning Loni Hancock, wife of the area's state assemblyman, Tom Bates.

Whatever its effect in other areas, the radicalization of Berkeley— especially the adoption of the state's most stringent rent control law—has discouraged private financial investment in the city, creating a shortage of rental housing, encouraging landlords to neglect their properties and forcing students to look elsewhere for quarters. And like Oakland, it was hit hard by the 1991 firestorm that swept through upscale neighborhoods in the hills.

Although Oakland and Berkeley are economically stagnant, the southern end of Alameda County, from Hayward eastward into the Livermore Valley, has more going for it.

The Hayward-Fremont area is getting some spillover development from the nearby San Jose-Silicon Valley area while the Livermore Valley is an extension of ContraCostapolis. Fremont seemingly acquired a new lease on industrial life when General Motors reopened an auto assembly plant in partnership with Toyota to produce a new car. The Association of Bay Area Governments, a regional planning agency, projects that the southern part of the county will account for more than 70 percent of Alameda County's job growth between 1985 and 2005 and also account for the bulk of the county's population expansion.

Although Alameda County's population is expected to grow by only 42 percent between 1960 and 2005—less than half the growth in the state as a whole—the Livermore Valley alone is expected to expand by 74 percent just between 1985 and 2005. Alameda County's actual growth in the 1980s was some 16 percent, about two-thirds of California's overall population expansion rate, and that growth, some 200,000 persons, was concentrated in the southern and eastern suburbs.

Perched virtually on the line that separates Alameda County from Contra Costa County is San Ramon, which was just another bedroom town until the owners of Bishop Ranch decided that there was more money in concrete than cows.

The still-growing Bishop Ranch complex, sprawled along Interstate 680, is a living lesson in how transportation access—in this case a beltway freeway— begets growth.

By late 1985, according to the Contra Costa County Planning Department, more than 5.5 million square feet of offices, warehouses, restaurants and hotels had been built or were under construction with another 2.3 million square feet being planned. Already, more than 20,000 employees are working or being moved into the complex by its tenants with another 7,500 scheduled.

Those who occupy complexes in Bishop Ranch are among California's largest private employers.

Pacific Bell has consolidated operations previously scattered throughout the Bay Area in a 1.8 million-square-foot complex. The move began in January -1985-and within a year 3,500 workers had been installed at Bishop Ranch with another 4,000 scheduled to be moved. The company says it expects to save $200 million by the consolidation.

As big as the Pacific Bell complex is—three times as large as the Transamerica building in downtown San Francisco, for example—it is matched exactly by the Chevron USA complex just across the street, which also is projected to house 7,500 employees.

More than jobs are moving to Bishop Ranch. Hotels and restaurants are being developed to handle the corporate tenants. And on the hills just east of the office-industrial center, homes are being built. One of those developments, Blackhawk, has become an ostentatious symbol of the new money moving into the area.

But Bishop Ranch is just a piece of the megalopolis that is emerging along Interstate 680, originally constructed as a beltway to route traffic around the Bay Area.

In three years, more than 3 million square feet of office space were constructed in Walnut Creek, giving the formerly low-rise city a mini-skyline and creating a backlash of complaints from residents about traffic and noise pollution.

Concord, too, is seeing an explosion of office development, most spectacularly a 3,500-employee, five-building complex housing Bank of America's data processing and other technological operations.

It's a pattern that has been repeated on a smaller scale throughout central Contra Costa County—corporations consolidating their operations and moving jobs into the suburbs.

Between 1985 and 1990 alone, Contra Costa County increased its employment by more than 20 percent, easily the most expansive economy of any Bay Area county. As the rest of the state suffered from job-destroying recession in 1991, Contra Costa had a modest 5.4 percent unemployment rate. Between 1980 and 1989, state employment data show, the county added 8,100 more jobs than it did workers, a sign that its socioeconomic role had changed from bedroom community to a destination of commuters from the new bedroom towns to the east.

Thousands of hotel rooms, shopping centers, upgraded airline service— Contra Costa is showing all of the signs of a new metropolitan area in the making, somewhat analogous to what is occurring in Orange County, another one-time bedroom community in Southern California. And like Orange County, it has experienced a slowdown in population growth even as it has seen a boom in jobs and traffic. The county's population expanded by some 22 percent, from about 650,000 to just over 800,000, during the 1980s but that's several points below the statewide growth rate.

As local traffic was overlaid by daily hordes of commuters coming into the county from residential developments to the north and east, the local road and highway system was choked and traffic jams became commonplace. But commuters were forced out of job centers—again like Orange County—because housing costs soared.

"They want their multimillion-dollar industries but they don't want to provide for the people who work there," 29-year-old single mother Marie DuVall said after being transferred into the area from Idaho by her company in the mid-1980s.

DuVall was forced to send her two children to her parents' home in Arizona and move in with a friend after trying unsuccessfully to find housing that she could afford on her $20,000 per year income.

ContraCostapolis has occurred because the local power structure has been dominated by pro-development forces—developers, bankers, newspaper publishers and politicians—hoping to cash in on the surge. But in 1985, there was a backlash. Anti-growth city councilmen were elected and ballot measures aimed at blocking development were adopted.

The most-noticed was a Walnut Creek measure aimed at stopping more office development until traffic problems ease, an unlikely occurrence in the near future. Its advocates said dense high-rise construction in the downtown area had created bumper-to-bumper traffic jams.

The message wasn't lost on local politicians who had favored go-go development in the past. Contra Costa County supervisors, known previously for their open-arms approach to development schemes, quickly ordered their staff to write a "growth management plan" and the Walnut Creek City Council drew up a list of building projects to be cancelled.

"This is an absolute signal to every middle-class suburban community in the Bay Area that if these issues are not resolved by the elected officials, the public will step in and do it," Concord Mayor Steve Weir, who fended off a challenge from a anti-growth leader, said after the November 1985 elections.

Larry Orman, director of People for Open Space, said what happened in Contra Costa County in 1985 is an example of increased militancy by residents of areas under heavy development pressure.

"People are as attuned to transportation and gridlock problems as they were to the high housing prices of the early 1980s," Orman said.

"It is an absolute milestone," said Evelyn Munn, a new Walnut Creek city councilwoman elected on an anti-growth platform. "It just shows it can be done, you can fight the money. I think it'll go right through the country."

The anti-growth backlash, however, sparked a backlash of its own. Dean Lesher, publisher of Contra Costa County's largest newspapers and by most accounts the county's most powerful figure, sued to overturn Walnut Creek's anti-growth law and won his case.

While most of the media attention has been devoted to the rapid development of central Contra Costa County, there are two other pieces that have problems of their own.

Richmond, a largely black industrial city on San Francisco Bay, saw its school system gain nationwide notoriety when it was pushed to the brink of bankruptcy in the late 1980s. And eastern Contra Costa County, including the one-time industrial cities of Antioch and Pittsburg, began experiencing their own surges of growth—residential subdivisions for the most part—and local leaders even mounted an effort to break off and form a new county, complaining that their needs were being ignored.

Despite its well-publicized legal and political battles, Contra Costa did muster enough unity to pass a local sales tax measure to improve highways but was torn apart again by a state proposal to punch a new freeway—a toll road to be financed by private investors—through the eastern and largely unpopulated fringes of the county. Environmentalists argued that the new freeway would just bring more growth to an area already overburdened.

The growth debate notwithstanding, there continues to be enormous pressure to move jobs and people out of the central cities into the suburbs. And if developers are blocked in Contra Costa, they'll go where they are welcome—perhaps to Solano County, just across the Carquinez Strait.

Solano County is the geographic bridge that connects the Bay Area with the burgeoning Sacramento metropolitan area and is feeling development pressure from both directions.

Western Solano—Vallejo, Benicia and environs—is part of the Bay Area, another of the blue-collar industrial communities that dot the inner reaches of San Francisco Bay.

Vallejo's economic mainstay has been a large naval shipyard but in recent years, as heavy industry throughout the Bay Area has declined and commuters have pushed outward in search of affordable housing, Vallejo's economy has broadened into services to support a steadily growing population and, in perhaps the most dramatic development, into tourism.

Tourism in Vallejo? The mind boggles. But Marine World-Africa USA, a major Bay Area theme park, was driven off its site south of San Francisco by the value of its underlying land for other development purposes and relocated on a golf course in Vallejo near Interstate 80, touching off a boom in related development nearby.

The winds of change also are blowing in Benicia, one of California's most historic towns. Although it's just across a bridge from the explosive growth in Contra Costa County, until recently Benicia has existed in a kind of vacuum of consciousness.

If anything, Benicia seemed to be a town on the skids after an Army ammunition depot closed in the 1960s. But artists discovered the city's historic charm and cheap rents and created a thriving colony, and in more recent years there are signs of economic and civic renewal. The old Army depot, now converted into an industrial park, is filling up with warehouses, a refinery and light industry, and commuters have discovered a community with a small-town feel, relatively low housing costs and easy access to freeways.

"We're getting growth pressure," said Arlette Cortright, an assistant city planner. Already, only a quarter of the city's workers work in Benicia, the others commuting to outside jobs.

Benicia and Vallejo are evolving slowly from blue-collar industrial towns to white-collar bedroom communities and it's a process that regional planners believe will accelerate during the latter part of the century.

Eastern Solano County, the area closest to Sacramento, is still mostly farmland, but many farmers believe that pressure from developers will force them into sales, especially of land nearest the I-80 freeway that connects Sacramento with the Bay Area. Already, large housing developments are transforming Dixon from a farm town into a commuter town.

In mid-Solano County, the Fairfield-Vacaville area, the conversion from an agricultural economy to an industrial-commuter economy already is well-advanced. The huge Anheuser-Busch brewery at Fairfield, the county seat, is a monument to the central location of the area and to the development pressures that transportation access brings.

"If you look at the change just in the past year, you can see it," Solano County's planning director, Bob Pendoley, told a visitor in between appointments with developers anxious to cash in on the Solano County land boom in the mid-1980s.

Aware of the chaos that has accompanied rapid development in the Santa Clara Valley and Contra Costa County, Pendoley said Solano hopes to learn by the examples. "We're doing it differently," he said.

Solano saw its population nearly double between 1960 and 1985 with the heaviest growth coming in the Fairfield-Vacaville area. And it had one of the state's highest rates of growth—45 percent—in the 1980s. Pasture land is being converted into subdivisions and industrial parks and a major "factory store" shopping center along I-80 testifies to developers' belief in the economic future of the area. By the late 1980s, six major commercial and office park developments—the latter aimed at housing back-office operations of such major employers as Bank of America—were being processed on sites along I-80 near Vacaville. The 1989 earthquake in the immediate San Francisco Bay Area hastened plans by banks and other major institutions to shift back-office operations to less earthquake-prone areas and Vacaville has become a major site for that shift.

The pro-development attitude of the local power structure was demonstrated in mid-1985 when the county Board of Supervisors rejected a "right to farm" ordinance pushed by local farmers anxious about development pressure. A few weeks earlier, however, local voters defeated by a 2-1 margin a proposal to create a new city called Manzanita on 886 acres of grazing land north of Vacaville. Opponents said it would drive up local government costs.

Fairfield, attempting to control the growth, has expanded its city limits well into the surrounding rural area. The city's population, 59,483 in 1980, is projected to pass 100,000 by the end of the century and the growth in Vacaville will be only slightly less spectacular. An area just east of Vacaville, at the juncture of Interstates 80 and 505, was transformed from farmland into a major retail shopping complex in just a few years.

Overall population projection figures by the state Department of Finance for the East Bay demonstrate graphically the development of the suburban counties and the relative stagnation of Alameda County.

In 1960, the three-county area had 1.5 million people with nearly a million of those in Alameda. By 1990, the counties' population had approached 2.5 million and it's likely to pass 3 million by 2000, with Contra Costa and Solano accounting for most of the growth as Alameda's population increases only slowly.

Among other things, the tilt to the suburbs—a smaller-scale version of what is happening in Southern California—is changing the politics of the region.

Suburbanites tend to be more conservative politically than central-city dwellers. The Walnut Creek area already had a Republican bent and as Vallejo, Benicia and other former blue-collar industrial towns change their economic orientation, what had been Democratic strongholds may become fertile ground for the GOP.

Even within Alameda County there are signs of change as the liberal Democratic areas of Oakland and Berkeley remain relatively stagnant in population and the county's suburban, Republican-voting eastern half continues to grow.

Those demographic trends have put the squeeze on the region's long-dominant Democratic politicians as reapportionment redraws political maps. Vallejo, a pocket of dependably Democratic voters, has become such a prize that Democratic politicians fight among themselves to have the city in their districts. At one point in the 1980s, Vallejo was attached to the congressional district of a San Francisco politician—attached only by water. Likewise, the heavily black communities along the eastern shore of San Francisco Bay have been carved up to bolster the loyal voting margins of Democratic state and federal legislators who feel pressured by the faster-growing, GOP-voting suburbs.

NORTH BAY
Ripening on the vine

T HREE DECADES AGO, SANTA ROSA AND EUREKA WERE THE MAJOR CITIES OF the so-called "Redwood Empire," a term devised by local boosters to spur tourism in the coastal counties north of San Francisco. They were about the same size—25,000-30,000 in population—and had seasonal economies revolving about tourists, lumber and agriculture.

Eureka hasn't changed much during the ensuing 30 years. Indeed, it hasn't changed much in nine decades. Santa Rosa, however, has blossomed into a mid-sized city of more than 100,000 and is headed, regional planners say, for 200,000 by the end of the century, by far the largest city north of the San Francisco-Sacramento axis.

With its wineries, hordes of tourists, high-tech industry, sprawling suburbs and traffic problems, Santa Rosa typifies the incredible transformation of the three-county region immediately north of the Golden Gate. Sonoma, Napa and Marin counties, once a sleepy region of wooded hills, picturesque river valleys and pleasant little towns, now is one of California's boom areas. And its growing pains are reflected in crowded streets and highways, in overburdened water and sewage treatment systems and in local political upheavals.

The very qualities that attracted so many to live north of San Francisco Bay are being threatened by their popularity.

"I would never have visualized that Santa Rosa would get this big this fast," Pud Bertoli, a member of a longtime local farm family that sold its apple orchards to developers, said as the city began to boom in the 1980s. "It's all

screwed up. You hate to see something you were born on go to hell but what
are you going to do?"

Others throughout the region echo those sentiments with the most virulent
anti-growth advocates being, ironically, the newest of the newcomers, wanting
to shut the door.

Eric Koenigshoffer, who came to Sonoma County in 1972 from Southern
California, was elected to the county Board of Supervisors a few years later by
contending, "Short-term people, myself included, are people who took flight
from less desirable areas and are sensitive to the whole concept of what poor
planning and over-development means."

Koenigshoffer was part of an environmentalist coalition that briefly seized
control of the Sonoma County political structure in the 1970s but got caught
up in a pro-development backlash that opened the door to investment, resulting
in an explosion of homes and industry that continues unabated. Sonoma was,
by far, the fastest growing of the three counties during the 1980s, adding nearly
90,000 persons to its population, a 30 percent expansion.

It is growth that leapfrogged over Marin County, directly north of the
Golden Gate, which had a virtual moratorium on new development throughout
the 1970s and 1980s and saw its population grow by just 3 percent in the last
decade, a tenth of Sonoma's rate and one of the slowest of any urban or
suburban area in the state. And it is growth that had taken an odd turn in
neighboring Napa County, expansion of wineries and tourist-related businesses but only slow increases in permanent population. Napa's growth in the
1980s was 12 percent.

In 1960, Marin and Sonoma had virtually identical populations (148,000)
and were still evenly matched in 1970 at 207,000. But by 1980, Sonoma had
grown to more than 300,000 while Marin remained at 222,800 and by 1990,
the gap had widened even more—388,000 to 230,000. By 2005, the state
Department of Finance estimates that Marin will have expanded to just
245,600 while Sonoma will be more than twice as populous at 542,900.

To many, Santa Rosa is another San Jose in the making—a sleepy
agricultural area becoming a fast-growing suburb and industrial center. But if
that's true, it's also true that Santa Rosa is handling its spurt of growth far more
intelligently. San Jose, for example, allowed its downtown to deteriorate. Santa
Rosa's is thriving with department stores, public buildings and other amenities.

Transportation capacity is being strained and sewage treatment facilities are
running over capacity. But there is a local willingness —a leadership capacity—to deal with the side effects of growth that was decidedly lacking in San
Jose during its explosive period.

What has happened in Sonoma County is a microcosm of what's happening
throughout the Bay Area, a dispersal of people, housing and jobs to the outer
suburbs and a lowering of concentrations in the central cities. Regional
planners estimate that as Sonoma County's population expands by 50 percent
from about 300,000 in 1980 to nearly 500,000 by 2000, the number of

employed residents will nearly double and household income will increase by a fourth in constant dollars.

As the local economy continues to mature, fewer Sonomans will be commuting to jobs outside the county and, if anything, people will be coming into Sonoma from other areas to work—a trend evident in Marin County as well. But achieving a closer balance of jobs and workers will take years and Sonoma County's general plan assumes that the number of residents commuting to jobs outside the county will continue to increase at least until 2005, when it reaches 40,000. And that puts a major strain on highways serving the area— highways that were not built to accommodate such numbers in addition to local traffic.

Sonoma County boomed because Marin County's residents didn't want the boom in their picturesque communities and imposed policies, such as a refusal to develop new water supplies, that amounted to a moratorium on growth. As the Bay Area economy began to expand outward in the 1970s, it passed over Marin and settled in Sonoma, the next stop up the line on Highway 101. And Sonoma County leaders were receptive to that growth.

It's a phenomenon more visible in Petaluma, the southernmost community in Sonoma County, than in Santa Rosa, the county seat.

It's been scarcely a generation since Petaluma was best known as the "Chicken Capital of the World" and the site of an annual arm-wrestling contest. But in the 1970s, Petaluma began growing houses rather than chickens and in the 1980s, the attractive little town began acquiring the trappings of upscale suburbia, much like nearby Marin County.

"We're a town in transition," city manager John Scharer told a reporter in 1987. "When I came here in 1961, the downtown was a disaster. Now there is a renaissance going on. New people have moved here and are changing the character of the city, Maybe it is becoming yuppified but it's in a positive way."

At first, Petaluma resisted development pressure by imposing a stringent limit on housing development—500 new units per year. Developers responded with a lawsuit and the Petaluma law became a test case of local anti-growth efforts with nationwide implications.

Federal Judge Lloyd Burke declared the law to be unconstitutional in 1974.

"No city," Burke said, "can regulate its population growth... The City of Petaluma violates the right of people to travel, to do business."

But in 1975, an appellate court overturned Burke, saying that growth regulation "is rationally related to the social and environmental welfare of the community..."

The U.S. Supreme Court refused to review the ruling. Petaluma won its case and growth- restriction laws have become popular vehicles in other communities. It's questionable, however, whether it has materially softened the impact of development pressure.

Nevertheless, one impact of such growth limits—whether directly, as in Petaluma, or indirectly, as in Marin County—has been to drive up the cost of housing and therefore make it available only to a white overclass. In 1979, a University of California, Davis, study of Petaluma said typical home prices had risen from $25,000 in 1969 to $90,000 in 1979 and that the growth limit had added about $7,000 to the cost.

Despite the growth limit, Petaluma has evolved from a city of chickens and eggs into a community of commuters, with as many as half of the residents traveling to jobs outside the area, mostly along heavily congested Highway 101. Efforts to promote more jobs in the city have not been highly successful, in part because of Petaluma's anti-growth reputation.

Elsewhere in Sonoma County, however, there has been broad expansion of jobs, both industrial and white collar, although not enough to cope with the growth of population—hence, the continued growth in commuters.

Two Hewlett-Packard plants and a smattering of other high-tech installations are hallmarks of the socioeconomic transformation of the area that occurred after the anti-growth, environmentalist movement was shattered by a conservative, pro-development backlash.

William Kortum, an environmentalist county supervisor, was recalled in 1976. But as late as 1984, the development battle was still being waged via a local initiative aimed at preserving farmlands from developers. It was opposed by farmers and was defeated by a wide margin—further evidence that local political sentiment continued to favor expansion.

Infrastructure—especially transportation and sewage treatment—is the major constraint on development of the Santa Rosa plain into one of the state's major urban centers.

Santa Rosa began dumping untreated sewage into the Russian River after its plant reached capacity in 1984. And Highway 101 between San Francisco and Santa Rosa often resembles Southern California's Santa Monica Freeway at rush hour, with traffic backed up for miles.

A "101 Corridor Committee" of local government and state officials in Marin and Sonoma counties has been working on improvements in the area's primary transportation route, but state highway money is scarce and there is no consensus locally on whether the freeway should be expanded or alternatives, including curbs on development, should be explored—a reflection of the widely varying attitudes toward development in the two counties.

The conflict was concisely described in a 1989 report on urban trends in California issued by the Greenbelt Alliance:

"Beginning in 1983, 26 representatives of the towns and counties connected by this strip of highway began working together to study ways of improving transportation and land use through the corridor. Within a couple of years, the land use concern had fallen away and by 1988, the Highway 101 committee was looking at only two transportation facility packages.

"But Sonoma County, frustrated by Marin's unbalanced jobs/housing ratio and eager to place a sales tax on the ballot to widen the highway within its boundaries, has struck out on its own and may scuttle the long, painstaking process of coordinating the two counties' transportation efforts."

Western Sonoma County, including its rugged coastline, has escaped much of the growth pressure that's been concentrated on the communities strung out along Highway 101. It remains agricultural and rural with a sharp tinge of counterculturism and strongly resists development. That creates something of a political split. The eastern portion of the county tends to vote conservatively while the west—including the gay-dominated resort community of Guerneville—is far more liberal.

As Sonoma County has exploded with development, Marin remains pretty much what it always has been: an affluent bedroom for San Francisco.

"The population mix is moving in the direction of the more affluent with the moderate- and low-income households finding housing choice in Marin very limited," says a 1982 Marin County planning report. "Because housing costs are rising faster than incomes, the housing problem is becoming steadily more severe."

A severely curtailed local water supply was the basis—or excuse, in the eyes of critics—for a virtual moratorium on new housing development in Marin during the 1970s. It had the effect of driving up the prices of existing housing units, both rentals and owner-occupied homes, and encouraging developers to move northward into Sonoma.

Marin is, by any measure, California's most prosperous county—even if that prosperity is the result of exclusionary social and development policies. Its average household income of $39,000 in 1985 was the highest of any county in the Bay Area and is one of the highest of any area in the nation. And by 1990, it had risen even higher to the $40,000-plus range. Its unemployment rate, 3.7 percent, was the lowest of any county in mid-1991, as was its percentage of residents on welfare, just 1.3 percent. The water shortage that plagued the area during the 1970s, and assumed critical proportions during an extensive statewide drought, neatly dovetailed with the dominant local attitude of preventing large-scale development in the area.

Marin County residents like their quaint little towns and the anti-outsider mentality is especially virulent along the Marin County coast. The residents of one small town routinely destroy highway signs that would direct motorists to their community. There's a certain snobbery attached to that attitude—and a certain degree of unspoken racial and socioeconomic elitism. In the name of preserving environmental values, Marin County has created a monochromatic ghetto of affluence. The 1990 census revealed that nearly 85 percent of Marin's residents are white.

The high cost of housing—the median home price was $330,000 in 1990—has, moreover, excluded "young families and the elderly" from living in Marin, says the 1982 county planning report.

Even middle-income families have trouble finding affordable housing in the county. "Young people are being driven out," county Supervisor Al Aramburu said in 1991. "When they go to college, they don't come back." And

for those who have below-median incomes, housing is almost non-existent—
although there are tiny pockets of the poor who have Marin County addresses.

Each morning a little drama is played out in Marin County. The affluent
local residents leave their rustic, redwood-sided homes (even though, ironically, Marin is a hotbed of save-the-redwoods fever) and commute to San
Francisco and elsewhere to work at high-paying professional and managerial
jobs.

But as Marin County's residents cross the Golden Gate in their Volvos,
Audis and Mercedes-Benzes or by bus or ferry, thousands of others commute
northward—or westward from Contra Costa and Alameda counties—to work
in low-paying service jobs in stores, shops and offices that maintain Marin
County's affluent lifestyle. Some of them work in a Corte Madera supermarket
that offers 14 kinds of ice cream, venison flown in from New Zealand and
chemical-free beef from Colorado—certified by the market's $400,000 chemical
tester.

And although the county's population is growing very slowly, the number
of jobs in the county is growing fairly rapidly.

The Association of Bay Area Governments has estimated that Marin's
employment base will expand by 82 percent between 1985 and 2005, even
though the number of households will grow by only 17,000. And the organization predicts that "job growth will worsen the housing market situation
because of increased pressure on the local markets to provide affordable
housing..."

Chris Fitzgerald, a Marin County planner, put it another way in a 1985
interview: "Everybody wants the jobs and nobody wants the workers."

The accuracy of that observation was underscored after a private developer
acquired the former Hamilton Air Force and proposed a complex of housing
and jobs.

The issue wound up on the ballot in Novato, the city whose boundaries
encompassed the former military installation, in 1989 and voters killed the
project by a 2-1 margin despite a strenuous and expensive campaign. And at
least some of the opposition came because a portion of the development was
to be devoted to moderate-income housing.

Already, Marin County service employers such as fast food outlets are
having difficulty recruiting enough workers and, as Fitzgerald says, "From
Oakland, they can't get here."

Marin's ability to resist development will continue to be tested. There's a
backlash of resentment among officials of other Bay Area counties that Marin
has sealed itself off and many local interests think it's time to develop new
water supplies and allow at least a measure of development. The advent of
regional government may force the county to accept what critics say would be
a "fair share" of the region's housing development and thus cut down on the
long commutes in and out of the county that already have choked Highway 101
with traffic. But "development" is still a secular sin to many in Marin, who

complain about the traffic but don't recognize the relationship between it and the county's policies that allow job growth but discourage housing for workers.

It was the underlying issue in a 1991 debate over whether the county should bring more water into the county from the Russian River in Sonoma County. A bond issue was placed on the ballot to develop the additional water supply but opponents charged that its passage would remove an anti-development tool that had worked effectively for two decades and by a narrow margin, Marin voters defeated the bond measure, thus opting for continued restrictions on

Focus on North Bay

Area .... 2,982.5 sq. miles
Percentage of California 1.9%

Population
(with percentage of California total)

	1960	1970	1980	1990	2000	2005
Marin Co.	148,000	207,000	222,800	231,200	243,600	245,600
Napa Co.	66,400	79,400	99,200	111,700	127,600	135,900
Sonoma Co.	148,600	206,500	301,500	392,000	494,300	542,900
TOTAL	363,000	492,900	623,500	734,900	865,500	924,400
CALIFORNIA	2.3%	2.5%	2.6%	2.5%	2.4%	2.4%

Ethnic composition
(1990 Census)

	Anglo	Latino	Asian/Pacific	Black
Marin Co.	84.6%	7.8%	3.9%	3.3%
Napa Co.	80.8%	14.4%	3.1%	1.1%
Sonoma Co.	84.3%	10.6%	2.6%	1.4%
CALIFORNIA	57.2%	25.8%	9.1%	7.0%

Economic Data

	Unemployment rate (Aug. 1991)	Taxable sales (1990 per capita)	Personal income (per capita) 1984	Personal income (per capita) 1989
Marin Co.	3.7%	$10,656	$21,970	$35,137
Napa Co.	6.2%	$8,979	$14,567	$20,690
Sonoma Co.	5.4%	$9,569	$13,115	$20,109
CALIFORNIA	7.2%	$9,400	$14,593	$19,229

Political data

	1964	1972	1980	1984	1988
Voter registration (Democrat-Republican)	53-44%	53-39%	50-35%	52-27%	54-34%
Presidential vote (Democrat-Republican)	62-38%	44-56%	39-53%	48-52%	57-43%

Sources: State Department of Finance, 1990 Census, employment Development Department, Board of Equalization, Center for Continuing Study of the California Economy and the Secretary of State's office.

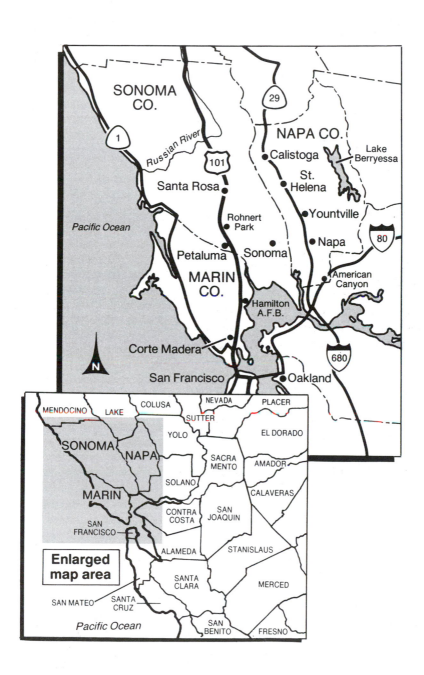

growth over the possibility of even more severe water shortages.

Marin's exclusionary policies are often cited by proponents of regional government and state growth-management policies. It's unfair, they say, that Marin should continue to develop its employment base while refusing to allow housing. It's likely that some kind of parity rules—job development would have to be accompanied by housing—will be imposed either by the state or by a new regional government in the San Francisco Bay Area, thus presenting Marin and other anti-growth areas with either/or decisions.

Growth pressure has taken still another form in Napa County, whose leaders attempt to strike a balance between the boosterism of Sonoma and the exclusionism of Marin. The population is growing faster than Marin's and slower than Sonoma's—some 12 percent in the 1980s—but the big issue in Napa is the monster created by the popularity of the Napa Valley as a readily accessible tourist attraction—more than 2 million visitors a year who come to taste the wine, eat in the restaurants, sleep in the inns and resort hotels and buy in the stores.

Three decades ago, the quiet valley supported a few wineries. But that was before the explosion of interest in wine-drinking that began in the late 1960s, before the wineries along Highway 29 began putting in "tasting rooms" to accommodate wine lovers and before the valley became choked with weekend visitors.

Eventually, in communities such as Yountville and St. Helena, bumper-to-bumper weekend traffic became the norm as tourists sought respite from city pressures amidst the vineyards.

Yountville, previously known as the site of the state's home for aged veterans, acquired one restaurant for every 100 citizens and so many antique and curio shops that it took a catalog to list them.

They still grow grapes and make wine in the Napa Valley, but one senses that the authentic character of the region has been tarnished by the rush to exploit it—not unlike what has happened in Monterey, Carmel and other tourist-oriented areas of the state. The epitome may have been reached in 1985 when it was discovered that one "winery" was nothing more than a wine store built to exploit the tourist trade.

The area is deeply divided over the issue—between those who want to put brakes on the tourist trade and those who want to cash in on it.

The establishment of dozens, perhaps hundreds, of bed-and-breakfast inns—many in residential neighborhoods—has created a backlash among nearby residents who resent the traffic that the inns bring.

Established local merchants, moreover, resent the rent hikes that commercial landlords are imposing as they find tourist-related tenants.

The backlash, too, had a political impact, found in such places as St. Helena, where a new city general plan was aimed specifically at curtailing tourist-related business.

"There was a big undercurrent of distrust about tourism and what it would do to the city...but at the same time they weren't dealing with it very well," said Gary Gouvea, a planner hired by the city to work on the document.

The general plan sees tourism "as sort of the bad guy, to the extent that it would displace local serving business," says Gouvea.

"The general plan says St. Helena's primary goal should be to perpetuate its role as a rural agricultural center. We have a great many older people who don't have a great deal of income."

Those older residents are having difficulty coping with rapidly rising housing costs associated with St. Helena's popularity.

"Tourism won't go away," said Jack Davies of Schramsberg Vineyards. "We saw to that a long time ago. It's up to us to minimize the impact on the local community, industry and environment."

Clearly, however, there is more than a little resentment among long-term local residents at the wine industry's cultivation of tourism that, in their view, has gotten out of hand.

"The minute you set out to attract tourists, you have a problem," Yountville restaurateur Don Schmitt said as the tourist boom shifted into high gear in the mid-1980s. "We're getting beyond the point now where tourists are blending in."

The vintners who created the Napa Valley's unique charms are themselves divided over how to deal with the tourist crush. Land prices soared as subdividers sought to build pricey residential developments and plush resorts amid the vineyards—sometimes so high that growing grapes became uneconomical and wine industry meetings have become heated debates over land use issues, as well as the more traditional matters such as grape prices.

The proposed creation of a "wine train" to bring more well-heeled visitors into the valley for weekend winery tours in 1988 touched off a firestorm of political controversy that reached into the state Legislature as pro- and anti-tourism forces clashed. There were community debates and demonstrations that symbolized the valley's lack of consensus over what its future will be— a rural, agriculturally oriented area or a world-class tourist destination.

If Yountville, St. Helena, Calistoga and the other hot Napa Valley tourists spots have been feeling the pressure of weekend visitors, it is not being felt in the county's seat and largest city, Napa. It remains a quiet community of stores, homes and parks, scarcely changed in a quarter-century, even though its population has expanded somewhat.

The generally slow growth in the county's population, despite the wine and tourism booms and in sharp contrast to neighboring Sonoma, is "a reflection of the history of the community," said Tony McClimans, a senior county planner.

"There is a mindset different between Napa and Santa Rosa," said McClimans. While Santa Rosa has been dominated by pro-development forces, "a sizable contingent in Napa felt there is something about the character of the Napa Valley that is different than other places and worth saving."

Politically, that attitude has expressed itself in a series of local laws and programs aimed at limiting population growth and forcing development into existing cities, preserving the countryside for agriculture. In 1974, for example, an informal plebiscite indicated that three-quarters of the population favored a slow-growth, pro-agriculture land use policy—a finding repeated in 1978. And in 1980, the adoption of a county ballot measure put legal limits on growth in the unincorporated area.

The expansion of the wine industry allowed that attitude to manifest itself without paying an economic penalty, as did the area's relative lack of proximity to the Bay Area population centers. Napa County—except for the American Canyon region in its southern corner—is a bit too far and isolated for commuters. The state Department of Finance expects that Napa's moderate level of growth will continue into the next century, with its population increasing from 111,700 in 1990 to 135,900 by 2005.

Politically, the North Bay always has been a mixed bag with legislative representation running from liberal Democrats to conservative Republican and politics often hinging on local issues and causes, such as environmental protection.

If anything, however, it has been trending somewhat rightward in recent years, especially in the fast-growing and increasingly dominant Santa Rosa area, which is exhibiting the conservative tendencies common to newly minted "edge cities."

Several liberal Democrats who held legislative seats in the area were ousted by Republicans and the wary Democratic Party hierarchy carefully redrew legislative lines to place only the more liberal coastal area in Democratic districts. But Democrats scored a comeback in 1990 when legislative staffer Mike Thompson upset Republican state Sen. Jim Nielsen, who had drifted a little too far to the right to suit local voters. Marin County, meanwhile, has drifted a bit to the left in more recent years as anti-growth environmentalism became its dominant religion.

South Bay:
A chip on its shoulder

W HEREVER ONE TRAVELS IN CALIFORNIA TO TALK WITH LOCAL LEADERS ABOUT economic trends, one hears a similar refrain.

"We'd like to get some new payrolls," they will say, "but we don't want to be another San Jose."

It's the paradox of a city that was at the center of an entirely new industry— computers—that transformed the global economy as it changed the socioeconomic and physical landscape of the area south of San Francisco but was almost destroyed in its headlong growth.

San Jose, California's oldest city and its first capital, has re-emerged in the late 20th century as the state's third-largest municipality and the largest in Northern California with the potential for world-class status—even if it exists in the cultural shadow of San Francisco, 50 miles to the north.

Only in recent years, however, has San Jose taken on some of the trappings of big city status, such as first-class hotels, museums and major league sports. And it has just begun to transform its downtown area, which was devastated by the fast growth of suburban shopping centers in the 1970s.

The revival began under the city's dynamic young mayor of the 1980s, Tom McEnery, who was fond of referring to San Francisco as a "dying city" and promoting San Jose as the emerging municipal power of Northern California because of the go-go growth of the Silicon Valley computer industry.

McEnery's successor, Susan Hammer, has had to cope with a slowing Silicon Valley economy but has vowed to continue the civic renewal that has included one of the state's new trolley systems, a children's museum and several new high-rise buildings.

"We're never going to have the Golden Gate Bridge, Coit Tower or cable cars, but we are the city of the future," Hammer said as she assumed the mayorship in early 1991. Referring to the projects begun under her predecessor, Hammer said, "Our task is to continue that expansion, but also manage our growth."

The prime point of rivalry between San Jose and San Francisco to date is the Giants baseball team. As efforts to build a new baseball park in San Francisco has failed, Santa Clara Valley leaders have attempted to lure the team south with offers of new facilities—although those efforts developed a hitch when Santa Clara County voters in 1990 rejected additional taxes to pay for a new stadium.

The San Francisco-San Jose rivalry is a very recent development because San Jose had been a sleepy backwater for most of the 20th century, even though it had played a prominent role in California's 19th century settlement.

Most of California's coastal cities developed around missions established by evangelical Spanish priests, but San Jose was a town first, founded in 1777 along the banks of the Guadalupe River, and didn't acquire a mission for another two decades. By most accounts, it was California's first city and quickly became one of its most prominent, long before San Francisco and Los Angeles were more than crude camps. Among other things, it was the site of California's first state college, San Jose State, which still is a major part of the downtown area. When California became a state, San Jose was its first capital and even after the government was moved elsewhere, it continued to prosper as the center of a fertile agricultural valley, although its relative prominence declined as other cities evolved.

For most of the 20th century, San Jose was known mostly as a large farm town in which canning and other forms of food processing were the most prominent industries. Its two claims to fame beyond its borders were the Winchester House, a 160-room mansion with staircases leading nowhere whose eccentric owner, a member of the Winchester firearms family, believed that she would continue to live as long as she continued to build, and the Rosicrucian Egyptian Temple, the center of a cult founded on belief in ancient Egyptian rituals.

San Jose began bursting out of its cocoon in the 1960s because railroad tycoon Leland Stanford had decided 70 years earlier to convert his northern Santa Clara County farm into a university, named for his son. By happenstance, Stanford University generated research into computers and the ability of the silicon chip to raise their efficiency and lower their costs. Stanford engineers such as David Packard founded the first of what became hundreds of "high-tech" companies that exploded in the 1970s, changing what had been the Santa Clara Valley into Silicon Valley. Tens of thousands of jobs drew hundreds of thousands of people into the area and the boom was on.

The Association of Bay Area Governments has calculated that 87 percent of the Bay Area's new jobs in the 1970s were generated in the Santa Clara Valley, declining only slightly to 81 percent in the 1980s. The number of high-tech firms in Silicon Valley expanded from 905 in 1977 to 3,146 in 1987. As employment mushroomed, housing prices skyrocketed and, increasingly, the valley's workforce has been made up of commuters from even more distant suburbs, some of them as far away as the San Joaquin Valley.

Population growth in Santa Clara County slowed in the 1980s to 16 percent, less than two-thirds the statewide mark, as its role as a job center matured and housing prices rose to a median quarter-million dollars for a single-family home, forcing workers to commute from outside. And much of that growth was not in San Jose or the older communities of northern Santa Clara County, but in Gilroy, Morgan Hill and other towns on the fringes. The transformation was especially dramatic in Gilroy, the one-time "Garlic Capital of the World" that became a suburban haven whose homes range upward to the million-dollar-plus category.

But just as San Jose has developed the political will to deal with its internal problems, after years of neglect, it also must contend with the sobering fact that the economic future of the local high-tech industry may be limited.

As the silicon chip market went into a oversupplied slump in the mid-1980s, massive layoffs became commonplace in the hundreds of firms that had popped up in scarcely a generation—and there was an increasing trend for companies to expand their plants in areas with less daunting housing prices and traffic. By 1984, almost 280,000 workers were employed in Silicon Valley high-tech firms but four years later, the number had dropped by 20,000.

"It (Silicon Valley's high-tech industry) supports a thriving Bay Area economy," said Raymond Brady, the top researcher for the Association of Bay Area Governments, "but it also leaves the region in a fragile position and wide-open to the `Detroit syndrome.' Major disruptions in the high-tech industries could affect other areas of the region's economy."

Almost daily, it seemed during the mid-1980s slump, local newspapers carried accounts of massive layoffs at what had been considered to be solid high-tech companies. Production line workers—who never were paid very highly in the first place—and affluent technical and managerial experts alike felt the pinch, putting a dent into the hard-working, hard-living lifestyle that had become the peninsula's trademark.

A 1,509-person survey of Silicon Valley attitudes commissioned by the San Jose Mercury-News in early 1985 revealed a work-obsessed culture that would have put the Pilgrims to shame. Work weeks of more than 50 hours a week were standard and more than a third of those questioned said their work lives created family stress—a finding reflected in the area's high divorce rate and high incidences of drug use and personal bankruptcy.

"The currency of Silicon Valley is cocaine," San Jose's former police chief, Joseph McNamara, told an interviewer.

By the late 1980s, however, newspapers were reporting that the life's-a-party attitude in Silicon Valley was changing radically as the industry came to grips with a more competitive climate. The lavish Christmas parties and other trappings of an industry awash in money were abandoned and managers assumed control of many companies from their free-spirited founders, such as Tandem Computers president Jimmy Treybig, whose motto had been "We never run out of beer."

"Silicon Valley's individual entrepreneur is fast becoming extinct," The Sacramento Bee reported in a look at the changing culture of the region. "No

Focus on South Bay

Area .... 3243.8 sq. miles
Percentage of California 2.0%

Population
(with percentage of California total)

	1960	1970	1980	1990	2000	2005
San Benito Co.	15,500	18,400	25,200	37,000	49,600	55,100
San Mateo Co.	449,100	557,100	587,700	652,100	712,700	726,900
Santa Clara Co.	658,700	1,072,600	1,299,100	1,502,200	1,502,200	1,822,500
TOTAL	1,123,300	1,648,100	1,912,000	2,191,300	2,479,100	2,604,500
CALIFORNIA	7.2%	8.2%	8.1%	7.3%	6.8%	6.7%

Ethnic composition
(1990 Census)

	Anglo	Latino	Asian/Pacific	Black
San Benito Co.	51.2%	45.8%	1.8%	.5%
San Mateo Co.	60.4%	17.6%	16.2%	5.2%
Santa Clara Co.	58.1%	21.0%	16.8%	3.5%
CALIFORNIA	57.2%	25.8%	9.1%	7.0%

Economic Data

	Unemployment rate (Aug. 1991)	Taxable sales (1990 per capita)	Personal income (per capita) 1984	Personal income (per capita) 1989
San Benito Co.	10.1%	$6,650	$11,151	$14,897
San Mateo Co.	3.9%	$12,028	$20,331	$26,881
Santa Clara Co.	5.3%	$11,925	$17,344	$23,662
CALIFORNIA	7.2%	$9,400	$14,593	$19,229

Political data

	1964	1972	1980	1984	1988
Voter registration (Democrat-Republican)	55-41%	55-37%	52-34%	52-34%	51-36%
Presidential vote (Democrat-Republican)	64-36%	46-54%	37-50%	45-55%	53-47%

Sources: State Department of Finance, 1990 Census, employment Development Department, Board of Equalization, Center for Continuing Study of the California Economy and the Secretary of State's office.

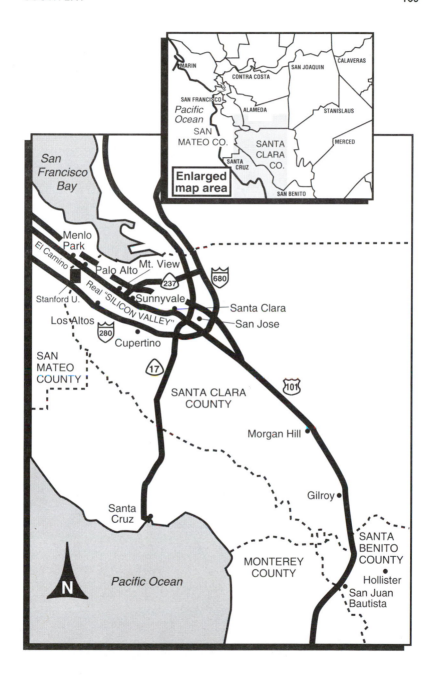

Graphic courtesy *The Sacramento Bee*

longer can the lone genius working in his garage become a millionaire 50 times over like Apple Computer's co-founder, Steve Wozniak."

Small, would-be entrepreneurs complained that the pool of venture capital was drying up and carefully dressed accountants and business managers were taking over from the blue-jeaned computer nerds who had founded the industry.

"What was once a place of mavericks has now become a giant, often oppressive bureaucracy," one newspaper quoted Mike Malone, a writer who specialized in tracking the high-tech industry. "Employees have begun to feel like numbers and each year the brass ring seems further away."

Santa Clara County had experienced a growth of more than 8,000 jobs in 1989 but saw a net decrease in 1990 and employment continued to be soft into 1991 as the high-tech industry felt the combined effects of recession and a sharp cutback in military spending, which had evolved into a major source of Silicon Valley income in the 1980s.

Silicon Valley is still a very important economic resource but experts are saying that it needs a new burst of creativity and entrepreneurship.

Frederick Cannon, a senior economist for Bank of America, has predicted continued sluggishness in the local economy during the 1990s. "Maybe it will be the silicon and gene-splice valley someday," he said, referring to efforts to create a biotechnical industry in the area.

Silicon Valley's rapid industrialization put immense pressure on the local housing market, driving up prices for even the blandest of tract homes to levels well beyond the ability of production workers to afford.

As the San Jose Mercury-news editorialized in 1991, "In the bad old days of the 1960s and 1970s, cities like Palo Alto and Sunnyvale and Santa Clara grabbed the industry and the commerce and looked to San Jose to build the bedroom suburbs.

"In the 1980s, San Jose said: never again. The city slammed the brakes on homebuilding, meanwhile scrambling to lure industry to areas like North First Street. This has helped San Jose balance its municipal budget but it also has contributed to a severe housing shortage."

The rapidly ascending housing market forced workers to seek housing outside the area and local streets and highways were choked with commuters, a problem so intense that Santa Clara County was compelled to impose a new local sales tax just to build freeway extensions ordinarily financed by the state.

And in the mid-1980s, the area learned that what it thought was clean industry, without the visible pollution of an oil refinery or a steel mill, had its own set of environmental hazards.

The chemicals used to produce silicon chips and associated products had been dumped indiscriminately around the area, giving it one of California's worst toxic waste problems. The shock began when residents of a San Jose neighborhood near a semiconductor plant began noticing a high level of birth defects. Plant officials then discovered than an underground chemical storage plant was leaking, touching off a search that has uncovered dozens of other toxic sites throughout the area.

Santa Clara County, as it developed, had more federal toxic cleanup sites than any other county in the nation.

"It is tragically ironic," resident Loraine Ross told Newsweek magazine in 1985, "that the brains behind so many electronic innovations didn't realize the danger of storing powerful solvents in fiberglass tanks."

The problems—traffic, toxic pollution, soaring housing prices—hit just as the silicon chip industry itself was beginning its years-long slump. And the juxtaposition of those events has engendered not a little soul-searching over what industrialization and suburban expansion has wrought on the once-bucolic Santa Clara Valley.

"There was absolutely no direction in the City of San Jose," ex-Mayor McEnery acknowledged to a visitor to his office atop San Jose's high-rise city hall as he began the downtown renewal effort in the mid-1980s. "It was run by a series of power structures, most of which existed outside of city hall."

McEnery came from a family of long-time residents who have extensive interests in downtown commercial property.

"When I was born, San Jose was 60,000 people," he said. "It was a backwater through the 1950s."

When he became mayor in 1982, before he was 30, McEnery presided over a city that was more than 10 times as large, having expanded through the fields and orchards that once were the area's hallmarks.

It also was a city in which development interests had operated unchecked. Suburban shopping centers were draining the downtown business district dry of shoppers and the infrastructure of local services was being strained to the breaking point and beyond. "We killed the downtown," he said flatly.

McEnery enlisted high-tech executives and others in the local power structure in his "channeled growth" program aimed at restoring the core city.

"We're really trying to put our shoulders to the wheel with local government," said Peter Giles, president of the 90-member Santa Clara County Manufacturing Group, which is considered to be the county's single most-influential pressure organization.

The high-tech companies helped persuade voters to raise the local sales tax to fix up commuter freeways and are pressuring San Jose and nearby communities to be cooperative, rather than competitive, in land use planning.

When the Santa Clara Valley was a farming area with San Jose as its market center, large numbers of Mexican-American farm workers came for the jobs in fields and canneries and put down roots. San Jose's large Hispanic population, centered in the central city, has not fully shared, however, in the conversion of the local economy from agriculture to high-tech industry.

Although Hispanics represent nearly a third of San Jose's population, they are largely ignored in local decision-making—a reflection, in part, of the low level of political participation among Hispanics. It's a situation that permeates throughout the state, effectively barring Hispanics from major political influence.

"We get pacified," Abel Cota, an Hispanic community leader, told one interviewer. "They give us a little but we don't really have a say."

The Hispanic community arose in anger in 1985, however, when local school officials proposed to close 122-year-old San Jose High School to improve the school district's ethnic/racial balance. Ironically, Hispanics complained, it would remove the central magnet of their community.

There was anger, too, when ramshackle Victorian homes occupied by low-income families in the downtown area were seized for the new high-tech museum.

"The new high technology has raised housing prices so that the people who have lived here can't afford to do it anymore," said community organizer Sofia Mendoza. "These high-tech companies just expect to come in and knock people down. We're talking about human beings here."

State Democratic politicians pledge from time to time to create legislative districts for Hispanics in San Jose but so far, it hasn't happened and all of the area's representatives in Sacramento are white, although Japanese-American Norman Mineta is one of San Jose's congressmen.

More in cultural tune with the high-tech industry and its allies at city hall are San Jose's 70,000-plus Southeast Asia refugees, who display the Asian affinity for educational and technical achievement. A dilapidated section of downtown San Jose along East Santa Clara Street has become the city's "Little Saigon" and the one-time refugees, who began appearing in large numbers in the mid-1970s, have achieved a toehold of economic and political power.

Palo Alto, at the northern edge of Santa Clara County, has achieved a fame of its own—the home of Stanford University, arguably one of the finest, and most politically potent, universities in the world.

Palo Alto became such a desirable city in which to live—thanks largely to its collegiate atmosphere—that it began to experience in the 1980s a uniquely California phenomenon: the tear-down house. Speculators would pay inflated prices for small Palo Alto homes, tear them down and then build large mansions.

"I've lived in Palo Alto and Stanford since 1966 and it's changed too much," 39-year-old Steve Scoles told The San Francisco Chronicle in 1989 as the city hit the height of its real estate boom. "It used to have a small town feeling and now it's getting a really high-tech, yuppie feeling now."

In one year, more than 80 homes were demolished and replaced with larger houses that typically sell for a half-million dollars or more. What disturbed local activists most was that the homes being destroyed were often older, California-style bungalows and the new houses were large, lot-filling and sterile-looking.

The high-tech boom that made the Santa Clara Valley what it is today—both a model and an object lesson for other regions of the state—bypassed San

Mateo County, which connects San Francisco with the San Jose area. It remains what it has been for decades, a slow-growing island of affluence that's similar in tone to Marin County on the northern side of the Golden Gate. San Mateo County's population expanded by just 11 percent in the 1980s and its welfare and unemployment rolls are among the smallest in California. In mid-1991, just 1.74 percent of San Mateo's people drew welfare checks and fewer than 4 percent of its workers were without jobs—in the middle of a severe recession.

There's a lot of old money in San Mateo County, in the pricey bedroom towns such as Hillsborough, and a general feeling that things are just fine as they are and shouldn't be changed.

The northern end of the county—South San Francisco, Daly City, Millbrae—is filled with blue-collar families who vote Democratic, as is East Palo Alto, a black-dominated community that lies in San Mateo County but is adjacent to Palo Alto and whose residents have incomes that are a mere fraction of those in other communities of the region. But the power in the county rests in the oases of quiet affluence such as Hillsborough and Atherton, where San Francisco business executives have traditionally lived.

And yet, regional planners say, there is socioeconomic change underway in San Mateo County.

The dispersal of the economy has meant the construction of office complexes in the central part of the county, especially around Redwood City and especially along the edge of San Francisco Bay, while the picturesque San Mateo coast has become a refuge for wealthy commuters.

"With jobs growing at a faster rate than the resident labor force," ABAG said, "San Mateo should have an increase in in-commuting and/or a decrease in out-commuting over the projected growth period (1985-2005)." In its shift from bedroom community to employment center, San Mateo is emulating the experiences of other postwar suburbs, including Marin County to the north, Contra Costa County to the east and Orange County in Southern California. All have experienced sharp increases in housing prices and traffic congestion, and sharp decreases in population growth as they added jobs by the thousands, mostly of the white-collar variety.

On the other end of Silicon Valley, tiny San Benito County seems to be undergoing a population boom of its own—47 percent in the 1980s—as the dispersal of employment brings it into the commuter orbit. One developer in Hollister, the county's largest city and county seat, offered "big city homes at small town prices" which he defined as $190,000-up. "Hollister is perfect for commuters who want to come home to a small town atmosphere with rustic beauty, wide open spaces and scenic landscapes," the developer advertised and it was a message that seemed to catch on in the 1980s, driving the county's population sharply upward.

The upgrading of Highway 152, which connects the lower Santa Clara Valley with the San Joaquin Valley through Hollister, also is fueling the county's growth spurt. As the Pacheco Pass Highway, as the locals call it, becomes a freeway, it's expected to spark a commercial development boom as well.

San Benito has one of California's highest proportions of Latino residents—46 percent, according to the 1990 census—and is one of the few places where Hispanics have the potential to wield real political power.

The prospects of a real estate boom in San Benito County have sparked a backlash from those who would like to keep the pastoral area as it has been. San Juan Bautista, the historic old mission town just off Highway 101, has developed a reputation for wild and woolly politics—recall elections, fistfights and name-calling contests—as it wrestles with its future.

"You think Lebanon is bad," said a slow-growth city councilman, Robert Paradice. "You'll hear 25 points of view—and every one of them is the absolute truth."

Until now San Juan Bautista's single industry has been tourism—visitors to its mission and an adjacent state park devoted to California history. The town's downtown area has retained a consciously quaint, Old West atmosphere and the police chief of the 1980s often strode through town dressed in Western clothes, complete with six-shooter on his hip.

The three-county South Bay region, which had 2.2 million people counted in the 1990 census, will continue to grow, according to state population experts. The Department of Finance projects that its population will reach 2.6 million by 2005 with San Benito growing the fastest.

Politically, the San Francisco peninsula is a land of great contrast.

The more affluent pockets are steadfastly Republican, albeit of the protect-the-environment variety. Maverick Republican Pete McCloskey represented San Mateo County in Congress for many years and was succeeded by high-tech executive Ed Zschau and then by Stanford University law professor Tom Campbell who, like McCloskey and Zschau before him, immediately began running for the U.S. Senate. But northern San Mateo is solidly Democratic and San Jose is, too. In fact, San Jose represents one of the few bright spots in the state for improving Democratic Party fortunes.

The area has enjoyed a strong presence in Sacramento that brought an impressive amount of money into the region during the 1980s for new highways, light rail and other civic improvements. Two San Jose legislators, Assemblyman John Vasconcellos and Sen. Alfred Alquist, chaired the Legislature's two budget-writing committees, which ensured that local desires were heard. Alquist, for example, obtained state financing for a large state office building that bears his name.

As the area's southern extremity, in the Morgan Hill-Gilroy area, continues to grow, however, regional politics may become somewhat more conservative. And the large Hispanic population remains largely an untapped political resource, available to whichever party and whichever leader is successful in organizing it.

The future of Santa Clara and San Mateo counties, however, cannot be divorced from the future of high-tech industry.

With civilian demand for silicon chips receding and overseas competitors moving in on markets, many Silicon Valley firms turned to military contracts in the 1980s, including work on the so-called "Star Wars" space defense system.

If employment and population continue to expand, as local and regional planners expect, the negative effects of urban sprawl also are likely to increase. There is strong neighborhood resistance to high-rise, high-density housing development, thus pushing development even further away from the urban core and exacerbating traffic problems.

What's needed, many believe, is for a more regional approach to development that would replace the often brutal competition among South Bay cities to attract desirable and lucrative kinds of development, such as shopping centers and high-tech plants, and shun housing.

"Regional development," the San Jose Mercury-News has said, "if it includes revenue-sharing, would give everyone more flexibility."

Central Coast:
California's middle kingdom

In THE DAYS BEFORE FREEWAYS SLICED THROUGH EVERY CORNER OF CALIFORNIA and before the major cities were linked by jet commuter flights, San Luis Obispo was a very important spot on the map.

It was the mid-point on the two-day, 400-mile journey between San Francisco and Los Angeles. Clusters of crude cabins were built to accomodate the motorists and one of the operators devised the word "motel" as shorthand for motor hotel to save money on sign-painting, —and that hostelry on the northern edge of San Luis Obispo still accommodates guests.

More than a half-century later, California's idyllic Central Coast still finds itself tied by concrete umbilical cords to the state's two major metropolitan areas and feeling socioeconomic pressure on both ends.

At the northern end, in Santa Cruz and Monterey counties, the outward expansion of the San Francisco Bay Area is producing pressure for suburban-style development. At the southern end, in Ventura and Santa Barbara counties, the pressure from Los Angeles is even more intense. In the middle, San Luis Obispo County escapes the direct pressure for physical development from the metropolitan areas but generates its own demands from people who simply want to get away from urban life. And throughout the five-county region—especially in the picturesque coastal areas and old mission towns—there is pressure to alter what is authentic to cash in on the demands of tourists and urban refugees.

Overall, the population of the area virtually doubled between 1960 and 1980

116

from about 750,000 to nearly 1.5 million and by 1990 had hit 1.8 million. But during that period, Santa Cruz County—fueled by invasions of commuters, retirees, alternative lifestyle seekers and students at a new University of California campus—jumped from about 85,000 to well over 200,000 and it's expected to approach 300,000 by 2005, despite strenuous efforts of local anti-growth activists.

In 1960, Ventura County, with population and employment based in oil production and citrus ranching, had just over 200,000 persons. That had nearly doubled by 1970, passed the half-million mark by 1980, neared 700,000 by 1990 and is projected to approach a million by 2005, the state Department of Finance says.

There are local fears that the population and economic growth that Ventura County is experiencing could make it another Orange County—wall-to-wall suburbs—and erode the rural values that Venturans believe set their county apart from the rest of Southern California.

Maria VanderKolk, who was elected to the Ventura County Board of Supervisors in 1990 at age 26, spoke for many of her constituents when she told The Los Angeles Times: "The pressure here is what Orange County was feeling 15 years ago and it's going to be a challenge to make sure that doesn't happen again."

Some of the anti-Orange County feeling has been engendered by the efforts of developers from that county to move into Ventura in a big way, bringing with them the high-powered development politics that have long been their hall-mark.

The similarities between the two counties, one to the north of Los Angeles, the other to the south, are remarkable. Both were citrus and ranching counties with a bit of oil development before the great outward push from Los Angeles after World War II. But Orange County developed rapidly in the 1950s and 1960s while Ventura remained untouched until the late 1970s, when freeways made access into the southern and eastern portions of the county from the San Fernando Valley easier. The subdividers came first, followed by the industrial park and office complex developers.

The economic future of Ventura County looks so bright that developers have erected countless office and light industrial buildings on speculation, without firm leases from tenants. Land costs —low by Los Angeles stan-dards—make such speculation attractive.

Office consruction in Ventura County raced at an annual clip of 3 million to 5 million square feet in the late 1980s and by 1991, some 5.3 million square feet of office space was either approved or under construction. Upward of 100 companies have located in the Ventura Industrial Park alone.

The Simi Valley-Camarillo area of Ventura County has been dubbed "Gallium Gulch" for its concentration of companies working on advanced work on gallium arsenide chips, which many researchers believe will replace silicon chips as the computer breakthrough of the future. If it happens, Ventura

County could become as important a center of high-tech industry as Silicon Valley south of San Francisco has been.

The prevailing Ventura County political climate, like that in the remainder of Southern California, has tended to favor development over preservation of the agricultural land, although county planners attempt to steer urban development into existing city boundaries. There is an effort to develop tourism and slow-growth political movements have been established in some communities. And even Republican politicians, who ordinarily favor unbridled development, have called for slower growth.

"All of us are nostalgic for days when there were only a few hundred thousand people living in the county amid wide-open spaces," Republican Assemblyman Tom McClintock told an interviewer in 1987. "But I remember in 1965 there were no major hospitals in the Conejo Valley (Thousand Oaks) and no major shopping facilities. We give up something, but things change for the better."

McClintock said local governments have done a "meticulous" job of planning for growth. And population growth during the 1980s, as it turned out, was precisely that of the state as a whole, 26 percent.

Ventura, somewhat envious of the fame that neighboring Santa Barbara has achieved as a tourism center, is trying to lure Southern Californians to its attractions. Until 1983, Ventura had only five hotels with a total of 515 first-class rooms, but in 1984 five more were built, including the area's first resort hotel, and several golf-and-tennis resort hotels now lure conventions and affluent visitors from the rest of Southern California. Ronald Reagan's presidential library in Simi Valley is expected to become a major draw for visitors.

There is a decidedly different attitude a few miles to the north in Santa Barbara County, which takes its beauty for granted, where preservation of environmental values approaches the status of a secular religion and "development" is considered by many to be a profanity.

The trendy shops along Santa Barbara's self-consciously quaint main street testify to the existence of a moneyed upper crust. The median age, a full six years above that of Ventura County, attests to the absence of young commuter families and the presence of many retirees.

There is a smugness about the area that is reminiscent of Marin County— a sense that those who already have acquired their pieces of coastal paradise don't want to share it with interlopers, especially those who can't afford the price of admission.

Population data support the observation. Although Santa Barbara was only slightly less populous than Ventura in 1960, the latter boomed in the 1960s and 1970s and by 1980 had nearly twice as many people. In the 1980s, the population growth rate of both counties was nearly equal—24 percent in Santa Barbara, 26 percent in Ventura. But for the remainder of this century and the first part of the next, Ventura is expected to grow substantially faster than Santa Barbara.

Santa Barbara has been openly hostile to industrial development efforts. Instead, the county depends on the incomes of retirees from private and public pension funds, local service business, government and tourism to keep the economy moving.

And even expansionist efforts in those "clean industries" are viewed with suspicion, as Fess Parker, once television's "Davy Crockett" and now a Santa Barbara developer, learned when he proposed to build a hotel and convention center on a prime piece of Santa Barbara beachfront land.

The local environmental activists, who are vocal as any in the land, raised the specter of Santa Barbara's becoming what one called "a low-rise Waikiki." Local merchants and boosters said a convention center would bring in visitors and their money, but the opponents warned solemnly in one brochure that "conventioneers are different from traditional tourists (and) we could expect a marked increase in drunk driving and prostitution."

Ultimately, as have many issues in Santa Barbara, it came to a vote. And in March 1985, for the first time in a decade, Santa Barbara's voters favored a development—a new wrinkle in local politics that may have carried over in another election later in the year when they approved a county oil development program and rejected an anti-oil initiative, thanks in part to big campaign spending by oil companies.

Some of Santa Barbara's civic smugness evaporated when the community was devastated by two natural disasters—a fire that consumed expensive homes as it raged to the very edge of the city and a years-long drought that gave the land surrounding Santa Barbara a scorched look and led to serious consideration of such radical steps as desalinisation and importing water by tanker from Canada. Local anti-growthers looked upon the severe water shortage, perhaps the state's worst, with mixed feelings. Personal hardships aside, the lack of water dampened development plans, much as it did in Marin County, Santa Barbara's socioeconomic sibling north of San Francisco.

Actually, Santa Barbara may have some justification for fearing the effects of a tourist-conventioneer invasion. A couple of hundred miles to the north, on the even more scenic Monterey peninsula, tourism is having a socioeconomic impact that none of its boosters foresaw.

Monterey, with its quaint waterfront, its seedy and historic Cannery Row, its red-tiled Spanish colonial architecture and its sweeping vistas of Monterey Bay, had always been a prime tourist draw for Northern California. But it also retained its air of authenticity.

At the height of the Monterey sardine boom, 100 plants processed the tiny fish and writer John Steinbeck dubbed a stretch of Ocean View Boulevard "Cannery Row" in his 1945 novel that depicted the colorful and rugged life of the fishermen and cannery workers, describing the district as "a poem, a stink, a grating noise, a quality of light, a tone, a habit, a nostalgia, a dream."

Eventually, the sardines were fished out and Cannery Row became even seedier. But Steinbeck had immortalized it and it was inevitable that it would be exploited to attract visitors—and lose much of its authenticity in the process.

The transformation of Cannery Row symbolized the change in Monterey itself from fishing village to one of California's prime tourist destinations with shopping centers, restaurants and resort hotels. As the plans for a series of big

Focus on Central Coast

Area .... 11,698.2 sq. miles
Percentage of California 7.4%

Population
(with percentage of California total)

	1960	1970	1980	1990	2000	2005
Monterey Co.	195,300	247,800	292,000	358,800	419,500	445,200
San Luis Obispo Co.	81,900	106,600	156,900	219,500	287,600	321,100
Santa Barbara Co.	173,600	265,800	299,700	371,400	434,600	462,800
Santa Cruz Co.	85,000	124,500	189,400	230,800	273,800	294,000
Ventura Co.	203,100	381,400	532,000	671,600	824,200	895,400
TOTAL	739,000	1,126,100	1,470,000	1,852,100	2,239,700	2,418,500
CALIFORNIA	4.7%	5.6%	6.2%	6.2%	6.2%	6.2%

Ethnic composition
(1990 Census)

	Anglo	Latino	Asian/Pacific	Black
Monterey Co.	52.3%	33.6%	7.1%	6.0%
San Luis Obispo Co.	81.2%	13.3%	2.7%	2.0%
Santa Barbara Co.	66.1%	26.6%	4.1%	2.5%
Santa Cruz Co.	74.5%	20.4%	3.3%	1.0%
Ventura Co.	65.9%	26.4%	4.9%	2.2%
CALIFORNIA	57.2%	25.8%	9.1%	7.0%

Economic Data

	Unemployment rate (Aug. 1991)	Taxable sales (1990 per capita)	Personal income (per capita)	
			1984	1989
Monterey Co.	6.8%	$7,952	$15,049	$17,486
San Luis Obispo Co.	4.9%	$7,884	$11,553	$15,938
Santa Barbara Co.	5.3%	$8,518	$15,068	$20,135
Santa Cruz Co.	6.1%	$7,944	$13,436	$18,725
Ventura Co.	7.6$	$8,408	$13,352	$19,947
CALIFORNIA	7.2%	$9,400	$14,593	$19,229

Political data

	1964	1972	1980	1984	1988
Voter registration (Democrat-Republican)	55-42%	52-40%	48-38%	47-40%	45-42%
Presidential vote (Democrat-Republican)	59-41%	36-64%	35-60%	33-67%	46-54%

Sources: State Department of Finance, 1990 Census, employment Development Department, Board of Equalization, Center for Continuing Study of the California Economy and the Secretary of State's office.

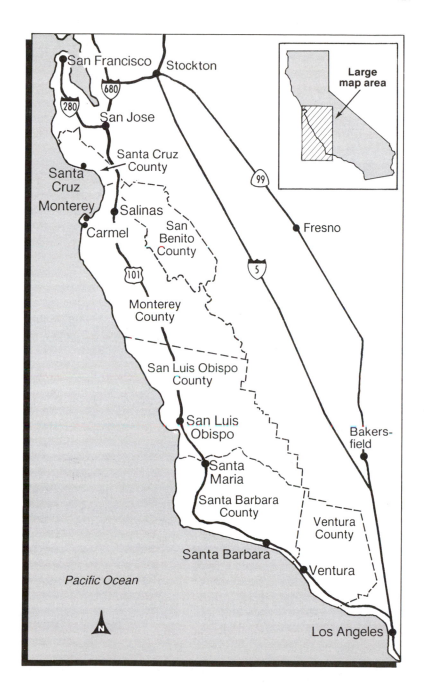

San Francisco Stockton

680

280

San Jose

Santa Cruz County

Santa Cruz

Monterey Salinas

Carmel San Benito County

99

Fresno

101

5

Monterey County

Large map area

San Luis Obispo County

San Luis Obispo

Bakersfield

Santa Maria

Santa Barbara County

Ventura County

Santa Barbara

Ventura

Pacific Ocean

N

Los Angeles

Graphic courtesy *The Sacramento Bee*

hotels raced through a compliant City Council, resistance developed among settled residents who worried—as have the residents of other tourist towns— that it was getting to be too much. In four years, Monterey acquired 970 new hotel rooms. The construction of the Sheraton Hotel, quickly dubbed "Sheraton General" for its hospital-like appearance, led to a local political revolt.

An elementary school teacher, Clyde Roberson, was elected mayor in the early 1980s on a pledge to slow down development and a newly realigned City Council imposed a moratorium on new hotels aimed at stalling some 1,500 rooms already in the planning stage.

There was a backlash from pro-development forces. To Burke Pease, former executive director of the Monterey Peninsula Chamber of Commerce, the moratorium was a "knee-jerk reaction" that failed to come to grips with the dependence of the local ecomomy—including the city coffers—on tourist dollars.

Neverthess, in May 1985, Roberson was re-elected as mayor handily, as were two members of his bloc on the council, and voters passed a measure to extend the city's hotel moratorium, plus an increase in the tax on hotel rooms.

"Now we can continue our new direction," Roberson said after his victory. "We will make this the best place on Earth to live."

The Monterey moratorium notwithstanding, a number of new hotels continued to rise in the downtown area and along Cannery Row to continue tourist expansion—a prospect that worried neighborhood activists such as Elizabeth Leeper, president of the New Monterey Neighborhood Association.

"We're a peninsula and we've got a lot of it locked up so there isn't a free flow of traffic," Leeper told a visitor to her Monterey home in the mid-1980s.

Indeed, on weekends the downtown area and nearby Cannery Row—which has long since packed its last sardine but now packs in tourists—are clogged with cars. If anything, it's worsened with the opening of the Monterey Aquarium at the south end of Cannery Row, a gift to the city from industrialist David Packard.

Monterey residents such as Leeper are proud of the aquarium but they are unhappy with the traffic congestion and other problems that visitors bring.

"The tourist thing is a bittersweet thing for us," said husband Ed Leeper. "Everybody loves the aquarium (which attracted 2.3 million visitors in its first year alone) but the Sheraton Hotel everybody hates."

"There was too much tourist development without a consideration of the infrastructure," his wife added. "You put a limit on the tourists by not building any more hotels."

As the 1980s gave way to the 1990s, tourism showed no signs of abating, the efforts of slow-growth advocates notwithstanding. The Monterey penin- sula receives an estimated 2 million tourists a year and local politics are dominated by the question: How many are too many?

While the descendents of sardine fishermen—most of them Italian-Ameri- cans—cash in on the tourist boom by operating restaurants, souvenir shops and other businesses, retirees and other relative newcomers, like the Leepers, agitate for limits on hotels and other tourist facilities. The Monterey Aquarium has proved to be a huge attraction and is laying plans for a $35 million expansion, one that some fear will bring even more hordes to the area.

Monterey's effort to limit tourist traffic has its counterpart in nearby Carmel, one of the nation's most unusual communities.

Carmel is Disneyland for rich people, packed with shops—or "shoppes" in the preferred local spelling—full of expensive clothing, antiques and gadgets to excite the jaded into parting with plastic or paper money. It abounds with restaurants, bed-and-breakfast inns and other facilities for visitors with money and the willingness to spend it. And it doesn't quite know how to handle its success.

Carmel was established as an artists' colony but it has become a tourist haven in which only the most successful artists can afford to live. On one hand, it encourages tourists. On the other, it provides but one public toilet to accommodate them.

The battle over Carmel and its ambiance has been under way for at least a half-century. Once, it was seriously proposed that a wall be built around the town to keep out visitors. The pages of the Pine Cone, the local newspaper, are filled with letters that debate such burning local issues as whether visitors should be allowed to eat ice cream cones on the street. Carmelites worry about such things a lot.

"Those who come to our Bach Festival, those who have the same feelings about protecting the environment we have are welcomed," then-Mayor Charlotte Townsend, a Carmel resident since the 1930s, said in 1985. "But we don't welcome people who eat ice cream cones or buy film and scatter their debris behind them."

Carmel has fewer than 5,000 permanent residents but on a busy weekend day may have 7,400 extra cars on its streets—a conflict that the town has yet to resolve and one captured in a bit of graffito scrawled on a statue of Father Junipero Serra, who founded the Carmel mission: "Tourist go home."

The battle of Carmel may not be over, but a significant skirmish occurred in 1986 when movie star Clint Eastwood, a Carmel resident and restaurant owner, challenged Townsend for the mayorship and won by a nearly 3-to-1 margin. Eastwood had campaigned on a platform of accommodating tourists and, if anything, his mayorship brought more of them to the town. Eastwood served for just two years, however, and after he retired, the anti-tourist forces once more took command. Among other things, they pushed through the City Council a law banning short-term rentals of homes, clearly aimed at forcing visitors to either stay away or stay in hotels.

The most isolated piece of the Central Coast is the Big Sur, a stretch of rugged coastline south of Carmel that has long been a Mecca for artists and expatriates and a test of skill for motorists as they negotiate winding Highway 1 through what to many is the most beautiful piece of coastal real estate in the nation. One of the major attractions of the region is the Hearst Castle, a complex of buildings and art built by the legendary newspaper publisher William Randolph Hearst. Today, it's owned by the state and open to the public.

If Carmel, south of Monterey, is hostile to tourists, on the north side, the sand dune cities of Seaside, Marina and Sand City have the welcome mat out for developers and tourists, trying to shed their images of being on the wrong side of the tracks.

Marina, which counted the soldiers at nearby Fort Ord in its population, was speeding toward becoming the largest city on the Monterey peninsula when, in 1991, the Pentagon announced that the venerable military base would be one of those closed as part of the post-Cold War reduction of military spending. It was a huge economic blow not only to Marina but other communities; Fort Ord, local officials quickly pointed out, accounted for a third of the local economy. As they battled politically to keep the installation open, local leaders scrambled to plan for its closing. The best scenario was that the base's expanses of oceanfront land would be developed into even more vacation facilities, but even the most optimistic see years of economic dislocation for the area.

On the northern shore of Monterey Bay, one finds a completely different set of socioeconomic and political imperatives.

Santa Cruz was a tourist town while Monterey still reeked of dead sardines—a place for residents of San Francisco and Oakland to escape from the summer fog and catch some sun on the beach. It was a working-class tourist town, with a boardwalk and a roller coaster and cheap motels. But by the early 1960s, as improving highways opened up other areas to tourism, Santa Cruz was losing its luster and local merchants were nervous about the future.

Someone hit on the idea of establishing a branch campus of the University of California at Santa Cruz to put the city on the map, local boosters thought, and provide a source of year-round jobs and customers.

An intensive campaign underwritten by local interests was successful and in 1965, the University of California, Santa Cruz, opened its doors on a wooded site at the northern edge of the city. It turned out, however, to have effects that the boosters never intended.

The extension of the vote to 18-year-olds and a change of law allowing students to vote at their campus residences, coupled with an invasion of counterculturists into the area in the late 1960s and early 1970s, radically changed the local political climate. What had been an isolated and conservative community moved more than a few notches to the left politically. The political change, moreover, created an intense debate over the future of Santa Cruz—the liberal-environmentalist bloc opposing development and the remnants of the conservative business community promoting it.

The former bloc defeated efforts to create a hotel-convention center complex near the beach in the mid-1970s and the waterfront area has continued a slow physical deterioration, although owners of the one major hotel, the Dream Inn, maintained expansion plans.

At the same time, the explosive growth of the San Jose-Silicon Valley area just across the mountains produced a different kind of pressure. It's estimated that as many as 15,000 persons commute each day from the Santa Cruz area to San Jose-Silicon Valley over a narrow, winding mountain highway.

Environmentalists have resisted efforts to upgrade the highway, fearing it will mean more development pressure in Santa Cruz. "They are telling people not to come here," Lionel Stoloff, manager of the Santa Cruz Chamber of Commerce, complained in the mid-1980s.

Those who wanted to isolate Santa Cruz from the rest of the world almost got their wish in 1989 when a severe earthquake clobbered the area, leaving much of the downtown business district in shambles. In the longer run, however, the earthquake may have only delayed Santa Cruz County's destiny to become an extension of the Bay Area, much as Ventura, on the southern end of the Central Coast, is being drawn ever-closer to Los Angeles.

One of every five Santa Cruz County workers already was directly involved in high-tech industry by the mid-1980s, a report prepared for the county planning department by UC-Santa Cruz Prof. Richard Gordon said—7,000 in firms within the county and 12,000 who commute across the mountains.

"The irony is that while (anti-growth) politics have been dominant in the county since 1975, that is precisely the time when the vast bulk of high-technology firms have developed here," Gordon said in a speech summarizing his findings, terming high-tech the "fourth layer" of the local economy behind tourism, government and agriculture.

The emergence of high-tech industry in Santa Cruz County may lead to a political counterrevolution. Those involved with the industry, both commuters and non-commuters, are decidely more conservative than the liberal-environmentalist bloc that dominated local politics in the 1970s and early 1980s.

While the heavily populated coastal strip debates how much and what kind of development should be allowed, the interior valleys of the Central Coast counties are caught up in the problems that confront 20th century agribusiness—the gap between farm prices and interest rates, the struggle of farm workers to unionize and the environmental hazards posed by pesticides.

From the vegetable fields of the Salinas Valley and the coastal plains to the cattle ranches of San Luis Obispo, agriculture has seen lean times in recent years.

Steinbeck chronicled the hard lives of migrant farm workers in the Salinas Valley more than a half-century ago—a struggle mirrored today in the up-and-down efforts of the United Farm Workers Union to organize workers into an effective economic force.

The Salinas Valley lettuce industry has been the chief target of those organizational efforts, which seem to rise and fall with the prevailing political mood in Sacramento and Washington. Most recently, those moods have been conservative and the UFW's efforts have been faltering.

The struggle in the fields has been reflected, too, in the efforts of Hispanic activists to organize their community into an influential local political power.

It's estimated that Salinas, the capital of the interior coast, is at least 40 percent Hispanic but Anglos have remained in firm control of the City Council and other local political institutions—thanks, in part, to at-large voting that makes it difficult to concentrate Hispanic political strength.

In the late 1980s, cracks in that wall began to emerge. The first developed not in Salinas but in Watsonville, a few miles to the north. A court ruled that Watsonville's system of electing City Council members at large disenfranchised Hispanics and ordered elections to be conducted from districts. The ruling reverberated throughout California's farm towns with their large Hispanic populations, and as far away as Los Angeles, where courts intervened to force the creation of Hispanic seats on the City Council and county Board of Supervisors.

Just as Hispanics began acquiring a measure of political power in the Salinas Valley, the basis of their economic sustenance began to erode. The large food processing plants that have been the backbone of the local economy began shutting down in the late 1980s and moving their operations to Mexico and other low-wage sites, eliminating the jobs of hundreds of mostly Hispanic local workers.

The political and socioeconomic storms that rage through the northern and southern ends of the Central Coast blow out before they reach the mid-point, the San Luis Obispo-Santa Maria area.

The overall impression is one of serenity and continuity—qualities that attract retirees and others wanting to escape from urban pressures.

Santa Maria, on the northern edge of Santa Barbara County, is growing steadily, thanks to the expansion of nearby Vandenberg Air Force Base, the West Coast spaceport. San Luis Obispo's economy, meanwhile, rests firmly on a multitude of bases—agriculture, tourism, a state prison, a state mental hospital and a state university whose students are nearly as conservative as the surrounding community and whose only sign of political activism came when the local City Council threatened to ban beer drinking in city parks. San Luis Obispo, moreover, became one of several smaller cities in California to experience a pheneomenon of the 1980s, the equity refugee migration.

Middle-aged empty-nesters would cash in the equity of their homes in soaring metropolitan real estate markets and move to San Luis Obispo and other communities where housing was cheaper and their accumulated savings would supplement lower-paying jobs or, in some cases, early retirements from urban rat races.

The arrival of so many newcomers with no visible means of support was a mixed blessing for the target communities. They were not burdens on schools or other public services but they tended to drive up local housing markets. The arrival of the urban transplants gave San Luis Obispo County the region's highest rate of population growth, 40 percent, during the 1980s and undercut the nickname—"SLO Town"—that college students decades ago laid on San

Luis Obispo. But its unemployment and welfare dependency rates remained blessedly below average—which is true of other Central Coast counties as well.

The attraction is not difficult to understand. San Luis Obispo may be California's most perfect blend of mild climate, social ambiance, recreational opportunity, economic stability, physical attractiveness and historic amenities. It has all of the qualities that made California so seductive to visitors in the first place, qualities that many other communities have lost.

Politically, California's Central Coast tends to be conservative, with an overlay of concern about environmental matters. Ventura, Santa Barbara and San Luis Obispo counties have Republican registration majorities, Monterey is a bit less conservative and Santa Cruz, with its latter-day bohemian flavor, can be downright radical in its politics at times. The northern end of the region elects Democrats to legislative and congressional seats while the south leans Republican but also tolerates a couple of Democratic state legislators who have established strong personal followings.

Sacramento:
The gangly adolescent

SACRAMENTO IS THE GANGLY ADOLESCENT OF CALIFORNIA CITIES—GROWING
fast, unsure of its identity, a bit afraid of adulthood and prone to making
mistakes.

California's capital also is its largest inland city whose rapid growth in the
last generation symbolizes the state's eastward development push, away from
overcrowded and expensive coastal enclaves and into the broad, flat interior
valleys.

"Sacramento was California's fastest-growing region, measured by jobs,
population and households in the 1980s, and should repeat that top ranking in
the 1990s," said the Center for the Continuing Study of the California Economy
in an analysis of 1990 census data.

Nearly 1.5 million persons already live in the Sacramento metropolitan
area—more than a fifth of them in the city itself—and as population climbs
toward 2 million by the early 21st century, there is an ever-lessening economic
dependence on government employment and an expanding private sector,
including high-tech manufacturing and financial services. In a sense, Sacramento is feeding off the San Francisco Bay Area, a two-hour drive to the
southwest, as large employers gravitate to an area with lower living and
business costs, fewer transportation bottlenecks and, most recently, less threat
of disruption from earthquakes. But that doesn't make Sacramento a suburb of
San Francisco; it is a distinctly separate community, even if its outer reaches
and those of its larger metropolitan neighbor are just a few miles apart and

marching toward each other along Interstate 80.

"Domestic migration has been the largest component of population growth in the 1980s," the Center for the Continuing Study of the California Economy concluded in its examination of Sacramento. "Many people came from within the state—particularly the Bay Area. Foreign immigration is not an important source of population growth. Natural increase will provide about one-third of the region's growth in the 1990s."

As it continues its explosive growth, Sacramento has acquired some big city cultural and social amenities, such as major league sports, and is actively seeking more. But it's also acquiring the negative effects of rapid urbanization, such as worsening rush-hour traffic, smog, submachine gun firefights between rival ethnic and drug gangs, a growing reputation for bizarre sex crimes and mass murders, and a strained infrastructure of public facilities. And, it is experiencing political conflict, pitting advocates of metropolitan expansion against a long-ensconced bloc—what one commentator has called the "civic gentry"—that wants to shield its "River City" from the joys and trials of big city status but exhibits little vision of what Sacramento should become.

The pro-growth forces seem to be winning the argument but it remains uncertain whether Sacramento also will develop the civic leadership and governmental organization to cope with the growth that is happening now and may even accelerate as the 21st century approaches. Efforts to consolidate the city and its 300,000-plus population with the sprawling, unincorporated suburbs have been rejected twice by voters and in many respects, albeit on a smaller scale, it is beginning to experience the balkanized, confusing and competitive proliferation of local governments that has plagued two predecessors in the high-stakes growth game, Los Angeles and San Jose.

The Sacramento metropolitan area includes all of Sacramento and Yolo counties and the western portions of two foothill counties, Placer and El Dorado. Sutter County, directly to the north, has shunned development that would make it, too, part of Sacramento's sprawl but that is destined to change as planners and developers lay out whole new cities in the fields and rice paddies of southern Sutter County.

Between 1980 and 1984, the Census Bureau said, the Sacramento area was among the nation's 10 fastest-growing urban regions, jumping 10.9 percent during the period. It's ranked as the 30th-largest urban area in the nation and in 1989, Newsweek named Sacramento as one of the nation's 10 best "second-tier" cities. U.S. News and World Report listed it as the fifth-hottest real estate market in the nation in a 1990 examination. In terms of population, it stands with cities such as Denver, Atlanta and Kansas City, but it has not yet achieved the independent identity of those cities, in part because of its closeness to world-famous San Francisco.

Sacramento County alone, just over a half-million population in 1960, doubled that by 1990 and could add another 300,000 by the end of the century.

Together, Sacramento and Yolo—a small, once-agricultural county to the west that is receiving heavy suburban development pressure—are expected to reach nearly 1.7 million in population by 2005. That's a 200 percent expansion from 1960, far more than the state as a whole is expected to see.

The city, however, is not growing as rapidly as the area as a whole, leaving the area with the highest proportion of unincorporated urban development in the state and creating its unique problem of confused governance.

A distinct unwillingness of city officials and local leaders to expand the city's boundaries into then-vacant land north and east of Sacramento after World War II laid the groundwork for the suburban explosion under a pro-development county government. And ultimately, it weakened the city's ability to affect critical land use decisions for the region. Ironically, therefore, the very urbanization that the civic gentry wanted to prevent was increased by its head-in-the-sand attitude.

The downtown business district was sucked dry by suburban shopping centers—including California's first one, built in 1945—and only in the last generation has it staged an even modest comeback. Stumbling efforts to rescue downtown from its dilemma, such as the ill-fated K Street Mall filled with concrete structures that resembled tank traps, came to symbolize the city's leadership vacuum, although the concrete was later removed for a softer look tied to light-rail transit.

The uncertainty over Sacramento's direction continues with a fierce political and economic struggle over development of the city's northern frontier, North Natomas, with a light-rail system that had a difficult time winning adherents as it ran up multimillion-dollar cost overruns and with a city government that stages fierce ideological debates over foreign policy issues but seems unable to make local decisions that stick.

The redevelopment of Old Sacramento as a living museum of the city's Gold Rush past has been a visual success, even if some of its commercial underpinnings are a bit shaky.

The state government—which operates without paying more than passing attention to local desires—has had both good and bad effects.

It built an ugly new state fairgrounds just outside the downtown area and has erected any number of sterile, slab-like state office buildings and garages in the downtown core. But it financed and built the impressive Railroad Museum in Old Sacramento and showed some architectural innovation during the 1970s, when futurist Jerry Brown was governor, and set aside state-owned land for housing to help create a "24-hour city." The reconstruction of the state Capitol itself has been an unqualified success, creating a turn-of-the-century museum that is both a working seat of government and a natural central focus for the city, and in the late 1980s, the Capitol became the centerpiece for an explosion of downtown office construction as local developers competed to erect the city's tallest building and the city adopted a more pro-development attitude.

By 1990, the city boasted of several skyscrapers worthy of the name and an almost-first-class hotel near the Capitol and had plans for more of both, although a national recession and credit crunch put a serious damper on downtown development plans in 1991 and developers complained that the city was imposing so many restrictions on them that they might gravitate to nearby West Sacramento. That aside, state government had provided a stable base of downtown employees that gave Sacramento opportunities that other cities could only envy.

At first it was just a spot where two rivers, the Sacramento and the American, joined. A few settlers lived along the rivers and the most important structure was John Sutter's fort a few miles to the east.

When a Sutter employee discovered gold in the Sierra foothills in 1848, however, Sacramento came into being as one of the most important cities of the West—the jumping-off point for the gold fields, the western terminus of the Pony Express and later the transcontinental railroad, the place where visionaries such as Leland Stanford planned an empire.

It wasn't long, though, before the state's political and economic power—and the men who wielded it—shifted to San Francisco and Los Angeles and for most of its history, Sacramento has been known as a quiet, almost sleepy, and dull center of state and federal bureaucracy, growing only as government grew. By the early 1970s, some 40 percent all workers in the area received public paychecks and Sacramento had earned the nickname "Big Tomato" for its best-known non-governmental product.

There was some economic diversification—a port to ship Central Valley produce to the outside world, a few food processing plants and canneries—but it was as the seat of state government, the regional headquarters of federal agencies and the site of two Air Force bases and an Army supply depot that Sacramento had its primary reasons for existence.

The economy during the first three-fourths of the 20th century was stable if unspectacular. The state bureaucrats and the military employees went to their jobs without fear of layoff, collected their paychecks and pensions and kept the new suburban shopping centers and grocery stores full of customers. Dull but dependable, that was Sacramento, a city of trees to shade its people from the fierce summer sun, of quaint old residential areas much favored by political types from the Capitol and of seemingly endless residential suburbs filled with bureaucrats and their families.

Things began to change in the mid-1970s. It wasn't anything that Sacramento did. It was simply that the coastal metropolitan areas were filling up, housing was becoming too expensive and developers and industrialists began looking at inland cities such as Sacramento, Fresno, San Bernardino, Riverside and Bakersfield, where employers could find inexpensive land and workers could find houses they could afford. Sacramento has the lowest-cost housing of any of the state's major metropolitan areas and that remains true even though it was one of the nation's hottest housing markets in the late 1980s. Median home prices jumped by a third in one torrid year.

High-tech companies opened plants in western Placer County and along

Highway 50 east of Sacramento. Professional and industry trade associations, consulting firms, lobbyists and law firms established Sacramento offices because of the Capitol—more than 500 trade associations alone at last count— and hired thousands of employees. Sacramento's central location encouraged warehousing and distribution facilities. Industrial and commercial parks were developed and Sacramento developed a mini-skyline of high-rise office buildings.

Government payrolls stagnated. By the mid-1980s, government employees had fallen from a high of 40 percent of the labor force to less than a third and the Menlo Park-based Institute for the Future projected a decline to about 25 percent by 2000 as private manufacturing, trade and services payrolls mush-

Focus on Sacramento

Area .... 2,049.3 sq. miles
Percentage of California 1.3%

Population
(with percentage of California total)

	1960	1970	1980	1990	2000	2005
Sacramento Co.	510,300	636,700	787,800	1,051,400	1,382,200	1,533,100
Yolo Co.	66,400	92,700	114,000	142,500	174,400	187,100
TOTAL	576,700	729,400	901,800	1,193,900	1,556,600	1,720,200
CALIFORNIA	3.7%	3.6%	3.8%	4.0%	4.3%	4.4%

Ethnic composition
(1990 Census)

	Anglo	Latino	Asian/Pacific	Black
Sacramento Co.	69.3%	11.7%	8.8%	9.0%
Yolo Co.	68.0%	20.0%	8.1%	2.1%
CALIFORNIA	57.2%	25.8%	9.1%	7.0%

Economic Data

	Unemployment rate (Aug. 1991)	Taxable sales (1990 per capita)	Personal income (per capita) 1984	Personal income (per capita) 1989
Sacramento Co.	5.7%	$9,915	$13,218	$17,462
Yolo Co.	5.2%	$9,892	$12,899	$17,779
CALIFORNIA	7.2%	$9,400	$14,593	$19,229

Political data

	1964	1972	1980	1984	1988
Voter registration (Democrat-Republican)	64-34%	62-32%	57-29%	51-32%	55-35%
Presidential vote (Democrat-Republican)	66-34%	50-50%	42-48%	45-55%	49-51%

Sources: State Department of Finance, 1990 Census, employment Development Department, Board of Equalization, Center for Continuing Study of the California Economy and the Secretary of State's office.

room and those of government stagnate or even decline.

Two of Sacramento's three major military installations, Mather AFB and Sacramento Army Depot, have been ticketed for closure by the Pentagon and the third and largest, McClellan AFB, is in some danger. At stake are tens of thousands of high-paying, stable civilian jobs and the military cutback is hastening the conversion of the region's economy from public to private. Some Sacramento planners envision that Mather, with its long runways built for B-52 bombers, might be converted into an international airport/trade center that would create thousands of jobs and relieve some of the pressure on San Francisco Bay Area airports—especially if supersonic transports begin connecting California with Asia and Europe.

Even without that development, Sacramento already has achieved a critical economic mass, becoming big enough to generate economic and cultural aspirations of its own. Slowly, almost imperceptibly, the old civic gentry's influence has faded and that of pro-development business executives expanded, although it has been narrowly focused on issues, such as land use, that immediately affect their pocketbooks.

The growth of private payrolls and the expansion of suburbia gave a more conservative, or at least pro-business, cast to local politics. Developers became the area's major campaign contributors and Sacramento began experiencing what other high-growth areas had experienced—intimate and sometimes scandalous relations between public officials and developers. Republicans

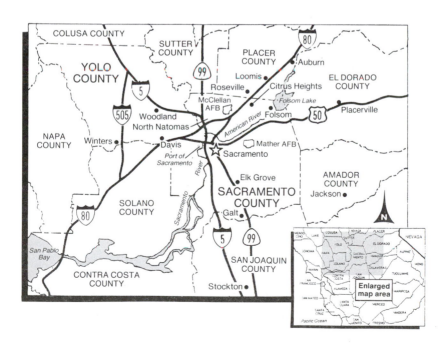

Graphic courtesy *The Sacramento Bee*

started winning elections in the suburbs of a city that once voted only for Democrats.

Karolyn Simon, a local environmental activist and county planning commission member, typlifies the ambivalent feelings that many have about the quickening pace of life in Sacramento.

"Part of what is happening to Sacramento is very, very exciting to me," Simon said as expansion hit high gear in the mid-1980s, mentioning such things as expanded theater, art, music and other cultural activities.

But, she quickly added, "We have to tread very carefully to make sure we don't destroy our quality of life. We have to determine whether we want to go beyond the cowtown mentality."

John Harvey Carter, a Sacramento architect and urban development critic, also worried aloud.

"Being against growth is like being against God and motherhood," he said, "but we're going to be another Los Angeles in 25 years with all the problems L.A. has. We're losing a certain sense of neighborliness and community."

Within a few years, much of what Carter feared was becoming true as Sacramento coped with gang warfare, drugs, a high murder rate and ethnic friction, even as construction crews busily transformed the downtown core into a forest of glass and steel towers.

The pro-growthers insisted that they could avoid the worst aspects of urbanization.

"If we are careful with our planning, we can sustain our quality of life," said Alan Ewen, who helped promote the expansion of the private economy for a number of years as head of the Sacramento Area Commerce and Trade Organization (SACTO). "We are not going to be like the Santa Clara Valley."

A local developer, Bob Slobe, put it another way in a 1989 Sacramento Bee article: "There's a chance, if we're not careful, of killing the goose that laid the golden egg."

Still another version of the same worrisome attitude came from county planner Robert Sherry as he outlined growth options to county supervisors in 1990: "I think we're uniquely situated historically and politically to accomplish something very exciting. We don't think we can afford to make a lot of mistakes over the next 20 years."

The war between pro-development forces and the go-slow establishment had any number of clashes, but the showdown battle was fought over the development of North Natomas in the mid-1980s—a battle still not resolved.

North Natomas, a 9,000-acre strip of land that connects Sacramento proper with its rapidly developing metropolitan airport along Interstate 5, is owned by a consortium of developers but had been set aside as an urban greenbelt by city planners.

The developers dangled the prospect of major league sports in front of the city by promising to build a major arena complex if they were given permission to place offices and other development on the land, too. The saliva production of local sports fans increased when the developers purchased a pro basketball team in Kansas City and moved it to Sacramento, housing it in a temporary arena just east of North Natomas on land controlled by county government.

In a sense, that temporary arena symbolized the leadership vacuum that afflicts the region. County supervisors had already sanctioned development on most of the land between the city and the airport, leaving the city with control only over a strip along I-5.

The advocates of contained growth may, in fact, have lost the battle decades earlier when the city's boundaries were not expanded into vacant fields.

The sports arena was the focus of the November 1983 mayoral race that pitted pro-development businessman Ross Relles against the personification of the local liberal/environmentalist establishment, Anne Rudin. Rudin won, but narrowly. It was a strong indication that the growth-control forces were weakening.

Nevertheless, as she assumed the mayor's seat, Rudin pledged to continue the fight against North Natomas development, saying, "We've been elected because of what we stand for."

Two years later, Rudin was fighting a rear-guard action as the adroit public relations work of the developers, coupled with more direct persuasive efforts aimed at the rest of the City Council, combined to turn the tide toward development of North Natomas and the creation, its promoters said, of as many as 65,000 new jobs. Rudin and other go-slow advocates were reduced to impotent fuming. Arco Arena, the permanent home of the Kings basketball team, was constructed and the developer/sportsmen, chief among them Gregg Lukenbill, went after football and baseball teams to occupy what they said would be a major sports complex. But by 1990, Arco Arena was still sitting in isolated splendor with further development delayed by a softening economy, the financial problems of the developers and by federal pressure to resolve the area's tendency to flood during heavy water years.

The battle over North Natomas demonstrated the fuzzy nature of political leadership in Sacramento, symbolized by the weakness of the mayor's office. Not only does the mayor have little more than symbolic authority over city affairs—the real power being wielded by a hired city manager—but he or she can't even speak for the majority of the metropolitan area's population.

One of the symbols of Sacramento's municipal adolescence is the weak governmental structure, which vests most administrative power in unelected professionals rather than elected officials. The effect is to sever the direct link between policy decision and administrative action and is exacerbated by the fact that responsibility is divided between a city government and a county government that controls a larger unincorporated area that lacks any semblance of a downtown core but nevertheless was declared a "pseudo-city" by an appellate court during one of the countless battles between county officials and advocates of suburban incorporation. The former fight bitterly to prevent suburban communities from becoming cities because sales tax revenues from commercial developments within any new cities would be taken from the county.

Political power is so diffused in Sacramento that it's sometimes hard to pin down who is responsible for what.

The five county supervisors are equals without a designated leader and govern communities that would be medium-sized cities of their own were they to be incorporated, and more than 100 independent governmental bodies provide transportation, fire, recreation, water, education, electric power and other services, each with its own governing body and own self-protective bureaucracy.

By default, developers and their partners in the financial community have become the true policy-makers for the region, deciding how it will grow by how they invest.

Phil Isenberg, one of Rudin's predecessors as mayor and later a state assemblyman, conceded that Sacramento should have pursued annexation more aggressively in the past to achieve more control over metropolitan development. But he also said he believes that the seemingly glacial pace of decision-making in Sacramento may be a blessing because it may avoid expensive mistakes.

"The decisions are being made but they are being made slowly," he said.

Lloyd Connelly, another former city councilman who joined Isenberg in the Assembly, said "Sacramento is clearly at the transition point from a very big town to a small city" but suffers from a lack of leadership because "the population base is outside the city."

Connelly advocates making the mayor's position a stronger one, bringing focus to a City Council that seems to be content to debate matters endlessly but come to few decisions. It was a council that couldn't agree on a position on the Persian Gulf War even weeks after the war was over and has waffled over what to do about the downtown area—a city that gained nationwide notoriety when it sought to officially find a new gender-neutral term for "manhole."

The list of snafus in local policy-making has been endless, including the K Street Mall, huge cost overruns in the light-rail system that was financed with diverted highway funds as a gesture toward local environmentalists, a short-sighted decision in the early 1970s to abandon suburban freeway routes that were needed to cope with the traffic of the 1980s and 1990s, long-delayed efforts to build a major hotel near the Capitol (one finished only with generous city subsidies) and fast-rising electric rates stemming, in part, from a nuclear power plant that was shut down more often than it operated and was finally closed for good by voters.

At one point in 1991, the city was encouraging suburban commuters to use light rail to reduce downtown congestion and reduce air pollution while one of its agencies slashed rates at city-owned garages to make parking and auto-commuting cheaper, the latter being a market reaction to the fact that the city had compelled developers to overbuild downtown parking, which put down-

ward pressure on competitive parking rates. To local critics of city government, it was just one more episode on a long list of contradictory edicts from
city hall.

Several attempts have been made to streamline the governmental morass,
most notably a city-county consolidation proposal in the mid-1970s and a
revised version placed before voters in 1990 to create California's third-largest
city.

The 1970s drive was shot down by the combined efforts of elected and
appointed officials of the area's many small special districts who disliked
losing control of their little public fiefdoms. Consolidation was revived in the
late 1980s in response to burgeoning efforts by several unincorporated
suburban communities to reorganize themselves as cities but it, too, was
rejected by voters in 1990 after a lackluster campaign failed to overcome fears
by both city-dwellers and suburbanites that they would be dominated by the
other. It became painfully clear that consolidation was not the result of some
comprehensive examination of local governance, but a political ploy aimed at
heading off the formation of new cities.

Glen Sparrow, who had been executive director of the city-county consolidation commission in the 1970s, coined the term "civic gentry" to describe
Sacramento's passive leadership in a lengthy monograph written on the
confused local government situation years later.

Sparrow quoted one Sacramento city manager as saying, "I don't know why
the council continues to meet weekly. They can take care of all their business
with four quarterly meetings a year. I can do the rest." It was an attitude that
several city managers exhibited.

As Sacramento entered the 1990s still fragmented but still growing, it
remained uncertain whether it would become the major city its numbers
implied it should be, or continue to suffer from weak civic and political
leadership. Developing that civic infrastructure may be more difficult in
Sacramento than in any other major metropolitan area of the state because of
its government-driven economy. While major employers traditionally nourish
the civic leadership cadre in most big league cities, Sacramento's major
employers are government agencies, thus depriving it of that natural base.

Yolo County, separated by the Sacramento River from Sacramento, has
faced many of its big brother's dilemmas as well.

The rich river bottomland of the county has been a magnet for large-scale
agriculture. But its proximity to Sacramento has created development pressure
that is slowly changing the nature of the county from rural to suburban.

"East Yolo," a jumble of unincorporated communities just across the river
from Sacramento, developed as a highway service center, full of motels and
cafes, and later as a port and warehousing center with an unsavory reputation
for catering to pleasures of the flesh. But in the late 1980s, local civic betterment
forces pushed through an incorporation plan that created the City of West
Sacramento and used the new city as a platform from which to launch

ambitious development schemes, focusing mostly on its Sacramento River frontage, that would take advantage of its proximity to downtown Sacramento's concentration of jobs and of the City of Sacramento's evident political confusion over development-related policy.

Woodland, the Yolo County seat, remains the most agricultural of the county's population centers, but it is beginning to show signs of urban-style development, of becoming an attractive option for commuters from Sacramento, less than a half-hour's drive away on Interstate 5, and beginning to see substantial warehousing and manufacturing operations. Another Yolo County farm town, Winters, is close enough to the San Francisco Bay Area and freeways that it, to, is beginning to experience growth pressure.

It is Davis, however, that is the major development battleground in Yolo County. Once a farm town that happened to contain a branch of the University of California system, Davis now is a full-blown college town with the convoluted politics typical of the genre.

The environmental movement came to Davis in the early 1970s and stayed. No city in California has exerted more effort to control its ambiance—from requiring solar power on new homes to encouraging the use of bicycles for transportation to trying to control its growth.

Davis created a very attractive, human-scale urban environment, but it also succeeded in making itself just that more inviting to Sacramento commuters and others, thereby creating even more development pressure for itself.

Davis dealt with that by clamping strict controls on development, trying, in effect, to make growth a crime. That then had the effect of driving up housing costs—supply and demand being in conflict—and making the city an island of Anglo affluence.

"Most people come to Davis from some place larger that they didn't like," City Councilman Jerry Adler told an interviewer in 1985. "They come and find a bucolic backwater that is very pleasing to them and they don't want it diluted."

But another Davis resident described the city's image another way. "Davis," said UC-Davis Professor Merline Williams, "has developed into a closed, elitist yuppie-town where only people with a certain income range can afford to live."

That's echoed by Davis newspaper columnist Bob Dunning, who once said, "The way we've structured the town, we may as well have a wall around it— a wall to keep the unwashed masses out. It's like, `I've got mine, now let's close the door.'"

The elitism that is an inevitable byproduct of such strong growth controls plainly worries many in the city. And it became the focus of a mid-1980s debate over the 50,000 population limit set in a 1982 city election.

The policy limited Davis to that number by 2000 but $1^1/_2$ decades in advance, the city was nearly there and city officials were showing signs of allowing the limit to rise—possibly as an annual number of new housing permits rather than a fixed overall population ceiling.

Councilman Adler said the 1982 limit means the city "exercised its political muscle without empirical support."

UC-Davis "is our growth generator," Adler argued. "To deny that is sophistry. We'll always have the growth generator as long as there is a university."

Those who opposed runaway growth in Davis seemingly locked their hopes into city law when the City Council limited expansion to 1.7 percent a year. But the council then turned around a approved development agreements for a 528-acre parcel on the eastern edge of the city, touching off a firestorm of criticism and leading to a ballot showdown in 1989. The anti-growthers lost big when voters ratified the plans from developer Frank Ramos, who had pledged to pursue the development through county government if the city spurned it. Most City Council members and most voters decided that having Ramos' development under city control was preferable; nonetheless, the political battle left Davis' once-solid slow-growth policies in disarray.

Both Davis and Sacramento are learning what other California communities have had to learn the hard way: trying to stop growth is almost self-defeating. At best, imaginative leaders can channel it and cope with its negative side effects, but it's still unclear whether the Sacramento area will accomplish what only one other fast-growing metropolitan region in California, San Diego, has done in the postwar era: move to big city—or, as local boosters put it, "world-class city"—status without choking on itself.

As the Sacramento Tomorrow Coalition, a local planning organization, put it in a 1990 report:

"Without a vision, the region risks becoming another casualty of rapid, unmanaged development."

San Joaquin Valley:
Soil, oil and toil

Hᴉsᴛᴏʀʏ ʀᴇᴄᴏʀᴅs ᴛʜᴀᴛ Gᴜʏ MᴀᴄLᴇᴏᴅ, ᴀɴ ᴇxᴇᴄᴜᴛɪᴠᴇ ᴏF ᴀ Fʀᴇsɴᴏ Fᴀʀᴍ chemical company, coined the term "agribusiness" in the mid-1940s.

He meant it to denote an agriculture that was more industry than a bucolic, slow-moving way of life, a scientific approach that incorporated advanced research and intensive, technology-heavy field techniques to squeeze the maximum yield from the land.

It was an agriculture that was then still evolving in California's elongated Central Valley but that has since matured into one of the wonders of the world, only to fall on hard times as the rest of the world began to catch up.

Even so, the numbers attached to agricultural production in the San Joaquin Valley—the intensely farmed lower half of the Central Valley—are staggering, adding billions of dollars to the state's economy each year. The output of Fresno County alone surpasses that of several states.

Even as agriculture expanded dramatically in the valley—helped by the construction of dams that plugged dozens of streams in the Sierra foothills and provided cheap water—there was a sense that it was dangerous to depend so much on one industry.

During the past generation, therefore, local leaders throughout the valley, from Bakersfield to Stockton, have undertaken serious economic diversification efforts and the state's high rate of population growth, coupled with a continuing shift to a dispersed, post-industrial economy, has opened up much of the valley to suburbanization.

The northern end of the valley, San Joaquin and Stanislaus counties, has become an extension of the San Francisco Bay Area and are among the fastest-growing regions of the state. The lower end of the valley, Kern County, is beginning to feel development pressure creeping northward from Los Angeles. And the middle—Fresno and environs—is developing a growth pattern of its own, based on an expansion of non-agricultural employment. The San Joaquin Valley, in short, is feeling the effects of a boom, one that is changing both the physical and social landscapes of a region long relegated to poor-relation status by Californians in the Los Angeles and San Francisco metroplexes. And as it booms, the San Joaquin Valley is becoming economically and politically more powerful.

Were it not for its economic dominance by agriculture, the San Joaquin Valley might be considered the most representative of California's major regions.

Its ethnic breakdown is characteristic of the state as a whole: mostly Anglo, dispersed among a number of easily identifiable ethnic groups, and with a substantial and fast-growing Latino population of about 30 percent and smaller black and Asian contingents. Its personal income levels are likewise near the norm. And its political profile—nominally Democratic but voting conservatively and often Republican—is a microcosm of the state. Because of that, the valley is often pivotal in statewide elections since Republican-leaning Southern California and the heavily Democratic San Francisco Bay Area tend to cancel each other out.

The San Joaquin Valley's population growth had been steady but unspectacular until the 1980s, when the boom began. In 1960, the eight-county region had 1.4 million persons or almost exactly 9 percent of California's population. By 1980 it had grown to 2.1 million and dipped to 8.7 percent but by 1990, it was 2.8 million and over 9 percent again. Over the next 15 years, between 1990 and 2005, the valley's population is expected to grow by another 50 percent to near 4 million and it will be more than 10 percent of California by then.

The valley's spectacular population growth has made it trendy, at least in academic and journalistic circles, with seminars and lengthy newspaper articles that explore the clash between its agricultural past and its urbanized future.

As Ed Blakely, a professor of urban planning at the University of California, Berkeley, put it in a paper delivered to one of those seminars in 1990:

"The great Central Valley has been no stranger to change. The valley's first great change was the conversion of its natural habitats to agriculture. For most of California's history, the Central Valley has been the world's premier irrigated garden, as its agriculture became the economic backbone for about one-sixth of the state's population.

"Today, the valley is undergoing a second great change—the transformation of an agricultural base to urban domination. The first change civilized it;

the second change brings confusion with respect to how the peoplescape will continue to develop. We don't want to destroy the valley, we want to create it. And in creating a new valley, there will be an essential interplay among agriculture, the people, the place and the resources."

By all accounts, the transition will not be a painless one. There are powerful elements within the valley—connected to agriculture, mostly—who resist the change. They see urbanization and economic diversity as pushing them out of business, conscious of what has occurred in other agricultural regions, such as the Santa Clara Valley, and bringing competition for labor, water and political power.

Although agribusiness—a combination of large farmers, their suppliers, their financiers and their political allies—came to dominate the San Joaquin Valley during the mid-20th century, it was not always so.

The history of the valley is one of succeeding migratory waves to whom the fertile valley represented new beginnings.

The original non-Indian settlers were small farmers from America's heartland who had been recruited by the Central Pacific (later Southern Pacific) Railroad to till the land that the railroad had received from the government as a subsidy for construction.

The railroad laid out the towns, giving them Spanish names or those attached to the railroad itself. Hanford, for example, was named for a railroad executive. Coalinga originally was "Coaling Station A" because a supply of low-grade but usable coal was discovered nearby _ a harbinger of the oil that later gushed from the hills surrounding the lower valley.

Those late 19th century farmers grew wheat as their money crop and fought with the railroad over its stranglehold on shipping rates. The fight turned violent during a shootout between farmers and railroad agents in what is now Kings County, a battle that went into the history books as the "Mussel Slough Tragedy" and inspired "The Octopus," Frank Norris' muckraking novel about railroad power.

The battle between San Joaquin Valley farmers and the railroad laid the groundwork for California's wave of political reform in the early 20th century that broke Southern Pacific's control of the state Legislature.

Armenians fleeing the genocidal impulses of the Turks settled in Fresno and became an integral part of the San Joaquin Valley's rich cultural heritage.

Even today, there are distinct settlements of Dutch, Mennonites and Yugoslavians in the valley. Immigrants from the Azores still trickle into the valley's dairy industry and there are a few Basques still tending herds of sheep and living in their distinctive homes on wheels.

Chinese-American neighborhoods in valley towns evolved from early railroad and field workers. There are enclaves of Japanese- and Filipino-Americans, descendants of early 20th century farm workers. And large numbers of Southeast Asian refugees settled in the valley during the 1970s and early 1980s.

One Tulare county town, Allensworth, was named for a black Union officer who led a group of immigrants to California after the Civil War and survives today as a living state monument.

The oil boom and the Depression brought countless tens of thousands of immigrants from Oklahoma, Texas and other Southwestern states, an exodus that was dramatically portrayed in John Steinbeck's "The Grapes of Wrath." Bakersfield, the center of the region's oil production, has a distinctive Oklahoma-Texas ambiance. Country singer Buck Owens founded a country music recording industry in the city.

In Stockton, at the other end of the valley, the eastern side is an almost undiluted settlement of immigrants and their descendants from Southwestern states—the result of a deliberate and racist policy of early 20th century land developers to recruit them rather than sell small truck garden plots to Japanese.

Mexicans began moving into the valley in the 1920s to work in the fields and tens of thousands remained to found a Hispanic community now numbering perhaps a half-million. And the larger cities in the valley acquired substantial black populations.

There are even a few—a very few—of the valley's original Indian inhabitants living on tiny, poverty-stricken reservations, called rancherias.

As the ethnic composition of the valley was enriched by the waves of migration—reflected today in the wide variety of ethnic restaurants and a body of literature from such writers as William Saroyan, John Steinbeck and Maxine Hong Kingston—so was its economic structure.

Wheat gave way to an astonishing variety of crops: cotton in the southern end, grapes and tree fruits in the middle, vegetables in the Sacramento-San Joaquin Delta. The agriculture intensified as more water became available from the network of government dams and canals. The marshlands of Tulare Lake were drained and became the very embodiment of agribusiness, holdings so vast that they were measured in sections, rather than acres, and operated out of corporate-style office complexes.

The J.G. Boswell Co., the largest privately owned farming operation in the world, grew cotton in the one-time lake, which periodically re-created itself when the winter rains and the spring runoff from the Sierra were too large for the dams to handle. Next door, the Salyer family operated on only a slightly smaller scale.

The Boswells and the Salyers fought for control of the lake bottom in court, but banded together against the outside world and became two of the most important sources of campaign funds for the state's politicians. Once, the Salyers tried to buy a state highway so that it wouldn't interfere with the runway for their private jet planes.

At another point, faced with the ruinous possibility that the 160-acre limitation on federally subsidized water would be enforced, the Tulare Lake agribusinessmen proposed to buy one of the government's dams to guarantee their water supply.

   The completion of the California Aqueduct, a monumental manmade river that takes Northern California water to Southern California, opened up even more acreage to cultivation on the west side of the valley. A new interstate highway down the valley provided even better access to the outside world.

   The valley's cities grew from small towns into substantial cities. Some, such as Fresno, even developed skylines and acquired at least a veneer of metropolitan sophistication. But even as it flirted with big city status, Fresno found itself parodied in a television network movie.

   With foreign and domestic markets for the valley's produce expanding and with bankers eager to lend on land that was rising in value, the future of San Joaquin Valley agribusiness seemed limitless. Trucking companies, farm equipment dealers, chemical firms and banks shared in the prosperity.

Focus on San Joaquin Valley

Area .... 27,561.2 sq. miles
Percentage of California 17.4%

Population
(with percentage of California total)

	1960	1970	1980	1990	2000	2005
Fresno Co.	368,500	413,800	516,900	673,900	855,500	942,700
Kern Co.	294,900	331,100	406,400	549,800	718,600	793,700
Kings Co.	50,500	66,700	74,200	102,500	124,300	134,900
Madera Co.	40,700	41,700	64,000	89,800	120,100	134,800
Merced Co.	90,900	105,000	135,600	180,600	236,000	266,400
San Joaquin Co.	251,700	292,100	350,200	483,800	621,700	686,300
Stanislaus Co.	158,300	195,800	267,900	3476,100	602,300	558,200
Tulare Co.	169,400	189,400	247,500	314,600	397,800	439,900
TOTAL	1,424,900	1,635,600	2,062,700	2,771,100	3,576,300	3,956,900
CALIFORNIA	9.0%	8.2%	8.7%	9.2%	9.9%	10.2%

Ethnic composition
(1990 Census)

	Anglo	Latino	Asian/Pacific	Black
Fresno Co.	50.7%	35.5%	8.1%	4.7%
Kern Co.	62.7%	28.0%	2.7%	5.3%
Kings Co.	53.6%	34.1%	3.4%	7.6%
Madera Co.	60.1%	34.5%	1.2%	2.6%
Merced Co.	54.2%	32.6%	7.9%	4.4%
San Joaquin Co.	58.8%	23.4%	11.6%	5.2%
Stanislaus Co.	70.5%	21.8%	1.6%	4.9%
Tulare Co.	54.6%	38.8%	4.0%	1.4%
CALIFORNIA	57.2%	25.8%	9.1%	7.0%

Economic Data

	Unemployment rate (Aug. 1991)	Taxable sales (1990 per capita)	Personal income (per capita)	
			1984	1989
Fresno Co.	8.9%	$8,517	$12,415	$14,872
Kern Co.	10.3%	$8,822	$11,984	$14,457
Kings Co.	9.9%	$54,679	$10,511	$12,938
Merced Co.	10.7%	$5,853	$11,738	$12,931
Madera Co.	11.8%	$6,497	$10,581	$12,578
San Joaquin Co.	9.2%	$7,872	$12,701	$14,465
Stanislaus Co.	10.4%	$8,874	$12,254	$13,858
Tulare Co.	13.1%	$6,830	$10,672	$13,235
CALIFORNIA	7.2%	$9,400	$14,593	$19,229

Political data

	1964	1972	1980	1984	1988
Voter registration (Democrat-Republican)	64-34%	61-34%	56-35%	55-36%	53-38%
Presidential vote (Democrat-Republican)	63-37%	43-47%	38-55%	40-60	44-56%

Sources: State Department of Finance, 1990 Census, employment Development Department, Board of Equalization, Center for Continuing Study of the California Economy and the Secretary of State's office.

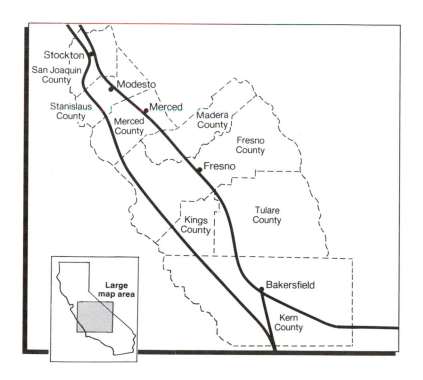

Graphic courtesy *The Sacramento Bee*

But in the mid-1980s, things began to change for agribusiness, change for the worse.

A strong dollar made California's agricultural produce more costly overseas and after peaking at $4.3 billion in 1981, farm exports dropped to $2.9 billion by 1984 and perhaps even further in 1985.

Domestic farm prices dropped and even the state's lack of a dominating crop failed to prevent the effects from being felt in the state, a rude awakening for those who thought that California-style agribusiness was immune to cyclic lows.

"We were wrong," California Farm Bureau president Henry Voss said as he watched farmers face serious financial peril on a broad scale for the first time.

Many farmers, having borrowed heavily at high rates, got caught in a squeeze that forced them into bankruptcy when prices and land values fell.

By 1986, Voss and other authorities were predicting that a quarter of California's 35,000 farmers faced the prospect of zero net worth.

"These are not speculators or people who were greedy," Voss said. "Many of these people are good farmers who made the right decisions, who were conservative in their operations. When the best farmers are faltering, we've got a problem."

Bill Allison, manager of the Fresno Farm Bureau, put it another way: "You've got a situation where land values are about 50 percent of what they were four years ago."

The steep decline in the farm economy had rippling effects throughout the valley and beyond. Equipment dealers folded and banks—some as large as Bank of America—were forced to write off tens of millions of dollars in bad loans that had been happily made when land values were soaring a few years earlier.

It hit the largest and the smallest. In fact, some economists concluded that the large farming operations, those that embodied the principles of agribusiness, were hit harder by the slump than the smaller family operations.

"The conventional wisdom is that during times of stress, you get a rush toward larger firms," Bank of American economist Fred Cannon said. "But, in fact, they're the ones that are now being squeezed."

Even giant J.G. Boswell slashed its workforce as the price of cotton fell and joined efforts to bring non-agricultural payrolls into Corcoran, its headquarters town in the Tulare Lake. The state, eager to find sites for new state prisons, decided to place one in Corcoran and another in Avenal, a one-time San Joaquin Valley oil boom town fallen on hard times.

There were a few exceptions. Citrus growers and premium wine grape growers continued to prosper. But for those who grew grapes for jug wines or raisins, things were bad.

Nor did it appear that things would be getting much better soon.

"I think we're going to see an increase in the number of people—the non-agriculturally oriented people now in agriculture—getting out," Fresno agribusiness consultant Allen Mather said.

A University of California study concluded that between 1980 and 1985, the decline of farm exports alone had cost the state 100,000 jobs.

Even a weaker dollar, however, would not mean a fully restored agricultural export economy. Demand for many of the commodities that California was shipping overseas also was declining because a number of the Third World nations, especially those in Asia, had become self-sufficient in food production and even were entering the export trade themselves to boost hard currency earnings. That was most noticeable in the decline in rice exports from the Sacramento Valley north of Sacramento but it affected San Joaquin Valley crops as well.

And just as the industry's economic position weakened, it was confronted with huge problems relating to the use and disposal of the chemicals that had helped spur production but also to the concentration of toxic agricultural wastewaters in the Kesterson wildlife refuge in the central portion of the valley.

Agribusiness did find better times later in the decade, although a drought that began in 1987 claimed its own share of victims, as did a record freeze that struck California in December 1990. The drought, the freeze and other negative factors left the valley with one of the state's highest unemployment rates—a situation that hit the largely Latino agricultural workforce especially hard. Even so, the northern part of the valley felt the effects of suburbanization as one-time vegetable fields and orchards began sprouting houses, part of California's great shift of population from coastal cities into inland valleys.

Cheap land, relatively inexpensive housing, a central location between the state's two major metropolitan markets and excellent rail and highway transportation access made the valley attractive to employers and home builders. During the 1985-88 period, traffic on Interstate 205, which connects the Modesto-Stockton area with the San Francisco Bay Area, increased by 42 percent as subdivision after subdivision opened to refugees seeking relief from Bay Area home prices. Even the tiny and seemingly isolated west valley farm town of Los Banos laid out subdivisions as its connector highway into the San Jose area was upgraded into full freeway status.

"Most (commuters) would like to have jobs without the commute," UC planner Blakely observed, "but valley wages are consistently below those of the Bay Area. The difference varies from a few percentage points to as much as 25 percent or more."

There are projections, meanwhile, for job growth in the Bay Area—especially the new suburban employment centers of the Santa Clara and Diablo valleys—that far outstrips housing production and that imbalance will continue to push home-seekers into the upper San Joaquin Valley.

As agribusiness' dominant position in the San Joaquin Valley economy softened, the non-agricultural segments took on a greater importance, although diversification has not always been easy.

Oil exploration and production in the lower valley picked up sharply in the late 1970s and early 1980s as the international OPEC cartel drove up prices—but that bubble, too, threatened to burst as prices tumbled in the mid-1980s.

"The problem with the Central Valley in-state is an image problem and people out of state don't know it exists," Barbara Hayes, a state economic development specialist who works on diversification programs for the valley, said. "When people say Central Valley, you think of flat land and little farm towns. But you've got affordable land and they're not little cow towns anymore."

Stockton has evolved from an agricultural town with some industry to an industrial city surrounded by agriculture and then into a suburban commuter city with some industry—and in the process has developed an unusual connection to Hollywood that has seen dozens of film production crews use the city and its environs for location shooting.

Hanford, one of the smallest of the valley cities, mounted an aggressive industrial development program in the 1960s to soak up the excess labor force left by the mechanization of agriculture and attracted several factories, including a 700-employee Armstrong Rubber Co. tire plant that, with a name change, survives as the only remaining tire factory in the state. Hershey Chocolate chose Oakdale, a tiny farm town in Stanislaus County, for its West Coast candy bar factory and it, too, employs about 700 persons.

Officials in Bakersfield, the valley city closest to Southern California, touted it as a site for industry to serve the giant market to the south with low housing costs and had several successes, most notably a Frito-Lay potato chip plant and a regional headquarters for State Farm Insurance that, when completed, will employ 1,000 workers.

"We feel Kern County, as the southernmost county in the valley and as the closest county to the Los Angeles market, is in the best position in the Central Valley for pure growth," said Jim Radoumis, manager of the local board of trade.

Indeed, Bakersfield was California's fastest-growing major city in the mid-1980s—a condition helped along by the early '80s oil boom that poured money into the community.

"It was diversity of opportunity that made Bakersfield...stand out," the Center for Continuing Study of the California Economy said of the city's population expansion, 6.5 percent in one year.

While the bust that followed the oil boom scarred the local economy, the late 1980s saw an economic rebirth as the Tehachapi Mountains, the psychological barrier between Los Angeles and the San Joaquin Valley as well as the physical one, was breached.

"I have talked to developers who have sold the entire subdivisions to people who work in the San Fernando Valley," Bakersfield planning director Jack Hardisty told The New York Times. The San Fernando Valley is 85 miles away, but by Southern California standards that's a medium-sized commute.

And if plans for a high-speed train linking Sacramento with Los Angeles through the valley are realized, Bakersfield might become a half-hour train ride from Los Angeles employment centers.

Visalia, in Tulare County, became known as America's most entrepreneurial city for its creative development projects that brought dozens of non-agricultural employers and hundreds of jobs to the community. At one point, the City of Visalia even owned its own minor league baseball team. But Visalia also discovered the downside of capitalistic government in 1991 when it was forced to take over a downtown hotel it had helped finance—and learned that it was worth only a fourth of what it had cost to build.

Merced County, meanwhile, pinned its hopes for economic diversification on persuading the University of California to establish a new campus. University officials tentatively chose Merced County for the first of three new campuses to serve enrollment demand but the state's shaky economic conditions in 1991 left it uncertain when the facility would be built. When—and if— the San Joaquin Valley campus is established, it would be a sign not only of first-class educational status for the region, but produce the spinoff benefits that most university communities enjoy.

The military also has valued the valley's wide open spaces. The Navy built its first-ever inland air base southwest of Fresno. And Lemoore Naval Air Station seems destined for even bigger things as the Navy and its jets are slowly squeezed out of heavily populated coastal bases around San Diego and San Francisco. The Air Force established Castle AFB near Merced—but later decided to shut it down as the Cold War came to an end.

Expanding non-agricultural payrolls was sought by local leaders to stabilize otherwise seasonal economies and provide pathways to the middle class for the valley's poor and ethnic minorities, but unemployment rates have remained high—typically above 8 percent in mid-1991—even in the face of superficial prosperity and five of the 10 California counties with the highest rates of welfare dependency in 1991 were found in the San Joaquin Valley. There remains, moreover, a decided caste system, both economic and political, in the region—Anglos on top and Hispanics and blacks on the bottom.

It's quite visible in the larger cities, where the more affluent Anglo residential areas spread northward while the poor and minorities remained locked into the south sides.

This development pattern, so common to valley towns and cities, is, a University of the Pacific researcher concluded, a result of the valley's prevailing winds from the north and northwest. Beginning in the 19th century, before indoor plumbing, the wealthier citizens always built their new homes upwind or north.

Ever since Cesar Chavez launched his farm worker unionization effort in Delano, a grape-growing town in Kern County, there have been recurrent hopes of organizing the region's large Hispanic population into a strong political force.

But those efforts have largely failed, as they have throughout California.

Fresno's Hispanic activists made a big push during the 1980 census to get as big a count as possible, predicting that the Hispanic proportion would turn out to be more than 40 percent and thus give the community a greater voice in political affairs. The Hispanic count in Fresno County turned out to be only 29.2 percent, however, and dreams of achieving political parity remained unrealized.

It was a shock to Carlos Rodriguez, who directed the Fresno County census.

"In 1970 it was 25 percent and that was when women from the Republican Ladies Club were doing the count and they were afraid to go into the barrios," Rodriguez said later. "This just doesn't get it."

Hopes arose anew with the 1990 census and it did produce a much-larger Latino count—well over a third in Fresno and most other valley counties. But it's still unclear whether the larger numbers will translate into real political power. The Mexican-American Legal Defense and Education Fund and other Latino rights groups pressed the Legislature and the courts to create legislative and congressional districts that would elect Hispanic candidates, but with very low levels of voter registration and wide distances between centers of Latino population in the valley, it's uncertain whether any political figures will emerge in the 1990s.

Hispanics are politically influential in small towns, such as Parlier, with clear Hispanic population majorities. But in the macro sense, they have failed to make a political dent and the valley remains politically dominated by agribusiness—a fact underscored by the obsequious attitude toward the industry displayed by state and federal legislators of both parties.

The region's most volatile and racially charged politics are found in Stockton, whose rigid racial patterns inspired a landmark school segregation trial in the 1970s.

Power blocs, many of them with ethnic cores, struggle endlessly for power in the city. One former mayor packed a pistol to City Council meetings and at least two mayors have been driven from office for malfeasance. Trials for official corruption are commonplace and the latest mayor took office on a pledge to clean out city hall and restore some luster to the city's image.

Stockton is, however, the only valley city in which blacks and Hispanics have achieved some degree of political influence.

With urbanization, or at least suburbanization, have come city-style problems such as drugs, gangs, crowded highways and smog.

"If you moved here from Los Angeles to escape the crime and drugs and for your kids to get away from all that, you made a mistake because it's all here now," Scott Irvine, a Modesto family psychiatric therapist, told The Sacramento Bee in 1990.

Government has had a difficult time catching up with the valley's rapidly changing social and economic trends. Most county governments are still dominated by farm-oriented supervisors and they jealously guard their power while newcomers fume over quality-of-life issues.

One positive step was taken in 1991 when a regional air quality district was formed, one that many believe will evolve into a form of regional government with broader powers. The valley's worsening smog situation, caused by increasing levels of auto traffic and the topography of the region, an elongated bowl surrounded by mountains that trap pollutants, provided the political impetus to overcome local rivalries. What Gov. Pete Wilson said when he signed the enabling legislation might well apply to other major issues facing the valley:

"Due to the physical layout of the valley, an air pollution problem in one county means an air quality problem in another. Since air quality problems affect the valley as a whole, it is only fair that they address them as a whole."

Mountains-Hills:
A new Gold Rush

HISTORICAL PURISTS MAY INSIST THAT THE HISTORY OF CALIFORNIA BEGAN WITH the Spanish explorers and missionaries who colonized the southern coast and began building missions. But California's preeminent economic and social position today stems directly from a sawmill worker's discovery on a January day in 1848.

He found gold in the gravel of the American River and within two years nearly 100,000 gold-crazed prospectors had made the arduous journey to California to seek their fortunes, thus putting an American stamp on what had just become a part of the United States after the Mexican War.

Gold no longer is a major factor in California's economy, although there are efforts underway to revive the industry. But the quaint, frozen-in-time towns of California's Mother Lode are experiencing a new land rush, born of the desire of urban Californians to get away from it all.

"It is clear," a 1981 report by the state Office of Planning and Research declared, "that the foothills have been rediscovered and this time the treasure is the land itself."

What happened to the region in the remainder of the decade bore out the observation. California's 11 central mountain and foothill counties experienced a population boom, growing more than twice as fast as the state as a whole, although the region still contains only a tiny fraction of the state's people and the growth was largely confined to the foothill portion. The more mountainous counties saw only modest population gains in the 1980s—which suited their residents just fine—and are expected to remain largely undeveloped until well into the 21st century.

In the western edges of the region nearest fast-growing Sacramento—Placer, El Dorado and Nevada counties—the boom is simply an extension of the suburbs, replete with block-after-block subdivisions and industrial development. County population gains of 50 percent or more were common in the 1980s and the state Department of Finance expects the trend to continue.

In the middle kingdom of the region, the foothills, it is a mixture of escapism and an economy that has evolved away from basic resources, such as timber and mining, and toward tourism and recreation.

And everywhere in the region, which encompasses more than 15 percent of California's land, there is concern that the very qualities that made the hills and mountains so attractive may be adversely affected by their popularity.

That concern is underscored by what already has happened to the region's most spectacular natural attractions—the visually and environmentally polluting overdevelopment of Lake Tahoe, the overcrowding of Yosemite Valley that sometimes makes it resemble more a parking lot in Sherman Oaks than an alpine retreat and the diversion of water to cities that left Mono Lake a shriveled remnant of its former self.

"Today," that 1981 state report said, "the sound of bulldozers and hammers echoes through the hills, to the delight of some and the dismay of others. Just about everyone is wondering how to accommodate the burgeoning population without abusing the land, infringing on constitutional freedoms, bankrupting local governments and destroying the qualities that brought people to the hills in the first place."

A decade later, they were still wondering and debates about growth and its effects had become a staple of foothill and mountain politics.

The boom touched off by the 1848 gold discovery didn't last very long and after experiencing that first wave of migration, California's upper reaches slid into a century-long slumber.

Most of the little mining towns nestled into the hollows, with colorful names such as Angel's Camp, Volcano, Fiddletown and Columbia, didn't become ghosts. They remained alive on the remnants of the mining industry, on employment in sawmills and on serving local ranchers. But their relative isolation from the remainder of the state insulated them from California's socioeconomic revolution that began in the 1930s and continued during World War II and the postwar era.

The population changed in tiny increments. The same families populated the same towns year after year, the offspring occasionally leaving to go to school or pursue careers unavailable in the hills, but nothing much changing. By 1960, the 11 counties had acquired only 165,500 residents, just over 1 percent of California's people, and a third of that was in the most populous county, Placer, whose population center, Roseville, was more a Central Valley railroad town than a true part of the hills.

One high mountain county, Alpine, could count only 400 souls in 1960, so tiny that in the early 1970s homosexual activists seriously contemplated an en masse migration that would allow them to take over local government. It didn't happen but it stirred up the county for months.

Most of the nearly 16 million acres of land in the region were empty, tied up in national parks, national forests and federally owned rangelands. But during the 1960s, the region began to experience the first stirrings of the second land rush to come. Better highways opened access and urban unrest encouraged Californians to look for unspoiled places.

Nevada County started seeing the first of what became a flood of urban refugees that created a combined artists' colony and high-tech oasis that is the envy of other foothill communities.

Charles Litton, founder of Litton Industries, became incensed at San Mateo County's business tax policies and moved his operations out of what would later become Silicon Valley to the outskirts of Grass Valley, laying the groundwork for a high-tech boomlet. Today, the Grass Valley Group, a maker of sophisticated video equipment, is the area's largest employer.

Poets and artists built subsistence homesteads at San Juan Ridge and created a colony that would eventually draw then-Gov. Jerry Brown into the community.

Today, Grass Valley and Nevada City are connected by a freeway, the population of the county has nearly quadrupled since 1960 and plans are being laid for big city-style shopping centers—even as the two Gold Rush towns continue a feud over image and power that has been underway for more than a century already.

"These foothill gold towns are only four miles apart on the map but that's just geography," journalist Don Stanley, a one-time Nevada County resident, wrote in The Sacramento Bee in 1987. "In character, in style and in resonance, they are distant beyond measure. Distant because so different. Always have been. Always will be."

Grass Valley is more commercial and modern. Nevada City, the county seat, is quainter and more arty.

As Stanley put it: "Put bluntly, Grass Valley thinks Nevada City is a plague of effete fools and idealistic eggheads. Nevada City thinks Grass Valley is redneck land, a place where destruction derbies are the entertainment of choice."

During the rowdier 19th century, partisans of the two towns would use guns, fists and knives to conduct their feud. Now it's done with words and politics. But however it's conducted, the Grass Valley-Nevada City feud is what one expects to find in a region with so much color in its history. It's the kind of authentic character that made the foothills so appealing to visitors from California's often interchangeably faceless urban areas—and why so many decided to remain.

Jack Lessinger, a retired University of Washington urban planning professor who has studied the phenomenon of urban migration to rural areas, called these new boom towns "penturbia," which translates into "fifth urban migration."

"During the first half of the 20th century, Americans migrated to the suburbs to preside like little kings and queens over one-sixth acre domains," Lessinger told The Los Angeles Times in 1987 as it surveyed the explosion in California's foothills. "Now the little kings and their mass consumption ethic are being supplanted by people I call 'caring conservers,' whose will to conserve extends to energy, investments, clean air and cultural artifacts."

These new refugees are put off by the complications and dangers of urban life, they cash in the equity in their homes and head for locales that have slower paces, cleaner air and cheaper real estate prices. They are not seeking primitive ways of life; they want shopping and cultural amenities. But they want them in friendlier surroundings.

The evolution of the California economy has contributed to the phenomenon. Computers and other tools allow professionals—architects, engineers, writers, computer programmers—to do their work in relatively remote locations and still remain in touch with urban-based employers and contractors. One foothill community in El Dorado County includes airplane hangars in its homes to facilitate airborne commuting to Sacramento and San Francisco—a situation that has made it especially attractive to airline pilots who fly out of San Francisco International.

"It's a quality of life attraction," said Tom Parilo, an assistant Nevada County planner, in a phrase heard often throughout the region. "I've seen people come up and drop out and change their lifestyles."

For all of those reasons, the huge levels of population growth in the foothill counties of California have not been tied to any burst of employment, although some communities such as Grass Valley-Nevada City and Roseville have seen an influx of high-tech jobs. And as California's employment and housing continues to march eastward away from the Bay Area, the foothills become even more attractive to commuters.

Roseville, born as a railroad town to serve Southern Pacific and its employees, has created a mini-Silicon Valley on its northern edge —just in time to compensate for huge cutbacks in railroad operations.

Hundreds already are working in high-tech factories along Highway 65, tens of thousands have been predicted, homes are being planned and despite a mid-1980s slump in the computer industry, the future of the area seems bright. A short freeway was authorized specifically to connect the high-tech industrial area with Interstate 80.

Roseville, moreover, has seen a spurt of suburban-style development — housing, subdivisions, shopping centers, restaurants, etc.—connected with Sacramento's outward bulge.

Nevada County and Roseville are exceptional in their ability to lure manufacturing industry; industrial payrolls have been hard to find for other

Focus on the Mountains-Hills

Area .... 24,580.3 sq. miles
Percentage of California 15.5%

Population
(with percentage of California total)

	1960	1970	1980	1990	2000	2005
Alpine Co.	400	500	1,100	1,100	1,100	1,300
Amador Co.	10,000	11,900	19,500	30,600	39,500	44,000
Calaveras Co.	10,400	13,700	21,000	32,500	45,600	51,800
El Dorado Co.	29,900	44,100	86,700	129,200	174,300	197,400
Inyo Co.	11,700	15,600	17,900	18,400	19,500	19,900
Mariposa Co.	5,100	6,100	11,200	14,500	18,500	20,800
Mono Co.	2,500	4,100	8,700	10,200	13,400	14,490
Nevada Co.	21,200	26,500	52,700	79,600	110,400	125,000
Placer Co.	57,500	78,000	118,400	175,600	238,700	267,400
Sierra Co.	2,200	2,400	3,100	3,400	3,700	3,900
Tuolumne Co.	14,500	22,300	34,300	49,000	64,300	71,600
TOTAL	165,400	225,200	374,600	573,100	729,000	817,590
CALIFORNIA	1.04%	1.1%	1.6%	1.9%	2.0%	2.1%

Ethnic composition
(1990 Census)

	Anglo	Latino	Asian/Pacific	Black
Alpine Co.	69.4%	6.6%	.4%	.4%
Amador Co.	83.7%	8.4%	.7%	5.6%
Calaveras Co.	91.5%	5.4%	.6%	.6%
El Dorado Co.	89.7%	7.0%	1.8%	.5%
Inyo Co.	81.1%	8.4%	.9%	.4%
Mariposa Co.	89.3%	4.9%	.8%	.8%
Mono Co.	83.7%	11.3%	1.1%	.4%
Nevada Co.	93.9%	4.2%	.8%	.2%
Placer Co.	88.3%	8.0%	2.1%	.6%
Sierra Co.	92.2%	5.5%	.2%	.2%
Tuolumne Co.	86.4%	7.7%	.7%	3.2%
CALIFORNIA	57.2%	25.8%	9.1%	7.0%

Political data

	1964	1972	1980	1984	1988
Voter registration (Democrat-Republican)	60-38%	55-39%	50-38%	47-40%	46-44%
Presidential vote (Democrat-Republican)	61-39%	43-57%	32-59%	27-73%	41-59%

Sources: State Department of Finance, 1990 Census, employment Development Department, Board of Equalization, Center for Continuing Study of the California Economy and the Secretary of State's office.

Economic Data

	Unemployment rate (Aug. 1991)	Taxable sales (1990 per capita)	Personal income (per capita)	
			1984	1989
Alpine Co.	11.6%	$13,997	$9,570	$22,315
Amador Co.	5.4%	$6,413	$11,717	$13,909
Calaveras Co.	9.1%	$5,036	$9,855	$12,806
El Dorado Co.	5.1%	$7,160	$11,048	$17,225
Inyo Co.	6.5%	$10,590	$12,407	$16,658
Mariposa Co.	4.0%	$7,363	$11,329	$14,260
Mono Co.	7.9%	$13,107	$11,403	$17,879
Nevada Co.	6.5%	$7,349	$10,090	$16,266
Placer Co.	5.9%	$10,235	$12,471	$17,822
SierraCo.	5.5%	$4,116	$10,756	$16,099
Tuolumne Co.	7.2%	$9,400	$14,593	$19,229
CALIFORNIA	7.2%	$9,400	$14,593	$19,229

Graphic courtesy *The Sacramento Bee*

parts of the 11-county region and, if anything, they have decreased.

In 1985, for example, Bishop's largest employer, a mining operation, virtually shut down operations, throwing more than 600 employees out of work and forcing some to commute to jobs in Los Angeles, more than 200 miles away. Elsewhere, lumber mills and gravel pits have closed. There seems to be little chance that their jobs will be replaced with anything comparable. When the state expressed interest in establishing a job-heavy prison in the Bishop area, a local protest quickly stopped it. It would, critics said, changed the quiet ambiance of the area.

The growth industries have been recreation, tourism and services to supply the newcomers who escaped from the city, moved into the region, and simply stayed, finding economic sustenance wherever they could.

"We have so many people from Southern California," said Tom McMahon, Placer County's planning director. "They want clean air, closeness to the mountains and a relatively short commute to work. It's a lifestyle they've always dreamed of in Southern California. Housing also is much lower in cost."

Placer and adjacent El Dorado counties exhibit all of the geographic and socioeconomic traits of the region—from the suburban-style development along their western edges through Mother Lode quaintness in the foothill cities of Placerville and Auburn to high-mountain vistas around Lake Tahoe.

The northern end of the lake is in Placer County, the southern in El Dorado and both—along with their counterparts in Nevada—have wrestled for decades with the problems posed by the lake's popularity as a recreational site and its environmental fragility.

Lake Tahoe is a case study in how bad planning, or no planning, can befoul a priceless resource.

When the construction of straighter, all-year highways made Tahoe more easily accessible after World War II, developers rushed in to take advantage. The cabins and lodges that the wealthy had maintained at the lake gave way to densely packed condominiums to accommodate the masses and small hotels and inns were replaced by garishly lighted high-rise hotels on the Nevada side, luring Californians with their floor shows and legalized gambling. The boom in skiing's popularity attracted millions of development dollars.

The jewel of the Sierra, whose cold blue waters had inspired generations of poets, suffered from sediment runoff and haphazard sewage disposal.

Environmentalists protested but politicians on both sides of the state line demonstrated a steadfast inability to resist the blandishments of development interests. The deteriorating condition of Lake Tahoe and its surrounding basin became a national scandal and challenged the contention that recreation is a "clean industry."

Finally, in effect, it hit bottom and the tide of public opinion turned against the developers. A two-state commission was formed in an effort to deal with the problems of Tahoe, but its Nevada contingent was still under the spell of casino-builders.

A California-only state commission was markedly stronger and environmentalists and their allies in state and local government were able to impose a building moratorium in the Tahoe basin, one upheld by a federal court of appeal in 1985. But, as with all development restrictions, the Tahoe moratorium had its downside—driving up the market for already-built homes and thereby pushing them out of reach for all except the most affluent who could profitably use the tax breaks accorded to second-home owners.

The moratorium also worked a financial hardship on those who had in good faith purchased building lots near the lake and suddenly found them to be nearly worthless.

California floated a bond issue to buy up the unbuildable lots and with environmentalists in the political driver's seat because of their victories in court, serious efforts are underway now to write master plans for the basin that will protect water quality while allowing a lower level of development. The courts have indicated that the moratorium will be lifted once environmentally protective plans are adopted by the bi-state commission.

It's too late for Tahoe to receive the same protected status as the nation's other scenic wonders, such as Yellowstone, Crater Lake and Yosemite, but optimists believe that the continued degradation of the lake's water quality can be stopped and perhaps even reversed.

Yosemite, the region's other great tourist attraction, is, however, proof that even national park status is not an iron-clad protection against environmental degradation. The park, as big as Rhode Island, has been California's premier recreational attraction for nearly a century.

It's that popularity—more than 3.5 million visitors each year—that poses the long-term threat to the park. As the visitor usage grew with the construction of better access highways, the Park Service and its concessionaire, a private subsidiary of the huge MCA entertainment conglomerate, built more and more facilities—parking lots, campgrounds, stores, etc.— to take care of the hordes.

The serenity that first attracted visitors was shattered by the sound of auto engines, the visual pollution of candy wrappers and smog. It was the city brought to the country.

Finally, in the 1970s, the Park Service awakened to what was happening to the Yosemite Valley and acted to do something about it. A new management plan, adopted in 1980, called for the deurbanization of Yosemite by the removal of manmade facilities to sites outside the valley and a sharp reduction in auto traffic.

There ensued a years-long battle over the plan's implementation, one that intimately involved the private concession firm, Yosemite Park and Curry Co. But in the late 1980s, the firm's political position began to erode (MCA's chairman, Lew Wasserman, had been a confidante of presidents). It was revealed that the company was making profits far beyond those estimated while paying the Park Service a tiny fraction of its income. And then MCA itself was sold to Japanese investors, raising the specter of foreign control of one of America's natural wonders. Quickly, the Japanese-based Matsushita Electric Industrial Co. agreed to sell Yosemite Park and Curry Co. to a non-profit national park foundation for $49.5 million, considerably less than one year's corporate income off the park and less than half of what MCA had previously said it was worth.

The expectation of Yosemite activists is that the new operator will be more inclined to support deurbanization of the park although its precise future remains unclear because California's incredible population growth is putting additional demand pressure on all recreational facilities. Yosemite's superintendent, Michael Finley, opened a 1991 conference on its future by listing "the most serious long-term threats to the very fabric of this park," which included Los Angeles-strength smog, acid rain, ozone damage and the physical impacts of millions of visitors.

"Driving to Yosemite is not a beautiful trip through the California countryside," author Alfred Runte told the conference. "It's a parade of billboards, freeways and truck stops."

Yosemite remains a question mark —a living laboratory to test the conflict between the environment and man's desire to be part of it, between solitude for the hardy few and recreation for the masses.

"Yosemite has most of the problems that face the parks only more so," said Ron Tipton, a specialist in parks for the Wilderness Society. "The parks have become isolated islands in a sea of civilization."

The flood of visitors that washed over Yosemite in the 1970s and 1980s, sparking concerns about its survival, was also experienced throughout the Sierra foothills.

Traffic along aptly named Highway 49, which connects the old mining towns, picked up as tourists abandoned the cities on weekends to find clean air, antiques and food and as many settled in permanently, sparking no little social and political conflict between the inbred hill-dwellers and those they called "flatlanders."

Often, the long time residents were the ones trying to cash in on the land boom while the newcomers were among the most adamant about controlling growth to protect their newly found rural lifestyles.

The population of the 11 counties jumped from 165,400 in 1960 to 225,200 in 1970 and then to 374,600 in 1980. By 1990, it had climbed past a half-million and it's expected to top 800,000 by 2005, the state Department of Finance projects.

Overall, the region is expected to experience a nearly 400 percent increase from 1960 to 2005 with only one county, Inyo, seeing less than a 100 percent gain.

The percentages are impressive, but they still will leave the region a tiny part of California, increasing from just over 1 percent in 1960 to just over 2 percent in 2005. That's about enough to support one of the 40 seats in the state Senate, which makes the area relatively insignificant from a political standpoint.

That insignificance, along with the region's massive resources of water, minerals, timber and scenery, have made it fair game for outside tinkering.

Examples are abundant throughout the region but the classic is what happened to Owens Valley on the eastern slope of the Sierra.

Early 20th century land barons in Los Angeles knew they could create vast fortunes if they could bring in water from the outside. The arid Los Angeles basin and the San Fernando Valley didn't have enough water locally to support more than a semi-rural agricultural economy.

There evolved, therefore, a secret conspiracy within the power elite of Los Angeles to acquire water rights in the pastoral Owens Valley on the Sierra's eastern slope and ship the water southward through an aqueduct across the Mojave Desert and into Los Angeles.

Secret agents were dispatched to tie up water rights and Los Angeles voters were persuaded to approve the necessary bonds. It laid the foundation for vast personal fortunes in Los Angeles as the San Fernando Valley and other areas were opened to development.

It made Los Angeles what it is today, for better or worse. But it also made the Owens Valley a virtual economic colony of the huge city to the south and left a bitter residue of suspicion among all Northern Californians about the rapacious intentions of the south that continues to manifest itself.

Mono Lake, another of the region's scenic wonders, became the focal point of controversy because the diversion of water to Los Angeles allowed it to shrink, thus eliminating valuable wildlife habitat as well as threatening its visual impact.

"Save Mono Lake" stickers were attached to thousands of California bumpers, signaling a political and legal war between environmentalists and Los Angeles that raged for years.

"We are trying to keep the lake filled with water," Ernie Peigne, a resident of the nearby town of Lee Vining, said as the battle raged in the mid-1980s. "If we don't, we're going to lose our town."

Mono Lake, with its eerie limestone formations, seems more suited to another planet than California. Its shrinkage was halted briefly by inordinately heavy runoff in the early 1980s, but the long-term prospects for its survival were not good unless more water was allowed to drain into its basin, created by a prehistoric volcanic upheaval.

Finally, in the late 1980s, a series of court decisions and a decided turn in public opinion compelled Los Angeles' watermasters to give ground and additional water began flowing into the lake—although the battle was not yet concluded.

Tahoe, Yosemite and Mono are symbols of the ongoing struggle between environmentalists and development interests over the future of California's foothills and mountains and also are symbols of how the region itself has spent more time fighting local battles than in shaping some vision for itself.

There is precious little regional planning or other political activity. The formation of the region's oddly shaped counties in the 19th century was a testament to its insular attitudes. One association conducts economic studies and other planning activities for four counties but the leaders of most are content to handle their own affairs and complain about what is happening in Sacramento and Washington.

To the mostly conservative politicians of the area, regionalism is a dirty word, one that implies some loss of local control over land use and other matters. But the counties experiencing the highest levels of suburban development are participating in regional planning in the Sacramento area.

The overall prospect for the area is more of the same: high levels of population growth and some job development in the lower elevations and little change in the higher-altitude counties such as Alpine, Sierra, Mono and Inyo.

Politically—although the small numbers don't count for much—the region is conservative and votes mostly Republican at the top of the ticket. A sign along Highway 395 in Mono County announces that the local chapter of the John Birch Society has assumed responsibility for keeping a two-mile stretch free of litter.

The only major political figure to emerge from the region, however, is a Democrat: state Insurance Commissioner John Garamendi, a one-time state assemblyman and senator who may run for governor some day. But most California politicians use the region not as a resource of votes but as a background for television commercials promoting their supposed concern for rural and natural values.

Northern California:
The empty corner

CAROLYN LEVAN, WHO MANAGES THE STATE EMPLOYMENT OFFICE IN ALTURAS, occasionally receives inquiries from persons thinking of moving to California's remote northeastern corner.

For many years, she sent them a form letter that quickly discouraged any but the most determined.

"Because of the weather and our relative isolation," LeVan told the inquirers in her letter, "Modoc County has had virtually no growth. One of the results of this lack of growth is the lowest wages in the state. In addition, there are no unions so that the minimum wage is the standard rather than the exception."

The letter continued for some length, expounding on the difficulties a job-seeker would encounter. "There is no manufacturing in the area and the majority of the stores are family owned and operated," she said. "There are no large chain stores or restaurants."

"I do not mean to paint a negative picture," LeVan concluded, "just a realistic one."

LeVan stopped sending the letter after a few years; for one thing, she stopped receiving more than a few inquiries each year because the word had gotten around. "We're not getting as many questions," she said in a 1991 interview. "But we're still a depressed area."

In a sense, LeVan's advice about Modoc County also could be applied to the other 11 counties that make up the vast and mostly empty expanses of

163

California north of Sacramento. "Empty," perhaps, is too bleak a word. The hand of man can be seen almost everywhere, even in the startlingly beautiful wilderness mountains of Trinity and Siskiyou counties. But one has to look for the people, scattered in dozens of small towns.

The 12 counties, with their 33,401 square miles of mountains and valleys, contain more than a fifth of California's land and are the source of much of the state's water and other vital resources. Yet, they contain only 2.2 percent of California's population—a fact that is driven home to local residents when it comes to a political showdown on the disposition of those resources.

No other major region of the state has changed so little in the last quarter-century. A traveler who would have wound his way along Highway 99 north of Sacramento in 1960 and repeated his journey a generation later would have found the same farm houses amid the same orchards.

Chico, one of two relatively major cities in the area, is somewhat bigger, thanks to growth in the region's only state university campus. And Chico has undergone something of political revolution and counterrevolution, thanks again to the presence of the college.

Redding, the other substantial city, acquired a veneer of 1980s-style commercial development because it is a natural stopping point for traffic along Interstate 5, the freeway that succeeded Highway 99 as the major north-south transportation link in the 1970s, 150 miles north of Sacramento. And it has experienced a population surge, thanks to an influx of urban refugees who traded the equity in their homes for serenity in the country. Redding's civic leaders have encouraged development; at one point, they produced an elaborate videotape and hired a well-connected lobbyist to seek establishment of a University of California campus.

But some in the area believe that the routing of I-5—perhaps the most important socioeconomic factor of the postwar era—was as much burden as blessing.

Prior to the advent of the interstate system, there were two Highway 99s north of Sacramento—99W that flowed through empty grain fields and cattle ranchlands and 99E that hit the Marysville-Yuba City area and Chico. The two highways then rejoined at Red Bluff.

Interstate 5 was placed along the 99W alignment, effectively bypassing Marysville-Yuba City and Chico. The latter continued to prosper because of Chico State University but the former withered on the economic vine as the highway traffic moved many miles to the west.

"Yuba County is always kind of passed up," county planning director Larry Brooks said in 1985.

When Rand McNally rated the Yuba City-Marysville area as one of the worst places to live in the nation, it angered local boosters, who quickly responded in kind. But it also pointed up why the lack of major highway access is a negative economic factor when it comes to competing for job-producing industry.

In the 1980s, Yuba County had the state's lowest median income and its highest rate of welfare dependency. By 1991, more than 11 percent of the county's 58,700 residents were welfare recipients and a whopping 10 percent of the labor force was unemployed.

Competition between Yuba City and Marysville, located on either side of the Feather River in different counties, contributed to the area's inability to attract new industry, and a chronic softness in the farm economy has hurt everywhere in the 12-county region.

More recently, however, a bi-county economic development operation has been established in hopes of getting the overflow from the burgeoning high-tech area northeast of Sacramento. And as the decade ended, so did years of local acrimony about the freeway route and that signaled what appears will be a burst of development in the 1990s, especially in the areas of Sutter County that are only minutes from downtown Sacramento.

Developers have ambitious schemes to convert thousands of acres of rolling Sutter County farmland into "new cities" that would be satellites of fast-growing Sacramento. A 1989 study commissioned by the Sutter County Board of Supervisors concluded that the southern part of the county could achieve a population of a quarter-million persons—and that's a prospect that generates intense anger among some rural residents.

One, 40-year resident Harriett Fritts, arose at a community meeting where the study was unveiled to accuse developers of wanting to re-create the sprawl of the San Jose area in Sutter County.

"You have fouled the nest over there," she said. "Now, you want to come here, foul it and move on."

Despite those kinds of sentiments, anti-growthers still appear to be a minority and pro-development policies got an implicit green light from voters in 1991 when they rejected an anti-development ballot measure.

Population experts in the state Department of Finance tend to agree that Sutter and Yuba counties will grow rapidly once the freeway access issue has been settled. They see the populations of Yuba and Sutter counties, which had been growing only graduallly since 1960, jumping sharply by 2005 to more than double their 1960 levels.

The fastest-growing spots in the area now, however, are Butte County, fueled by Chico's expansion and recreational-retiree development near Oroville Dam, whose construction was the other major economic development for the region, and Shasta County, whose biggest city, Redding, is the regional hub at the northern end of California's Central Valley, a center for shopping, medical care and other services.

Butte County's population, 83,200 in 1960, jumped to 144,900 by 1980 and 182,120 by 1990 and is expected to add another 65,000 by 2005. That's an overall increase of more than 200 percent in the 45-year period.

Shasta County, with Redding's highway-oriented development and continued recreational expansion of Lake Shasta, the state's largest man-made lake

Focus on Northern California

Area ....33,401.7 sq. miles
Percentage of California...21%

Population
(with percentage of California total)

	1960	1970	1980	1990	2000	2005
Butte Co.	82,200	102,500	144,900	183,900	226,700	249,000
Colusa Co.	12,200	12,400	12,900	16,400	19,600	20,700
Glenn Co.	17,400	17,500	21,500	25,000	28,800	30,400
Lassen Co.	13,600	16,900	21,900	27,800	33,400	36,000
Modoc Co.	8,300	7,500	8,700	9,700	10,700	11,100
Plumas Co.	11,600	11,700	17,400	19,900	22,300	23,400
Shasta Co.	60,400	78,000	116,800	148,800	186,500	202,400
Siskiyou Co.	33,000	33,200	40,000	43,800	48,400	50,300
Sutter Co.	33,700	42,100	52,600	65,100	78,400	84,100
Tehama Co.	25,500	29,600	39,100	50,100	61,700	67,000
Trinity Co.	9,600	7,600	12,000	13,100	13,800	14,300
Yuba Co.	35,100	44,400	49,800	58,700	69,100	73,500
TOTAL	342,600	403,400	547,600	662,300	799,400	862,200
CALIFORNIA	2.2%	2.0%	2.3%	2.2%	2.2%	2.2%

Ethnic composition
(1990 Census)

	Anglo	Latino	Asian/Pacific	Black
Butte Co.	86.9%	7.5%	2.7%	1.2%
Colusa Co.	62.1%	33.3%	2.0%	.5%
Glenn Co.	74.4%	20.0%	3.1%	.5%
Lassen Co.	79.4%	10.4%	1.1%	6.2%
Modic	87.6%	7.2%	.4%	.8%
Plumas Co.	91.2%	4.6%	.6%	.8%
Shasta Co.	91.1%	3.8%	1.8%	.7%
Siskiyou Co.	87.9%	5.9%	.8%	1.6%
Sutter Co.	71.6%	16.4%	8.9%	1.5%
Tehama Co.	86.7%	10.3%	.7%	.5%
Trinity Co.	91.0%	3.3%	.8%	.4%
Yuba Co.	73.7%	11.6%	7.9%	4.0%
CALIFORNIA	57.2%	25.8%	9.1%	7.0%

Political data

	1964	1972	1980	1984	1988
Voter registration (Democrat-Republican)	62-38%	57-38%	52-37%	49-39%	47-42%
Presidential vote (Democrat-Republican)	59-41%	41-59%	32-59%	36-64%	41-59%

Sources: State Department of Finance, 1990 Census, employment Development Department, Board of Equalization, Center for Continuing Study of the California Economy and the Secretary of State's office.

Economic Data

	Unemployment rate (Aug. 1991)	Taxable sales (1990 per capita)	Personal income (per capita)	
			1984	**1989**
Butte Co.	8.1%	$7,576	$11,084	$14,083
Colusa Co.	7.9%	$10,697	$15,416	$17,154
Glenn Co.	15.9%	$6,881	$12,389	$15,267
Lassen Co.	6.6%	$5,637	$9,996	$12,305
Modoc Co.	9.1%	$5,966	$11,310	$13,658
Plumas Co.	6.2%	$6,686	$10,068	$15,182
Shasta Co.	8.9%	$9,554	$10,859	$14,980
Siskiyou Co.	9.5%	$6,347	$10,543	$14,332
Sutter Co.	10.6%	$8,547	$12,216	$14,759
Tehama Co.	11.0%	$6,296	$10,155	$11,854
Trinity Co.	9.4%	$4,054	$8,491	$13,552
Yuba Co.	10.0%	$5,445	$10,463	$11,588
CALIFORNIA	7.2%	$9,400	$14,5931	$19,229

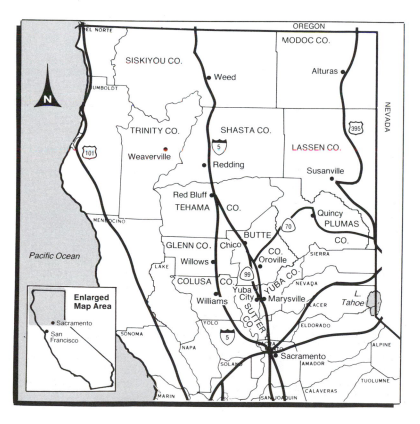

Graphic courtesy *The Sacramento Bee*

and the key to the entire Central Valley Project, matched Butte's growth rate in the 1980s.

Shasta County's population, 60,400 in 1960, hit 116,800 in the 1980 census, 147,036 by 1990 and is expected to top 200,000 by 2005.

The more rural parts of the area, cut off by weather, topography and poor transportation, are changing much more slowly, even though the region as a whole will have more than doubled its population between 1960 and 2005.

Towns such as Weaverville, Yreka, Susanville and Alturas have changed but little and show no signs of cashing in on the vast economic changes that are happening in the rest of California—or of experiencing the negative side effects of growth. Their economic and population stability mean relatively low levels of both unemployment and welfare dependency. Trinity County has achieved a certain fame—or infamy—for its frontier attitudes. Gold panners and marijuana growers—the two vocations are often combined in one person—pack guns and the quietude of the county's rugged mountains and narrow river gorges is occasionally shattered by gunfire as two of its residents settle their grudges the old-fashioned way.

Except for some expansion at the state's long-established prison in Susanville, the region has even resisted the state's intensive drive to build new penal facilities in rural, economically depressed communities. Prisons have been specifically rejected in some local communities.

Between bites of barbecued beef at a mid-summer picnic in the city park in 1985, Andy Anderson, a logger and Modoc County supervisor, talked about the slowness of change in the state's most remote corner.

"People come up from Los Angeles and they want to pioneer it," said Anderson. "But they want everything they ran away from and we don't have it."

One thing they don't have in Modoc County are a lot of jobs, as LeVan's letter to jobseekers points out.

They don't even have enough jobs to keep the young from moving out of the area.

"If a kid wants to better himself, it just isn't there," Anderson said, noting that the backbones of the local economy, lumber and cattle-ranching, had fallen on hard and perhaps unrecoverable times in recent years.

Anderson's own children left the area to pursue their careers and that syndrome explains why the median ages of those living in the most rural counties tend to be several years above those of the state as a whole.

Modoc County lost population during the 1970s—which was true of many lumber counties in Northern California—and only late in the decade did it recover to its 1960 level. The 1980s saw a modest spurt of population, but at a rate less than half the statewide average.

Anderson's logging business and other segments of the lumber industry throughout Northern California have been buffeted by a deep-seated, long-term recession that stems not from a lack of demand but from unbeatable competition from Canada, exacerbated by a strong dollar, by indirect subsidies from Canadian provincial governments and by perhaps the nation's strongest and most expensive environmental controls on lumber operations.

The demise of the lumber industry in this region is not as dramatic as that on the North Coast, but it's been a serious blow to a narrowly based economy nonetheless—and one made even worse because agriculture has been in a financial bind as well.

A 1989 economic survey by Chico State University's Irving Schiffman confirmed that outside of Chico and Redding, "the region—in general—is not doing very well economically" because of stagnant local industries.

"Rural areas tend to be very stagnant," said Mark Morelock, a Chico State economist who has examined the economy of the state's northern reaches, "with very low turnover of the labor force."

Even in relatively prosperous Chico, Morelock sees a trend—not unlike that in the remainder of California—toward growth in low-paying service jobs and high-paying professional positions but stagnation in the mid-pay industrial economy such as lumber mills and food processing plants.

That's creating what many economists believe will become a two-tier economy in the state, and it's especially apparent in areas such as northeastern California, where there is very little new industry coming to replace that which changing times is taking out.

"There's a real, definite change away from industries that offer middling employment—not a great job but a good job," said Morelock.

The loss of those kind of jobs, the backbone of the middle class, leads communities into trying what Morelock called a "very destructive economic development game."

Communities are pitted against one another in trying to offer tax concessions, low-interest financing and other direct and indirect subsidies to attract payrolls and often, Morlock said, it becomes a "zero-sum game" in which one community's gain is another's loss.

A prime example may be the movement of Chico-San, a producer of ricecakes, from Chico to Gridley, another Butte County community.

Chico-San, a subsidiary of the Heinz food conglomerate, was planning to leave California altogether and relocate in either New Jersey or Mississippi but was persuaded to remain by a shift to Gridley, which meant it could modernize its operations with direct and indirect government subsidies and obtain lower power bills from Gridley's municipally owned electric system.

That meant 90 jobs in Gridley, a town of 4,000. But it meant a loss of those jobs to Chico—the sort of thing that may happen when payrolls are being shifted around to take advantage of the best deal rather than being drawn into the area.

"The furor over that was tremendous," said Morelock. "It's one example of areas in the same county battling with each other."

Chico and other regional centers are continuing to acquire population, but the growth consists of "more and more professionals and more low-wage service people," as Morelock puts it, while the middle-class workers shrink.

"We're losing that and it is not being replaced," he said.

Chico, with its college community, joined in the nationwide hunt for high-tech industries that promise high payrolls and low environmental impact.

"We have Silicon Valley fever, too," said Morelock. "It's the belief we will be attractive to the myth of clean industry and high-paying jobs. But I don't think it is realistic to think we can get industry in general."

The city's relative transportation isolation, well east of Interstate 5, is the prime drawback to such industrial development—a lesson also learned by those in the Yuba City-Marysville area.

"If I-5 ran through Chico, there would be a lot more economic activity going on in Butte County," Morelock said.

Butte County's relatively high population growth, unmatched by job growth, strained county government coffers in the 1980s and forced it to the brink of bankruptcy. Only a last-minute bailout from the state kept Butte out of bankruptcy courts. County officials said they were being overwhelmed by health and welfare costs, many of them generated by newcomers. County supervisors in nearby Tehama County had made similar threats earlier—garnering national publicity for themselves in the process—and those in Lassen County voted in 1991 to defy the state's service mandates which, they said, were eliminating such local services as sheriff's patrols.

Those actions reflected a widespread antipathy in the region toward the rest of California, which is seen as politically tyrannical and interested only in grabbing or exploiting rural resources. In 1991, a state legislator who represents much of the region, Republican Assemblyman Stan Statham, and a group of dissident county supervisors proposed—seriously, they said—to split off the 27 northernmost counties of the state into a new state of "Northern California."

Concern about economic development—or the lack of development—in northeastern California led to the creation of a regional service center on the Chico State campus with Glenn County Supervisor Jim Mann as its sparkplug. Its aim is to foster regional cooperation and explore strategies that will lure economic development to the region.

Cut off from the development that feeds off interstate highway routes throughout the state, other cities in northeastern California are looking to government for economic benefits.

Susanville, the commercial center of the mountain portion of the region, has become something of a government center as well, with payrolls from a state prison that is expanding, an Army depot and regional offices for federal land and forestry management agencies.

The Department of Corrections is the city's largest employer with nearly 700 jobs and that will approach 1,000 when the expansion is completed.

Even though the prison brings some economic stability to the area—one that some other small, rural towns are trying to emulate by offering themselves as prison sites—it is not universally beloved by local residents.

When Gov. George Deukmejian paid a flying visit to Susanville in 1985 and toured the prison, he was confronted by pickets at the airport opposing the prison. As in other rural areas, the opposition comes from ranchers who believe that expanding prison facilities will disrupt their bucolic way of life.

"People think it will put some more money in the cash registers, that's all they think about," one of the protesters snapped.

But Mayor Helen Leve saw the prison as a bulwark against the seasonal nature of the ranching and timber economy, which allows unemployment to rise above 20 percent during winter months.

"We're not in a position to attract industry," she said. "We have to look for jobs in the near future. We can't wait indefinitely. We were terribly hit by the last recession."

A quarter-century earlier, the economic and political profiles of northeastern California were quite similar to that of the state's North Coast—a timber and ranching economy, a stable population of blue-collar workers who were nominal Democrats but voted conservatively and often for Republicans.

If anything, in fact, the northeastern section probably was a little more faithful to the Democratic Party than the North Coast, if the partisan identity of state legislators and congressmen was a guide. Conservative Democrats tended to get elected and stay elected for many terms, politicians such as Randolph Collier, who served in the state Senate for 38 years, Assemblywoman Pauline Davis and Congressman Harold Johnson.

Socioeconomic change—a decline in the lumber industry and an influx of counterculture immigrants—changed the political profile of the North Coast during the 1970s from conservative/Republican to liberal/Democratic.

The northeastern part of the state went the other way. It attracted relatively few counterculture types—although there is a marijuana industry in some remote areas—and its population remained stable. One by one, the local Democratic officeholders were replaced by Republicans and by the mid-1980s, all six politicians who represented the area in the state Legislature and Congress were conservative Republicans.

The rightward shift in regional politics was hammered home in 1984 when Republican-turned-independent Ray Johnson—the man who defeated Randolph Collier in 1976—was himself defeated by an ultraconservative Republican, John Doolittle, for one of the area's Senate seats.

The reasons for the starboard tilt in local politics are not clear because there has not been the vast socioeconomic change that would foretell a political evolution. Perhaps it is simply that the area always has been conservative and the Democratic Party's overall image became too liberal.

Nevertheless, there are odd little liberal pockets scattered throughout the area, mostly in the population centers. Chico, with its large college community, established itself as a hotbed of Tom Hayden-style "economic democracy" with liberals capturing control of the City Council. Among the council's actions were declaration of Chico as a "nuclear-free zone" and imposition of heavy fees on developers to pay for new classrooms. But in 1985, the conservatives struck back with a campaign operated by an aide to Doolittle, the conservative state senator.

The aide, John Feliz, provided professional campaign help and financing for a slate of challengers aimed at ousting the Campaign for Economic Democracy (CED), Hayden's political arm, from power.

The challenge succeeded. The liberals were toppled, including Mayor Karl Ory.

"Literally, what they faced in Chico was a popular uprising," Feliz said afterwards. "The choices were very clear. It was conservatives vs. the CED. It was a dynamic change."

Among other things, the 1985 election indicated that Chico State students had moved to the right politically—a phenomenon observed in other college towns in the state. The conservatives claimed, in fact, that they carried the college vote in Chico in 1985.

Jane Dolan was Chico State's student body president in 1972 and six years later, at age 27, she stunned the local political establishment by winning a county supervisor's seat.

For a time, Dolan represented liberal hopes of making a comeback in the area. She became something of a regional power in Democratic Party politics and toyed with running for the Legislature.

In turned out, however, that Dolan was coming into office just as the tide was turning the other way and she was left somewhat isolated—especially since the liberal defeat in the City Council elections.

"When I was first elected, I couldn't finish a sentence because the other four were horrified I was there," Dolan recalled. "The board was very pro-development but I didn't want to live in San Jose and I saw it coming. We had a real bad time."

Her ambitions cooled by reality, Dolan became content to remain in her supervisor's seat, concentrating on local matters. The Board of Supervisors consisted of three Democrats and two Republicans and had moved to the left, or at least to the middle, since her election. But she knew that she would have a difficult time running for legislative office.

"I can't win as a liberal Democrat," she said. "The political landscape in the north state is up for grabs."

Dolan and other liberals believe that over the next generation, the essential struggle will be to maintain environmental values in the face of development pressure, although the continued high unemployment rates indicate to pro-development forces that the opposite danger is a more realistic threat.

"I don't mind growing but I don't want to have streets you can't ride your bike down anymore," she said. "It will be a struggle to keep what we have."

Chico may be one of the few places in the north state to concern itself with growth pressure. With the exception of Butte and Shasta counties, whose growth roughly matched that of the state as a whole in the 1980s, northeastern California counties saw only modest population gains in the 1980s. Thus, its percentage of the state's overall population shrank to scarcely 2 percent.

If the politics of northeastern California are conservative in the macro sense, they are often eccentric in the localized sense.

The only black sheriff in the history of California, for instance, serves in very rural and very conservative Siskiyou County on the the state's nothern edge.

Plumas County's residents have been entertained for years by a long-running political power struggle between two factions that that has included recall elections and allegations of ballot box stuffing.

Lassen County officials has threatened periodically to secede from California and become part of neighboring Nevada, complaining that their interests are ignored by urban California. Lassen County residents are connected directly to Reno by Highway 395 and look to that Nevada city for shopping and other services.

Tiny Sierra County, meanwhile, has been feuding for decades over which of two towns, Loyalton or Downieville, should be the seat of county government. Downieville has the title now but Loyalton's loyalists never stop trying to shift it. And two women county supervisors feuded so bitterly with their three male colleagues that it resulted in formal sex discrimination charges. Overlaying both disputes is the fact that part of the county is in the foothills and the remainder is in the mountains with the residents of each part openly disliking those of the other.

It's the sort of dispute that occurs when an area becomes ingrown, without the influx of new blood from economic development and population growth.

North Coast:
Going to pot

IN THE MID-1950s, AT THE APEX OF THE POSTWAR BUILDING BOOM, THERE WERE more than 300 lumber mills in Humboldt County.

The cool, foggy North Coast of California echoed to the sound of chain saws felling the giant redwoods and cedars. The roads were clogged with log-laden trucks. The sawmills hummed as the logs were sliced into lumber and peeled for plywood.

On Friday and Saturday nights, the loggers, often still wearing their calk boots, packed into the High Lead, the Golden Horn and the other bars and their occasional fistfights spilled into "Two Street," as the locals called it.

Superficially, little has changed on the North Coast. The population of the four-county area, less than 200,000 in 1960, has edged up to about a quarter-million, not even enough to support one state Assembly seat. Freeway has replaced much, but not all, of the two-lane roadway along Highway 101, the main north-south link to the outside world. The Eel River still runs high and dirty in the winter and dwindles to a trickle in the summer.

The Victorian homes that abound in Eureka and other North Coast communities are as impressive as ever. The redwoods—fewer than before—still soar to the heavens and still inspire bitter political and even physical conflict between those who want to cut them and those who want to preserve them.

But the superficial stability belies deep-seated socioeconomic change.

The North Coast is one of California's rust belts whose basic industries of a quarter-century ago, lumber and fishing, have declined to mere shadows and whose population, despite scant overall growth, has undergone an evolutionary change.

Industrial decline has driven untold thousands of blue-collar workers out of the area to find jobs in more vibrant economies. As an entire generation of would-be blue-collar workers left the North Coast, they were replaced by urban refugees. Even so, Humboldt and Del Norte counties lost population during the 1960s and gained only marginally in the 1970s and 1980s—a trend that is expected to continue until well into the 21st century.

Nobody knows how many "hippies," as they were called at the time, moved into the area in the late 1960s and early 1970s. Thousands, perhaps tens of thousands, came in the ubiquitous Volkswagen vans and converted buses. They established communes, settlements or just extended households in little pockets throughout the region, but especially in southern Humboldt County and northern Mendocino County.

Some tired of the realities of Aquarian living and went elsewhere. But a substantial number remained, grew older, produced families and became an integral element of the North Coast.

During the first years of the hippie migration, there were frequent clashes with the redneck natives of the area. A sort of slow-motion war—sometimes with guns—developed.

But the advent of the commercially successful—if illegal—pot-growing industry during the 1970s coincided with the decline of the lumber industry, giving the once-despised hippies economic clout that local merchants could not ignore.

One woman, the wife of a policeman, recalled that the southern Humboldt grocery store in which she clerked was dying until a new owner put in merchandise, such as drip irrigation systems, that catered to the marijuana "garden" trade.

"Marijuana saved my job," she said with a trace of irony in her voice.

In terms of local acceptance, marijuana underwent three distinct phases.

At first, there was unbridled hostility. During the early 1970s, the local sheriff tried to stamp out the trade and several pot growers were killed by police raiders. A federal drug agent was even prosecuted—but acquitted—for the killing of one man.

But as the economic impact of marijuana increased, so did its social and political acceptance. There was a period of live-and-let-live during the late 1970s and early 1980s.

In the mid-1980s, the situation changed again. The local marijuana growers were accepted but during the late summer harvest season, they became targets for out-of-area robbers. The growers armed themselves and the area developed a reputation for Wild West violence.

Even the counterculture types who were not directly involved in the pot trade, therefore, welcomed renewed efforts by state and local authorities to stamp out the business, efforts that took the form of highly publicized, military-style expeditions into pot country during the summer harvests.

Wes Chesbro was a pony-tailed political and environmental activist 15 years ago. Later, he became a short-haired Humboldt County supervisor, albeit one of the Tom Hayden mold. But he welcomed the anti-marijuana campaign.

The violence was "scaring away legitimate business," said Chesbro.

Garberville, the unofficial capital of the pot trade, also is trying to change its image.

"We're creating a different image around here," said shoe store owner Tony Beebe, one-time president of the Garberville Chamber of Commerce. "We're trying to get rid of the negativity of the past few years and tell people that it's safe to come back."

What Beebe, Chesbro and counter-culturists who have put down roots want is an area that is prosperous because of small, non-polluting businesses.

"People who have chosen to stay here have started businesses and many are growing very rapidly now," said Chesbro, who ultimately gave up his seat on the Board of Supervisors to pursue another political career in Sacramento as the member of a state board that oversees recycling.

The area abounds with shops catering to tourists, small manufacturing businesses and others not dependent on natural resources.

It's questionable, however, whether that approach to the local economy will provide the numbers of jobs needed to prevent a continued exodus of blue collar workers from the area.

The lumber industry has continued its long slide from its high -point in the mid-1950s.

The causes for that are many. Despite strong demand for construction lumber during the first half of the 1980s, the American lumber industry was losing much of its market share to foreign competitors, especially Canadian companies.

A strong dollar, which makes imports cheaper, was one reason for the situation. But another, according to industry spokesmen, is that the Canadian provincial governments have indirectly subsidized their mills by providing raw timber at nearly giveaway prices. Throughout the Northwest, the lumber industry has been on the skids. The industry also has undergone a series of corporate shakeouts and extensive automation, all of which slashed payrolls.

But in California, the situation is aggravated by another fact of political life: It is the only major lumber-producing state in which lumber is not a major industry.

The North Coast has been blanketed by a series of environmental protection programs that, despite whatever other benefit they produced, made timber production so costly that much of the industry simply shut its doors.

"Regulation is a problem in the West in general, but California is in a class by itself," said Gerald Griffin, an executive with Louisiana-Pacific, one of the few large firms to continue operations in the area. "There are so many special interest groups at work in the Legislature and courts trying to beat business to its knees and eliminate jobs."

During the last 20 years, the North Coast lumber industry has gone through the creation and then expansion of Redwood National Park and the imposition of new state forestry laws, clean water laws, wild rivers protections, coastal controls and federal wilderness designations. As the 1980s evolved into the 1990s, the conflicts continued and even intensified with statewide ballot measure battles and legislative fights over forest practices regulation.

Each program was intended to protect the environment. Each one, however, was imposed without regard to the others and without any overall consideration of impact on the jobs of those who live on the North Coast.

The net effect was to make lumbering more expensive in California than in other states, to dry up the supply of logs and ultimately to eliminate thousands of jobs in the woods and in mills.

Indeed, many of the logs that come out of the North Coast woods today are trucked past boarded-up mills to the docks, where they are loaded aboard ships bound for Europe and Japan. One company even announced plans to ship semi-milled timber to Mexico for final finishing.

"If you take the logger's perspective, you're struck by the fact that 1954 was the peak of employment in the lumber industry and it's been declining ever since," said Humboldt State University economist Ted Ruprecht, who has made extensive studies of the local economy.

Unemployment rates are high, welfare rolls are packed and, as Ruprecht said, "Poverty is one of our big export industries" because of the influx of federal and state relief money. There are, however, poorer areas in California, principally inland agricultural valleys. The lack of population growth has cushioned the economic stagnation the area. The four North Coast counties have welfare dependency rates that are among the highest in California—over 8 percent in Del Norte County, for instance, in mid-1991—and above-average unemployment rates that sometimes hit double digits.

There always will be a lumber industry on the North Coast, but it will consist, Ruprecht and other economists believe, of small, highly automated mills that use relatively few workers.

The shakeout in the industry "squeezed a lot of the fat out" and "what you've got left is a rather productive industry," Ruprecht said.

That is of small consolation to Walt Newman, the business agent for Local 2592 of the Lumber and Sawmills Workers Union.

Newman, chain-smoking as he sat in his office on the outskirts of Eureka in 1985, had seen his local membership decline by two-thirds in the previous 10 years alone as the big unionized companies either pulled out or undertook thinly disguised union-busting campaigns.

The union scale in local mills was nearly $10 per hour but "a lot of young guys right out of school are willing to take $6," Newman said. That's what the non-union independents were paying and that's what the big mills were offering non-union help during the frequent labor disputes.

Like others tied to the area's industrial past, Newman was pessimistic. "It's going to be strictly tourists and retirees," he said ruefully.

Newman's pessimism of the mid-1980s was born out by events during the remainder of the decade. Lumber employment continued to wither, despite a

Focus on the North Coast

Area .... 9,439.7 sq. miles
Percentage of California 5.9%

Population
(with percentage of California total)

	1960	1970	1980	1990	2000	2005
Del Norte Co.	17,800	14,600	18,300	24,500	31,200	32,500
Humboldt Co.	104,900	100,200	109,000	119,800	130,200	131,600
Lake Co.	13,900	19,800	36,900	51,100	62,600	67,400
Mendocino Co.	51,000	51,300	67,100	81,000	95,400	102,200
TOTAL	187,600	185,900	231,300	276,400	319,400	333,700
CALIFORNIA	1.2%	.9%	1.0%	.9%	.8%	.9%

Ethnic composition
(1990 Census)

	Anglo	Latino	Asian/Pacific	Black
Del Norte Co.	78.0%	10.3%	1.8%	3.6%
Humboldt Co.	87.9%	4.2%	1.9%	.8%
Lake Co.	88.1%	7.2%	.9%	1.8%
Mendocino Co.	84.4%	10.3%	1.1%	.6%
CALIFORNIA	57.2%	25.8%	9.1%	7.0%

Economic Data

	Unemployment rate	Taxable sales	Personal income	
	(Aug. 1991)	(1990 per capita)	(per capita)	
			1984	1989
Del Norte Co.	10.5%	$5,750	$10,346	$10,242
Humboldt Co.	7.5%	$7,689	$11,215	$15,303
Lake Co.	7.9%	$5,751	$10,973	$14,690
Mendocino Co.	8.3%	$7,910	$11,273	$15,134
CALIFORNIA	7.2%	$9,400	$14,593	$19,229

Political data

	1964	1972	1980	1984	1988
Voter registration (Democrat-Republican)	60-37%	58-35%	53-32%	55-32%	56-32%
Presidential vote (Democrat-Republican)	65-35%	25-75%	36-52%	46-54%	56-44%

Sources: State Department of Finance, 1990 Census, employment Development Department, Board of Equalization, Center for Continuing Study of the California Economy and the Secretary of State's office.

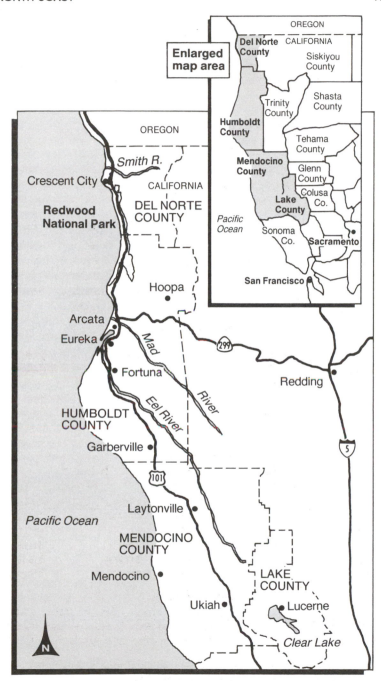

Graphic courtesy *The Sacramento Bee*

California home construction boom. The only bright spot, from the standpoint of some loggers, was a sharp increase in logging activity on some privately owner timberlands, especially those of the Pacific Lumber Co., the region's leading redwood products producer. But, at best, the logging outburst promised to be a short-lived phenomenon.

PL, as the firm is known in its company-owned town of Scotia, had been controlled by the Murphy family for generations but a corporate raider named Charles Hurwitz, using a junk bond financing scheme that involved jailed promoter Michael Milken and the later-bankrupt First Executive life insurance company, took over control in the late 1980s.

Immediately, the Hurwitz-controlled company accelerated logging of its old-growth redwood to retire the junk bond debt and that, in turn, sparked a years-long political controversy. Overnight, Pacific Lumber went from the darling of the environmentalists for its conservation-minded, sustained yield logging practices to the target of bitter denunciations from the Sierra Club and other organizations.

PL's logging, especially its plans to clear-cut a stand of virgin timber known as the Headwaters Forest, revived a dormant, but still bitter, political battle over private forestry practices and it was heightened even more by assertions that old-growth timber was the only home of the endangered spotted owl.

Earth First!, a radical environmental protection group, targeted the North Coast for confrontational demonstrations, which sparked counter-protests from loggers and lumber mill workers. Industry- and environmentalist-measures were placed on the 1990 California ballot and all were rejected. And the Legislature delved into the matter in 1991 as a series of bills imposing restrictions on logging was proposed.

As the controversy raged, a final—and bitterly ironic—revelation was made. Pacific Lumber's own retirees found their pensions endangered because they had been administered by the defunct First Executive company which had bought Hurwitz' junk bonds.

The outcome, and therefore net impact, of the logging practices controversy was still uncertain in mid-1991. Lumbermen were insisting that they would be driven out of the North Coast if proposed legislation was enacted and there was a possibility that another statewide ballot battle would be waged in 1992.

If nothing else, the controversy underscored the fact that while the North Coast contains less than 1 percent of California's population, its resources make it a continual focal point for the state's politics.

The area's colorful fishing industry, which never had a large impact on the economy, also has experienced a decline in recent years. Dozens of fishing boats are tied up in Humboldt Bay, having been seized by lenders for defaults on loans.

Marijuana, retail trade, government expansion (including growth at Humboldt State) and the infusion of government relief funds have eased the impact of lumber's decline somewhat.

Tourism, often touted by environmentalists as an alternative to lumber or other resource-based industry, has not taken up the slack.

Eureka and other North Coast communities are dotted with cute little bed-and-breakfast inns and even raunchy old "Two Street" has been redeveloped into a tourist-oriented "Old Town" with curio and antique shops in a pale emulation of Monterey or San Francisco's Fisherman's Wharf.

But tourism is even more seasonal than the lumber industry. Most of the North Coast is many hours' drive time from population centers and the summer weather along the North Coast tends toward the chilly, which discourages the high-spending, golf-playing kinds of tourism and convention business that support communities such as Palm Springs, Monterey and the Napa Valley. North Coast tourists tend to be middle-class people who stay in inexpensive motels or arrive in trailers or motorhomes, not high-rollers.

When the Sierra Club, the National Geographic Society and other major environmental groups promoted the creation of Redwood National Park in the mid-1960s, they tried to persuade local folks that it would promote a stable tourist industry to replace a cyclical lumber economy.

But if anyone envisioned something along the lines of a Yosemite or a Yellowstone, he was to be disappointed.

Although $1.4 billion was spent to acquire the park and provide minimal visitor facilities, much of it is inaccessible to all but the hardiest campers and backpackers. The timber companies, principally Arcata Redwood Co., took the money and departed, investing it in other businesses outside the area. But the people who used to work in their mills had their jobs eliminated and thousands were put on a special federal dole designed to ease the transition to other jobs that didn't materialize.

Later, when the park was proposed for expansion, the North Coast blossomed with bumper stickers saying "Don't Park My Job," pitting long-time locals against environmentalists for the umpteenth time.

Actually, the sales pitch about tourism was just a smokescreen worked on unsophisticated local residents by politicians and pro-park forces in Washington. The semi-secret master plan for the park, whose contents were discovered and reported by a local newspaper in the early 1970s, indicated that little or no tourist-related development was contemplated.

Officially, a half-million people visit the park annually, but that's only a seventh of the visitor load at Yosemite, for example, and even those figures are suspect.

"A half-million people coming through Humboldt County would be quite noticeable," said county Supervisor Anna Sparks, "especially on a two-lane road. We were promised over two million visitors by this time. I think it's more like 50,000—and we're thankful for that."

But even if the North Coast were experiencing a boom on tourism of the sort seen in Monterey or the Napa Valley, it would mean only low-paying service jobs.

The park's minimal or even negative economic impact on the area has made local leaders suspicious of adding more lands to the state or federal park systems. In 1985, county supervisors in Del Norte County voted 4-0 against a proposal to create another national park along the Smith River.

"Eighty percent of the county is already federal land and we can't afford any more," board chairman Glenn Smedley said.

If anything, Del Norte has been hit harder than Humboldt by the lumber industry decline.

Tourism is too seasonable and the Redwood National Park at the south edge of the county has "absolutely no economic impact," Smedley said.

Local boosters, desperately seeking something to replace the county's three declining economic mainstays, finally joined the parade of rural communities to Sacramento seeking pieces of a multibillion-dollar prison construction program. The result was a major prison complex north of Crescent City, named Pelican Bay and housing some of the state's most violent offenders. The new prison, with its several thousand employees, many of them recruited locally, had the desired economic impact. Prison guard salaries were twice those offered in local sawmills and a burst of housing and commercial construction attested to the new money flowing into the otherwise stagnant local economy. The inmates also were counted in the 1990 census, making Del Norte, at least on paper, one of the state's fastest-growing counties in the 1990 census.

Mendocino County, south of Humboldt, has experienced the same downward spiral of the lumber industry and the same rise and decline of marijuana. At one point, Mendicino County's agricultural commissioner proposed to count the pot crop along with grapes and other local commodities. But because it's closer to the Bay Area's population, tourism appears to be a more viable alternative.

The small towns along the spectacularly rugged Mendocino County coast, a three- to four-hour drive from the Bay Area, have seen a surge of affluent weekend visitors a la Napa—so many in some cases that local residents are worried about losing their solitude.

The wine industry has a strong foothold in the interior valleys of Mendocino and the largest city in the county, Ukiah, is close enough to the boom areas of Marin and Sonoma county to wait for some spillover effect.

Local leaders are promoting more development of Highway 101 to give the area vital access. "We're relying more and more on tourism and that needs transportation," said Al Beltrami, a veteran Mendocino County official. Mendocino's population growth, 20 percent in the 1980s, was twice that of Humboldt.

The fastest-growing of all the North Coast counties is Lake, which has no coast, save that of Clear Lake, California's largest natural body of fresh water. And that's because thousands of retirees have discovered its scenery, its mild climate and its relatively low cost of living.

The population of Lake County has nearly quadrupled since 1960 and the median age is 13 years above the state average.

Lake County even has experienced a mild surge in local employment—such as the relocation of a satellite claims processing center by Blue Shield. There are development efforts underway on large-scale gold mining and geothermal development as well. Some have even promoted the idea of having casino gambling on a large island in the middle of Clear Lake that would spark development of world-class tourist facilities.

The modest economic surge in Lake County serves mostly, however, to point up the lack of economic activity elsewhere in the region—what Mendocino County's Beltrami called "the Appalachia of the North Coast."

The latest of a long string of disputes over what kind of economy the region should pursue, pitting prodevelopment forces against environmentalists, revolves around offshore oil.

To some, such as ex-Eureka Mayor Fred Moore, offshore oil would be a godsend that would give young people a reason to remain in the area.

"Even now, we believe the majority is in favor of jobs," said Moore. "It is the vocal minority that is speaking (against offshore oil)."

The issue has bitterly divided the Humboldt County Board of Supervisors with then-Supervisor Chesbro leading the opposition to oil development.

The amount of oil to be developed off the North Coast "would be insignificant," said Chesbro, and not worth the environmental risk involved.

The area demonstrated an interest in the oil business when it tried to obtain an Exxon contract for construction of offshore oil equipment for other areas.

"The Koreans beat us by $100 million," said Kent Driesbock, who headed an embryonic program aimed at finding job-creating alternatives to lumber in Humboldt County.

Although that contract was lost, the effort resulted in the creation of a 131-acre industrial site on Humboldt Bay with all of the proper permits—a rarity along California's coastline.

"The pluses are that it is an economically feasible place to look at projects of this type," Driesbock said.

The unanimous opposition to offshore oil expressed by local state and federal legislators is indicative of a huge shift in political orientation for the area during the last generation.

As counterculture emigres put down roots and as blue-collar workers fled the area during the 1960s and 1970s, the political climate shifted. Historically, the area had been nominally Democratic but conservative, often electing Republicans to local office. Because of its industrial past and its scant population growth, the area had a conservative power structure that called the political shots, known as "the Ingomar bunch" for an exclusive men's club of that name housed in an ornate Victorian mansion in Eureka.

Things began to change in the early 1970s. Since 1972, when Democrat Barry Keene won a hotly contested Assembly race, Republican and conservative Democratic legislators one-by-one have been displaced by liberal-environmentalist Democrats. The most dramatic change occurred in 1982 when then-Assemblyman Doug Bosco ousted Republican Congressman Don Clausen, who had represented the North Coast for nearly 20 years. The ever-shifting political winds of the region blew away Bosco eight years later. Accused by liberals and environmentalists of abandoning them, Bosco lost his seat to a Republican challenger when liberals votes in droves for a Peace and Freedom Party candidate.

The local state assemblyman, Democrat Dan Hauser, almost suffered a similar fate in 1990 and immediately moved from being the political champion of the lumber industry to a crusader for logging reforms.

In 1973, local voters defied the Ingomar Club power structure and rejected a dam on the Mad River that would have provided more water for pulp plant expansion—and increased the value of land around the proposed reservoir owned by members of the power elite.

That would not—could not—have happened even a decade earlier.

Sources

Cᴀʟɪꜰᴏʀɴɪᴀ ɪꜱ ᴀ ꜰᴀꜱᴄɪɴᴀᴛɪɴɢ ꜱᴜʙᴊᴇᴄᴛ ꜰᴏʀ ʀᴇꜱᴇᴀʀᴄʜᴇʀꜱ ᴀɴᴅ ᴛʜᴇʀᴇ ᴀʀᴇ, therefore, a wealth of data available. Unfortunately, however, there is no central repository for those data. One must search for clues to the development of the state in a variety of locations, to wit:

The state Department of Finance, which acts as the economic arm of the governor's office, maintains active research into economic trends and has an office dedicated to detecting and reporting on changes in the state's population— an important basis for the allocation of public funds. The latest federal census information is available from the office as well.

Other state agencies also maintain valuable statistical records. The Franchise Tax Board collects data about personal and corporate income; the state Board of Equalization does the same for property and sales taxes, the latter an especially value economic indicator. The secretary of state's office maintains records on voter registration and voting patterns that provide clues to an area's political evolution. And the Employment Development Department charts unemployment statistics and trends relating to employment by type of industry on a county-by-county basis.

The County Supervisors Association of California has produced a book packed with economic and other data about the state's 58 counties. Another standard reference is the California Almanac, published by Presidio Press and Pacific Data Resources.

U.S. Census Bureau counts the population every 10 years and produces a steady stream of reports based on that census data throughout the decade. Census materials— including a detailed, county-by-county breakdown of economic, demographic and ethic data—are available from the state Department of Finance's Sacramento office.

Invaluable sources of data, as well as expertise, are the regional planning agencies. Those rural areas are able to do only scant original research but those in the major population centers are goldmines of data. Leaders are the Association of Bay Area Governments (ABAG), headquartered in Oakland, the Southern California Association of Governments (SCAG), located in Los Angeles and covering all Southern California counties except San Diego, and the San Diego Association of Governments.

Closely allied with the regional planning agencies are the county planning departments to be found everywhere in the state. County planners, more than almost anyone in government, keep track of economic developments within their areas and usually maintain statistical libraries about their areas.

Private think tanks and data banks, too, are valuable research resources. The Center for Continuing Study of the California Economy, based in Palo Alto, produces a series of reports dealing with economic and population trends in the state. The Population Reference Bureau in Washington has taken a special interest in California's demographic trends. Its report on California population and economic trends by demographers Leon Bouvier and Philip Morton is a basic resouce, and the bureau also has done reports on Hispanic and Asian population trends that deal with the entire nation but naturally focus much of their attention on California. The Rand Corporation in Santa Monica often focuses its research on California, and Rand demographer Kevin McCarthy is considered to be a leading expert on the state's changing profile.

Some of the most valuable, but least known, research on California is being done on college campuses. It's a rare state university or University of California campus that does not have someone—an economist, a political scientist, a geographer, etc.— who has made extensive studies of local development patterns.

Finally, the editors of California's newspapers are an inexhaustible source of information about what's happening in their communities— with backup from their extensive libraries of clippings.